David,

Let's integrate the

pension revolution

with the governance

revolution!

Keith

Jan 22 2007

"Yet another revolution in pensions! This one is about the very future of private pensions, their design, benefits, funding and the distribution of risk. As we would expect from Keith Ambachtsheer, this book combines perceptive and informed assessment of the issues with a way forward. This is nothing short of Drucker's world re-written for the twenty-first century."
—Gordon Clark, Professor of Geography and Director of the Oxford University Centre for the Environment, Oxford University, U.K.

"Financing retirement income has reached crisis proportions around the world. Keith has thought as much as anyone about how to best redeem and redefine societies' vital, yet frail structures for delivering income to workers once they retire. Here in one place you get the benefit of that accumulated wisdom."
—Richard Ennis, Co-founder and Chairman, Ennis Knupp + Associates, U.S.A., and Editor, *Financial Analysts Journal*

"I have known and worked with Keith for many years and look forward to the next chapter in his analysis of the pension fund business. I anticipate a thought provoking "solution" which will no doubt impact how many of us think about our business going forward."
—Nancy Everett, President and Chief Executive Officer, General Motors Asset Management, U.S.A.

"While I don't necessarily agree with all of Keith's pension revolution conclusions and proposed solutions, I do believe there is great value in seriously considering the issues. This thought-provoking book makes a substantial contribution to promoting that highly desirable end result."
—Gary Findlay, Executive Director, Missouri State Employees' Retirement System, U.S.A.

"A cure for pension ills? Founded on problems so well defined and incorporating relevant factors so well described in his earlier works, Keith's Pension Revolution *is surely an excellent prescription. Whether it is a cure is up to those of us with oversight responsibilities."*
—Michael Grandin, Corporate Director and former Dean, Haskayne School of Business, University of Calgary, Canada

Founded in 1807, John Wiley & Sons is the oldest independent publishing company in the United States. With offices in North America, Europe, Australia and Asia, Wiley is globally committed to developing and marketing print and electronic products and services for our customers' professional and personal knowledge and understanding.

The Wiley Finance series contains books written specifically for finance and investment professionals as well as sophisticated individual investors and their financial advisors. Book topics range from portfolio management to e-commerce, risk management, financial engineering, valuation and financial instrument analysis, as well as much more.

For a list of available titles, please visit our Web site at www.WileyFinance.com.

Pension Revolution

A Solution to the Pensions Crisis

KEITH P. AMBACHTSHEER

BICENTENNIAL
1807
WILEY
2007
BICENTENNIAL

John Wiley & Sons, Inc.

Published by John Wiley & Sons, Inc., Hoboken, New Jersey.
Published simultaneously in Canada.

For general information on our other products and services or for technical support, please contact our Customer Care Department within the United States at (800) 762-2974, outside the United States at (317) 572-3993 or fax (317) 572-4002.

Wiley also publishes its books in a variety of electronic formats. Some content that appears in print may not be available in electronic books. For more information about Wiley products, visit our Web site at www.wiley.com.

Library of Congress Cataloging-in-Publication Data:

Ambachtsheer, Keith P.
   Pension revolution : a solution to the pensions crisis / Keith Ambachtsheer.
      p. cm. – (Wiley finance series)
   ISBN-13: 978-0-470-08723-7 (cloth)
   ISBN-10: 0-470-08723-4 (cloth)
   1. Pension trusts. 2. Pension trusts—Management. 3. Pension trusts—Investments. I. Title.
   HD7105.4.A63 2007
   331.25′22—dc22

                                                    2006024003

Printed in the United States of America.

10 9 8 7 6 5 4 3 2 1

*To Peter Drucker, who foresaw the pension
revolution thirty years ago
and
To Virginia Atkin, who provided the inspiration
to see this project through.*

Contents

Preface: Peter Drucker's Pension Revolution: Here at Last   xxiii

Introduction: Why a Pension Revolution Now?   xxvii

The Trouble with DB Plans   xxvii
DC Plans Are Not the Answer Either   xxviii
Expert Pension Co-ops   xxix
TOPS Tipping Points   xxx

PART ONE

The Pension Revolution: Touchstones

CHAPTER 1
Are Pension Funds "Irrelevant"?   3

An "Unreasonable" Actuary?   3
Exley's Four Irrelevance Propositions   4
So What Is Relevant?   4
Responding to Exley   6
Relevant Pension Funds: Building the Case   6
Managing Retirement Income Risks   7
Leveling the Informational Playing Field   7
Getting the Execution of the Idea Right   8

CHAPTER 2
The Pension Revolution—Are You a Believer Yet?   9

A Revolutionary Reordering of the Pensions Firmament   10
From Fuzzy Pension Deals to "Risk-Sharing Co-ops"   10
Toward Pension "Business Models" That Work: The Risk
Issue   11
Toward Pension "Business Models" That Work: The Scale
Issue   12
The Pension Governance Issue   13

Two Role Models 14
    PGGM 14
    SunSuper 15
Great Treasures? 15

CHAPTER 3
After the Perfect Pension Storm: What Now? **16**

From Vegas to Oxford: In Search of Answers 16
Do Nothing or Something? 17
The Corporate Context: Two Basic Choices 18
New DC Plan "Business Model" Also Needed 19
The Industry/Public-Sector Pension Context 19
The "Fair Value" Question 20
Better Public Pensions Policy 21

CHAPTER 4
Beyond Portfolio Theory: The Next Frontier **22**

Investment Theory's Next Frontier: The Academic View 22
Investment Theory's Next Frontier: Two Further
    Considerations 24
The Next Frontier: "Integrative Investment Theory" 25

CHAPTER 5
The United Airlines Case: Tipping Point for U.S.
Pension System? **29**

The United Airlines Case 29
A Good Question and Two Very Different Answers 30
ERISA's "Sole Interest" Rule 31
Lessons from Abroad 32
Searching for "Supreme" Answers 33
The UAL Case in Context 34

CHAPTER 6
Peter Drucker's Pension Revolution After 30 Years:
Not Over Yet **36**

Two Unfashionable Themes 36
Politico-Agency Issues 37
Pension Contract and Risk Issues 39
Investment Beliefs 40
Pension Fund Governance 40
Still Much Work to Do 41

CHAPTER 7
Winning the Pension Revolution: Why the Dutch Are Leading the Way   **42**

The Globe's Number One Pensions Country   42
Culture, Compactness, and Leadership   44
Regulatory Leadership   45
Research Leadership   46
A Remaining Challenge: Solving the Organization Design
   Puzzle   46
What About the Other Pensions Countries?   47

CHAPTER 8
Pension Reform: Evolution or Revolution?   **48**

A Pension "Tipping Point" Indeed   48
What Should Happen?   49
Pension Reform in the United States   50
Pension Reform Elsewhere   51
Pension Reform: Evolution or Revolution?   52

PART TWO

Building Better Pension Plans

CHAPTER 9
Can Game Theory Help Build Better Pension Plans?   **57**

Pension Games   57
Why do Pension Game Switches Occur?   58
Who Are the Stakeholders and What do They Want?   59
Sources of Risk in Pension Schemes   60
Mitigating Micro Risks   60
Can We Mitigate Macro Risks?   61
Is Investment Risk Worth Taking in DB Plans?   61
Can Game Theory Build Better Pension Plans?   62

CHAPTER 10
If DB and DC Plans Are Not the Answers, What Are the Questions?   **63**

From Answers to Questions   63
Ultimate Pension Questions and Their Consequences   64
Underwriting Pension Mismatch Risk: Any Volunteers?   64
Should Pension Mismatch Risk Be Minimized?   66
Pension-Delivery Institutions   67
Benchmarking Traditional DB and DC Plans   67
The Way Ahead   68

CHAPTER 11
Human Foibles and Agency Dysfunction: Building Pension Plans for the
Real World   **69**

    Some Fundamental Questions First   69
    Back to First Principles   70
    Human Foibles   71
    Agency Issues   72
    Counteracting Human Foibles   73
    Minimizing Agency Costs   74
    TOPS, Employers, and Public Policy   75
    TOPS and DB Plans   77

CHAPTER 12
DB Plans and Bad Science   **78**

    Science and the Design of Pension Contracts   78
    The TOPS Contract   78
    Taking on Investment Risk: Implications   79
    Is Investment Regime Risk Insurable?   80
    Intergenerational Bargaining   81
    Robust Course-Correction Mechanisms Required   82
    The Flawed DB Model   82
    Bad Science   83

CHAPTER 13
Peter Drucker's Pension Legacy: A Vision of What Could Be   **84**

    Two Handshakes to Remember   84
    The Melbourne Message   85
    TOPS: Neither DC nor DB   86
    TOPS and Investing   87
    TOPS and Governance   87
    TOPS and the Real World   88
    The Drucker Visit   89

PART THREE

    Pension Fund Governance

CHAPTER 14
Reinventing Pension Fund Management: Easier Said than Done   **93**

    A Paradigm Shift?   93
    Novelties of Fact   94

Novelties of Theory   94
Pension Industry Responses   96
Crossing the "Innovation Chasm"   97

CHAPTER 15
Should (Could) You Manage Your Fund Like Harvard or Ontario
Teachers'?   **99**
Four Things in Common   99
Legal Foundations: Solid or Not?   100
Governance and Management: Understanding the
    Difference   101
Investment Beliefs: Theirs or Yours?   102
Investment Processes: Like Wall Street?   103
Should You Manage Like HMC or OTPP?   104
Could You Manage Like HMC or OTPP?   104

CHAPTER 16
"Beauty Contest" Investing: Not Dead Yet   **106**
"Déjà Vu All Over Again"   106
Why "Beauty Contest Investing" Is Ugly   108
Integrative Investment Theory   108
Investment Beliefs   109
Managing from the Inside Out   110

CHAPTER 17
Eradicating "Beauty Contest" Investing: What It Will Take   **112**
The Ugliness of "Beauty Contest" Investing   112
A Two-Pronged Eradication Strategy   113
What Corporations Must Do   114
What Investing Institutions Must Do   114
A Debilitating Pension Fund Governance Problem   115
Light at the End of the "Beauty Contest" Tunnel?   117

CHAPTER 18
High-Performance Cultures: Impossible Dream for Pension
Funds?   **118**
Thinking and Acting Like Goldman Sachs   118
New Research Results   119
Specific Governance and Management Challenges   121
In Conclusion   122

CHAPTER 19

How Much Is Good Governance Worth?   **124**

Governance Quality and Organization Performance Should
    Be Related   124
A Road Map for the Journey of Discovery   125
The Pension CEO Score and NVA Metrics: The Data   126
Pension CEO Scores Meet NVA Metrics   127
Further Insights   128
The Value of Good Governance   129

PART FOUR

Investment Beliefs

CHAPTER 20

The 10 Percent Equity Return Illusion: Possible Consequences   **133**

Consequential Miscalculations   133
Why 10 Percent Doesn't Work   134
Painted into an Awkward Corner?   136
Consequences   137

CHAPTER 21

Stocks for the Long Run? . . . or Not?   **139**

A Debate with Jeremy Siegel   139
How Investment Theory Became Investment Practice   140
What Is Wrong with These "Proofs"   141
What if "Reality" Is Not a Random Walk?   141
Investment Regimes, Dividend Yields, and ERPs   143
The Post-Bubble Blues Decade   143

CHAPTER 22

**"Persistent Investment Regimes" or "Random Walk"? Even
Shakespeare Knew the Answer**   **145**

The Ambachtsheer-Siegel Debate Revisited   145
History on Our Side   146
The Investment Returns Story: How to Tell It   147
The "Investment Regime" Game: Spot Today's Well Before
    It's Over, and Tomorrow's Before It's Gone on Too Long   148
"Regime Spotting" versus "Random Walk": Which Is More
    Useful?   149

Theory on Our Side, Too 150
Fellow Travelers 150

CHAPTER 23
The Fuss about Policy Portfolios: Adrift in Institutional Wonderland 151

Tempest in a Teapot ... or Not? 151
Duality in Finance: A Brief History 152
Financial Duality in Pension and Endowment Funds:
    Building the Conceptual Framework 153
New Insights from the CEM Database 154
Enter Organizational Dysfunction 155
Decisions by Default 156

CHAPTER 24
Shifting the Investment Paradigm: A Progress Report 157

The "Policy Portfolio" Debate Continues 157
A Lens to See the World 158
Why the "Old" Lens Distorts 158
A Varying Equity Risk Premium 159
A New Lens 160
A Higher Level of Thinking 161
Glimmers of Light 163

CHAPTER 25
Whose "Investment Beliefs" Do You Believe? 164

Writing an "Investment Beliefs" Statement 164
Inferring Beliefs from Actions 165
Measuring Predictive Ability 166
What about Market Timing and Strategic Asset Allocation? 167
Expected ERP Powerful Predictor 167
Enter Woody Brock 168
In Conclusion 169

CHAPTER 26
Our 60-40 Asset Mix Policy Advice in 1987: Wise or Foolish? 171

Why Roll the Clock Back 20 Years? 171
Leibowitz's Immunization Campaign 172
Investment Beliefs in 1987 173
Investment Beliefs in 1997 173
The Right Kind of Active Management 174
Wise or Foolish? 175

CHAPTER 27
"But What Does the Turtle Rest On?" A Further Exploration of Investment Beliefs   177

"But What Does the Turtle Rest On?"   177
The Efficient Markets Hypothesis: Fact or Fiction?   178
The Three Strikes against the EMH   179
Economists and "Operationally Meaningful Theorems"   180
The Adaptive Markets Hypothesis   180
The AMH's Five Practical Implications   182
The AMH and Integrative Investment Theory   182

CHAPTER 28
Professor Malkiel and the New Investment Paradigm: Raining on the Parade?   184

Raining on the "New Paradigm" Parade?   184
The Bases for Malkiel's Skepticism   185
An Alternative Conclusion   186
Winning Evidence   187
The "Good Governance" Boost   188
We're Both Right   189

CHAPTER 29
The "Post-Bubble Blues Decade": A Progress Report   190

Another Nail in the IID Coffin   190
Why Non-IID Logic Wins   191
Investment Regimes in the Real World   192
What Seems to Actually Be Happening?   193
Some Actual Numbers   194
The Bottom Line   195

PART FIVE
Risk in Pension Plans

CHAPTER 30
Rethinking Funding Policy and Regulation: How Should Pension Plans Be Financed?   199

The Devil in the Details   199
How Many Course-Correction Tools?   200
Making Financing Decisions: In Whose Interest?   201

An Analytical Framework for Assessing DB Plan Financing
   Decisions   202
"Rational" Explanations   203
Four Principles to Fund By   204

CHAPTER 31
Funding Policy and Investment Policy: How Should They Be Integrated in DB Pension Plans?   **206**

Principles to Fund and Invest By   206
What Makes DB Pension "Contracts" Risky?   208
Should DB Funding Target Calculations Assume That More
   Risk Means More Return?   208
Is Current "Accepted Actuarial Practice" Unacceptable?   209
What Is an "Acceptable Level of Certainty"?   210
Surplus Ownership   211
Cleaning Up Our Act   212

CHAPTER 32
Resurrecting Ranva: Adjusting Investment Returns for Risk   **213**

Resurrecting RANVA   213
RANVA in 1998   214
Measuring RANVA in the Real World   215
The 2000 to 2004 Experience: Lessons   216
Remaining Barriers   217

CHAPTER 33
Adjusting Investment Returns for Risk: What's the Best Way?   **219**

Resurrecting RANVA   219
The "Cost of Market Volatility" Approach   220
The "Cost of Insurance" Approach with Risk Buffers   222
The "Cost of Insurance" Approach with Put Options   223

PART SIX

Measuring Results

CHAPTER 34
Pension Plan Organizations: Measuring "Competitiveness"   **227**

Pension Plan Organizations and "Legitimacy"   227
"Provider of Choice" for Which Services?   228

Benchmarking Pension Services 229
Costing the Benefit Administration "Business" 229
The Benefit Administration Cost Equation 231
Build or Buy? 232

CHAPTER 35
Measuring DC Plans as "Value Propositions": The New Imperative for Plan Sponsors **233**

Silk Purses from Sows' Ears 233
Measures of "Prudence" 234
The "Own-Company Stock" Phenomenon 234
Understanding DC Plan Total Returns 235
DC versus DB Plan Cost Performance 237
Other DC Plan Performance Metrics 239
"Value Proposition": Yes or No? 239

CHAPTER 36
Measuring Pension Fund Behavior (1992 to 2004): What Can We Learn? **240**

A Well-Endowed Database 240
Current International Investment Policy and Implementation
    Style Differences 241
Ten-Year Investment Policy and Implementation Style
    Trends for U.S. Funds 242
Did Active Management Add Value? 243
The Selection "Alphas": Good News and Bad News 244
Is There Also a Payoff from Actively Managing Pension Fund
    Costs? 247
Two Important Lessons Learned Thus Far 249

PART SEVEN

Pensions, Politics, and the Investment Industry

CHAPTER 37
Whither Security Analysis? **253**

Bubble, Bubble, Toil and Trouble 253
Fortune Trashes Wall Street 254
Is Better Regulation the Answer? 255
Reversing the Financial Food Chain 256

What Is Security Analysis, Anyway? 257
Even Good Security Analysis Needs Context 257
Effective "Buy-Side" Structures 258
In Conclusion 259

CHAPTER 38
Pension Funds and Investment Firms: Redefining the Relationship **260**

Who Are the Simbas of the Pension Investment Kingdom? 260
The Money Flood 261
A Question of Governance 261
Enter the Anthropologists 262
A Call to "Excellence" 263
What Do "Excellent" Pension Funds Look Like? 264
A Supplier-Driven Market 265
The Tiny Equity Risk Premium Factor 265
"New Paradigm" Pension Funds: What Kind of Investment
    Services Do They Want? 267
New Pension Fund–Investment Firm Partnerships 270
Could You Be a "New Paradigm" Player? 271

CHAPTER 39
**The New Pension Fund Management Paradigm: Feedback from
Financial Analysts** **272**

Test Driving the New Paradigm 272
Pension Politics and Economics 273
Pension Plan Governance 276
The New Pension Fund Management Paradigm 277
Putting the Paradigm in Practice 278
Performance Measurement 281
Did the Yardsticks Move Forward or Backward? 282

CHAPTER 40
**Reconnecting GAAP and Common Sense: The Cases of Stock Options
and Pensions** **283**

Closing the Information GAAP 283
When Are Employee Stock Options "Expenses"? 284
The Common-Sense Solution in Action 285
Current Pension Accounting Rules Defy Common Sense, Too 285
Sensible Pension Accounting Rules 287
Common Sense in Action 288
Carpe Diem 289

CHAPTER 41
Is Sri Bunk?   **290**

SRI and Zen   290
What Is "Socially Responsible Investing"?   290
A Slippery Slope?   291
Sustainable Investing   292
Assessing the Sustainability of Dividend Growth   293
From Saying to Doing: A Case Study   294
Redefining the SRI Revolution   294

CHAPTER 42
Alpha, Beta, Bafflegab: Investment Theory as Marketing
Strategy   **296**

Giving Alpha and Beta a Rest   296
The Beautiful Art of Language   297
The Myth of "Absolute-Return Investing"   298
Investment Theory with the End in Mind   298
The Critical Role of Fund Governance   299
Pension Revolution   300

CHAPTER 43
The Turner Pensions Commission Report: A Blueprint for Global
Pension Reform   **302**

Pension Wisdom from the United Kingdom   302
Turner's Recommendations   303
The Power of Integrative Thinking   303
Blueprint for Global Pension Reform   304
NPSS Governance, Management, and Investment
    Options   307
Moving Forward   308

CHAPTER 44
More Pension Wisdom from Europe: The Geneva Report
on Pension Reform   **309**

Eight Hands, Four Economists, and One Point of View   309
Powerful Pension Policy Implications   310
Labor Markets and Human Capital   311
Optimal Risk Sharing   312

Optimal Pension Fund Organizations 313
A Powerful Pension Vision 314

PART EIGHT

The Case of PERS

CHAPTER 45
PERS and the Pension Revolution: Active Participant . . . or Passive Bystander? **317**

Alyson Green's New Job 317
History of Workplace Pensions 319
The 1976 to 2005 Period 319
Governance–Organizational Issues at PERS 320
Finance–Investment Beliefs 321
Pension Contract–Risk Issues at PERS 321
Is a Higher Contribution Rate the Answer? 323
More Drastic Action Indicated 324
Spreading the Pain Evenly 326
Is Risk-Sharing an Essential Pension Plan Feature? 327
Getting from Here to There 329
Devising an Action Plan 329

CHAPTER 46
Advice for Alyson Green: How PERS Can Join the Pension Revolution **331**

Case Discussion Summary from October 25, 2005 331
The PERS Situation 332
The PERS Debate 332

In Conclusion: A Call to Arms **335**

Preface:
Peter Drucker's Pension
Revolution: Here at Last

Peter Drucker's prescient pensions book *The Unseen Revolution: How Pension Fund Socialism Came to America* was first published in 1976. A decade later, I would write my own pensions book, *Pension Funds and the Bottom Line*. Another decade later, I co-authored a second book, *Pension Fund Excellence*, with Don Ezra. So chronologically, this new book, *Pension Revolution*, is right on schedule, arriving almost 10 years after *Pension Fund Excellence*, 20 years after *Pension Funds and the Bottom Line*, and 30 years after Drucker's original book, *The Unseen Revolution*. Why this third book now? Because I believe that the adverse events of the first half of this new decade have finally created the winning conditions to realize the pensions vision Drucker first articulated 30 years ago. The serious design shortcomings of traditional defined benefit (DB) and defined contribution (DC) pension plans have now been bared for all to see, as have the shortcomings of an investment paradigm based on the belief that "in the long run" heavy weightings in equities will always save the day. Rather than responding constructively to the events of the last five years, most pension plan sponsors, legislators, and regulators around the globe, as well as most experts from the actuarial, accounting, and legal professions have done little more than wring their hands as the foundations on which the old pension paradigm was constructed have crumbled.

Of equal importance is the light that the 2001 to 2005 experience has shed on the pension fund "legitimacy" question that Drucker raised 30 years ago. Even in pension plans where there is understanding that the old pension paradigm is dead, and that a new pension paradigm is needed, change for the better has been slow and difficult to achieve. Why? Sometimes internal principal-agent conflicts between managers and workers have gotten in the way, usually in corporate DB plans contexts. Sometimes game theory-related conflicts have broken out between various pension plan stakeholder groups, usually in public sector DB plan contexts. These agency-related blockages to improving pension arrangements are often exacerbated by pension laws, as well as by regulatory and governance processes that are still not up to the task. These realities suggest that Drucker's 30-year old "legitimacy" question has yet to be answered affirmatively. But now there is a difference. The 2001 to 2005 experience has shown the old pension paradigm to be fatally vulnerable to adversity, and in urgent need of renewal. This book offers a response to these realities that is both revolutionary and thoroughly practical at the same time.

I wrote my first book in 1985 as a practical decision guide for the pension trustees and executives of corporate pension plans. However, the book's final chapter was titled "The Private Pension System Challenge: Achieving 'Legitimacy.'" In it, I reiterated Drucker's warning from 10 years earlier that pension systems do not exist in a political vacuum. If independently and expertly governed, pension funds can become the enlightened means by which workers secure their retirement through ownership of the means of production, and by which new retirement savings are converted into new wealth-creating capital. Through this virtuous process, the historical contradictions between capitalism and socialism would finally fall away. On the other hand, poorly governed pension funds, in the hands of agents with their own agendas, have no hope of achieving the "legitimacy" required to play the dual role of providers of retirement income, and owners of the means of production. Drucker warned that the "enlightened" outcome was by no means assured. It would only come about if the "independently and expertly governed" condition became a general pension fund rule, rather than the exception.

The launch of my 1985 book was followed by the launch of KPA Advisory Services Ltd., my advisory publication *The Ambachtsheer Letter*, and CEM Benchmarking Inc. The goals of the businesses and the publication were to offer strategic research and advice on pension governance, finance, and investment issues consistent with both Drucker's "legitimacy" vision and with my own evolving views on pension finance and investment theory, and to benchmark the organizational performance of pension funds. As time passed into the 1990s, I found myself returning time and again to the central importance of Drucker's "legitimacy" requirement and its implication that pension funds should be established as well-governed, "arm's-length," single-purpose entities. It was the interactive process of research, debate, discovery, and hands-on advisory assignments that led to the second book with Don Ezra in 1998 titled *Pension Fund Excellence: Creating Value for Stakeholders*. While this book provided valuable new information and opinion into areas such as investment beliefs and pension balance-sheet management, its most valuable and lasting contribution was to provide new insights into the agency and governance issues that continued to confound much of the globe's pension fund "industry" through the 1990s, and continues to confound it to this day.

Through a series of 44 chapters originally written as letters for clients of KPA Advisory Services, this new *Pension Revolution* book tells the story of my personal transformation from a pension "evolutionary" to a pension revolutionary over the course of the last five years. With the editorial assistance of Caroline Cakebread and my friends at Wiley, the organizational skills of Ann Henhoeffer, and the technical assistance of Hubert Lum, the letters have been updated, edited, and converted into a logical sequence of chapters organized into seven broad themes. These themes range from the politics of pensions, to building better pension plans, to addressing pension agency and governance issues, to articulating believable investment beliefs, to managing risk in pension plan contexts, and to measuring results in ways that matter. Each chapter has its own stand-alone message, and thus can be read on its own merit. Reading the chapters chronologically within each theme allows readers to see how the key ideas within each theme have evolved over the course of the last five years. The structure of the seven part themes themselves resulted from taking an integrative approach to first articulating the status of the pension revolution early in the twenty-first century, and then to showing how it can now be brought to a successful conclusion by consciously building true pension fund "legitimacy." The results are indeed revolutionary. A new, conflict-free pension design named TOPS: The Optimal Pension System emerges. Clearer guidelines for resolving internal and external agency issues are identified, as are sharper, more effective pension governance principles. Investment beliefs reflecting both common sense and new academic research are deduced. Risk is connected to uncertainty about future consumption, and then made operational through risk budgets. Performance measurement is connected to what should be managed. Revolutionary indeed!

A final section of the book pulls all of the "legitimacy" elements together through a case study of the Public Employee Retirement System (PERS), a very typical public sector DB plan grappling with a very typical set of plan design, agency, governance, risk measurement, management, and disclosure issues. The case description and discussion are among the first tangible fruits of the newly founded Rotman International Centre for Pension Management (ICPM) at the University of Toronto. Sponsored by 17 of the globe's thought-leading pension organizations, ICPM's mission is to apply integrative thinking and research to helping pension organizations raise their "legitimacy" in the eyes of their own stakeholders and of the public at large.

Peter Drucker would be pleased.

Keith Ambachtsheer
Toronto, Canada
September 2006

Introduction:
Why a Pension Revolution Now?

There is now a broad consensus that the workplace pension systems in most of the developed world are sick, and that they will require strong medicine if they are to generate adequate pensions for workforces in the years ahead. Leading spokespersons of the business, labor, government, and professional communities in the North America, Europe, and the Pacific Rim have all been voicing similar concerns about workplace pension coverage, adequacy, and security in their respective countries. The proportion of the workforce covered by pension plans is too low. Many pension arrangements will not produce adequate pensions. Corporate employers are closing their traditional defined benefit (DB) plans, which provide guaranteed pensions according to a predefined formula. Many of the DB plans that remain now have insufficient assets to cover their liabilities.

THE TROUBLE WITH DB PLANS

Just as there is a consensus that workplace pension systems around the world are sick, so are there strong views on what the cure is. Many commentators continue to say the answer is to reverse the decline in the use of DB plans. DB plan enthusiasts point out that widespread adoption of this form of pension arrangement would cure the workplace pension systems' coverage, adequacy, and security ills in one fell swoop. While I agree with the consensus that the globe's workplace pension systems are seriously ill, I disagree that the cure lies in placing a DB chicken in every worker's pension pot. Why? The chapters in Parts One and Two of this book show that workplace-based DB plans suffer from a fatal flaw. How? By socializing risk bearing without clarity about how, and by whom the very material risks embedded in DB arrangements are borne. The chapter "Can Game Theory Help Build Better Pension Plans?" reminds us that game theorist John Nash taught us decades ago that such fuzzy "contracts" will eventually deteriorate into adversarial win-lose games.

So we should not be surprised that when financial surpluses appear on DB plan balance sheets, there are fights about who "owns" them. In corporate contexts, the surpluses of the 1990s frequently led to ownership disputes between plan members and shareholders, with regulators and even the courts having to step in to arbitrate these tiffs. When surpluses turn to deficits at times of financial distress, plan members duke it out with corporate bond and shareholders about how the financial pain should be allocated. The chapter "The United Airlines Case: Tipping Point for U.S. Pension System?" cites the recent United Airlines saga as a classic example of this outcome. A number of the book's chapters, and the Case of PERS in Part Eight, indicate that things are generally more subtle in public-sector contexts, where current generations of taxpayers and public servants quietly skim off surpluses at the expense of future generations. A good example was the easy decision by the teachers' federation and the provincial government of Ontario, Canada, to "spend" the teachers' pension plan surpluses of the 1990s on better pensions and lower contributions. At the end of 2005, despite relatively good investment results, the plan reported a serious $32 billion balance-sheet deficit. So now there are far more difficult decisions to be made about who "owns" the current deficit, and how it should be eliminated. Beneath all these game theory-based actions lies the common thread that collective risk-bearing arrangements such as DB plans do not eliminate risk. They merely offer opportunities to shift it from the strong to the weak.

This DB plan risk conundrum is further explored in Part Five of the book. The risks embedded in DB plans cannot be managed if they are not understood. Understanding them is far more challenging then most people realize. What specifically are the financial guarantees embedded in a DB pension arrangement? Are they nominal or inflation indexed? If assets are insufficient to cover the accrued liabilities, how is the difference made up? Do benefits get reduced? Contributions raised? Both? Neither? Are these measures contingent on uncertain future events? Can modern contingent claims valuation techniques throw new light on these questions? The chapters in Part Five address these challenging questions.

DC PLANS ARE NOT THE ANSWER EITHER

If not DB chickens, what *should* we stuff in the pension pots of workers around the world? There are strongly held views that defined contribution (DC) plans are the answer. Here employers and workers make contributions into employee pension accumulation accounts, with employees typically allocating contributions among a dozen or more investment options. It is certainly true that DC arrangements eliminate most of the DB plan ambiguity about risk bearing and asset ownership. However, Part Two chapters such as "Human Foibles and Agency Dysfunction: Building Better Pension Plans for the Real World" point out that the typical DC plan has three serious flaws of its own. First, behavioral finance research confirms that most people are hesitant, inconsistent, even irrational planners and decision makers regarding their own financial future. Second, informational asymmetry and misaligned interests with regard to the global for-profit financial services industry drive a material wedge between workers and the retirement money they do accumulate. The result is that many workers pay too much for retirement-related financial services in relation to their true economic value. These excessive fees paid over a working lifetime are another important factor why so many workers are under-achieving their pension goals. The third DC plan flaw is that these arrangements leave plan members bearing the full burden of longevity risk. Surely we should not expose the many millions of retirees around the world to the material risk of outliving their money.

So if broad workforce coverage with either traditional DB or DC plans is not the best cure for the world's workplace pension system ills, what is? Well, we know that on the one hand, such a cure must avoid the collective risk-bearing traps that eventually turn traditional DB plans into multistakeholder fist fights or "musical chairs" risk-shifting games. On the other hand, the cure must also effectively deal with the human foibles, agency, and longevity risk baggage attached to traditional DC arrangements. Through a number of chapters in Parts One and Two, the book introduces TOPS: the optimal pension system, a cure that is both revolutionary and thoroughly practical at the same time.

TOPS addresses the human foibles problem through auto-enrollment, and "auto-pilot" mechanisms that dynamically adjust individual contribution rates over time, and ties the optimal investment policy for each individual participant to their age, all with the goal of delivering a target pension within reasonable bounds. The point of the "auto-pilot" mechanisms is that these adjustments to contribution rates and investment policy are made automatically over time, without requiring any intervention by TOPS participants. Similarly, TOPS deals with longevity risk by including the purchase of deferred life-annuities over time as part of the "auto-pilot" investment policy design. As the annuity portfolio is priced and managed in accordance with insurance company principles, there will be no fist fights over the ownership of any balance sheet surpluses or deficits.

EXPERT PENSION CO-OPS

To address agency issues, TOPS arrangements are run by arm's-length, expert pension co-ops in order to manage the inherent conflicts and too-high costs the for-profit financial services industry brings to the table. The design, management, and operational issues of these financial institutions are addressed in Parts Three, Four, Five and Six of this book. The expert pension co-op concept was a critical element of Drucker's 1976 vision of the pension revolution. He astutely recognized that if pension funds were mere captives of the pension plan sponsors, they were unlikely to play their critically important role in launching and sustaining the revolution. Instead, pension delivery institutions needed to be set up as strong, arms-length, expert organizations with the sole mandate to create value for plan participants. Parts Three and Eight especially address the design and governance implications of this requirement. The key is for pension funds to be able to manage from the inside out, rather than being managed by external agents from the outside in for their own purposes.

Part Four integrates a different kind of revolution into the pension revolution story. To be effective, expert pension co-ops need to operate with investment beliefs that are relevant, research-based, and responsive to new information and insights. Based on observed behavior, the investment beliefs of most of the globe's pension funds cannot pass this important test. Instead, the beliefs of many funds seem to be based on historical rules of thumb, anecdotes, and what they are told by the for-profit financial services industry they should believe. Not surprisingly, such secondhand beliefs suit the financial services industry far better than it does pension fund beneficiaries. Expert pension co-ops are revolutionaries in the sense that they don't play this conventional wisdom game. Instead, they develop their own investment and skill beliefs from first principles, and fortify them with the best and newest available research results. Parts Five, Six, and Eight go on to address the related questions of how expert pension co-ops should define, measure, and manage risk, and how they should measure and report investment results.

TOPS TIPPING POINTS

If TOPS, with its auto-pilot and expert co-op features, is such a great idea, why doesn't it exist already? But it does! A number of the chapters reference the Teachers Insurance and Annuity Association–College Retirement Equities Fund (TIAA-CREF), the $350 billion retirement system for over three million current and retired U.S. college education and research employees, and in which Peter Drucker himself was a participant for many years, runs on TOPS principles. Through worklife-long employer-employee contributions as high as 18 percent of pay, millions of TIAA-CREF participants have converted sufficient pension capital into life annuities to live comfortably the rest of their lives, decade after decade. Founded through a Carnegie grant in 1918, it may well be the most successful workplace pension plan of all time. By mandating that all workers participate in a workplace pension plan, the Dutch and the Australians have become highly motivated to build effective TOPS-type pension arrangements based on industry and regional affiliations, and they are becoming increasingly successful at it. Having said this, TOPS-type pension arrangements are still more the exception than the rule around the world.

Public policy neglect is one reason. The Dutch and the Australian politicians have been astute to exploit the benefits of mandatory participation in fully funded workplace pension plans. Because of 100 percent workplace coverage and reasonable pension adequacy, there is no longer a need to finance and maintain large national Pillar 1 pay-go social safety nets. Also, because everyone has to play, much greater national attention is focused on such issues as optimal pension plan design and implementation. So the TOPS solution naturally emerges, stabilizing lifetime consumption patterns across the economy, while at the same time creating a new class of independent, wealth-creating, long-horizon investors. North Americans haven't even begun to talk about the pros and cons of mandatory workplace pension participation. Which brings me to another reason for current "no TOPS" condition in most of the developed world: a systemic failure to apply integrative thinking to solving pension problems. It has been sad experience to watch some of the finest minds in global pensiondom earnestly attempt to "fix" DB plans so that these arrangements will become not only manageable and sustainable, but wildly popular as well. It is hard to imagine a more futile exercise.

Having said that, the British have shown some recent signs of life. The essay "The Turner Commission Report: A Blueprint for Global Pension Reform" in Part Seven observes that two years ago, the U.K. Treasury commissioned a study to assess the status of workplace pensions in the United Kingdom, and to recommend measures to improve the system. The Turner Pensions Commission tabled its final report and recommendations on November 30, 2005. Its most important recommendation by far was to auto-enroll (with an "opt-out" clause) the entire U.K. workforce not already covered by a workplace pension plan, in a National Pension Savings Scheme (NPSS) with an 8 percent contribution rate. The Commission estimates that lifetime NPSS participation, plus the basic Pillar 1 state pension, would provide the median British worker with a 50 percent income replacement rate upon retirement. The NPSS would adopt many of the *TOPS* principles set out above. For example, the Commission recommends auto-pilot mechanisms to implement a life-cycle investment policy and to convert retirement savings into life annuities. It also recommends that the NPSS be set up as an arms-length, expert pension co-op. A subsequent White Paper issued by HM Treasury suggests that the key Turner recommendations are on their way to becoming government policy.

A final note of optimism. The winning conditions for a successful global workplace pension revolution have never been more favorable than today. There is a growing consensus across the globe that something must be done. The Dutch and the Australians have already demonstrated the societal value of broad-based workplace pension plan participation. The British are seriously considering it. TOPS, the optimal pension system, has already been invented and successfully road-tested. Across the globe, it could be adopted at the national level, at regional levels, at an industry-by-industry level, or at the individual employer level. What we need now is leadership that will make Peter Drucker's vision of a workplace pension revolution a reality at last. The goal of this book is to provide the inspiration and show the way.

The Pension Revolution:
Touchstones

"Revolution: a dramatic and far-reaching change."
The Oxford Dictionary

Are Pension Funds "Irrelevant"?

"The reasonable man adapts himself to the world; the unreasonable one persists in trying to adapt the world to himself. Thus all progress depends on the unreasonable man..."

George Bernard Shaw

"... a propensity to dabble in unproductive financial risks inside pension funds can crowd-out investors with appetites for genuine entrepreneurial risk-taking..."

Jon Exley
Chair, Finance and Investment
Theory Working Party
Faculty of Actuaries, United Kingdom

AN "UNREASONABLE" ACTUARY?

We had never met Jon Exley, but greatly looked forward to the occasion. The occasion turned out to be the first-ever Colloquium sponsored by the Rotman International Centre for Pension Management, University of Toronto, in October 2004, where we invited Exley to present his "unreasonable" views. He did so, based on an earlier paper presented to the U.K. Faculty of Actuaries Finance and Investments Conference titled "Pension Funds and the U.K. Economy." It is an intellectual tour de force not often associated with members of the actuarial profession. More importantly, it thoroughly trashes almost every piece of conventional wisdom that the global pension finance and investment industry has accumulated over the last 25 years.

This chapter tells the tale of Exley's trashing, and then proves the wisdom of Shaw's observation that there is indeed much to be learned from the "unreasonable man." Specifically, we show how Mr. Exley's nihilisms light up the path toward more productive pension schemes that can enhance economic welfare.

EXLEY'S FOUR IRRELEVANCE PROPOSITIONS

In the 1958 mother of all "irrelevance" propositions, Franco Modigliani and Merton Miller showed that the total value of a firm should not be affected by its capital structure. Similarly, Exley argues the value of pension debt is unaffected by whether it is secured by a portfolio of bonds or of shares. The impact of a pension fund's asset mix is on the riskiness of the securities issued by the pension plan sponsor. The more mismatching risk on the pension balance sheet, the riskier these sponsor securities become, and the higher the expected return that will be required for individual investors to hold them. This higher required return (i.e., higher cost of capital/lower security price) offsets any gain that might be earned on the pension balance sheet by undertaking mismatching risk. Therefore, asset mix is irrelevant.

Many observers see pension funds as natural long-horizon investors because pension liabilities typically have long durations. However, Exley argues that is the wrong focus. What matters are the horizons of the investors holding the securities of the pension scheme sponsors. It has already been noted that it is they who bear the pension plan balance-sheet mismatching risk. If the investment horizons of these investors are short, then so are the investment horizons of the pension funds they have indirectly invested in.

Can an equities rationale be developed for pension funds by arguing that equity returns "match" the liabilities of final-earnings pension schemes over the long run? Exley says "no" for two reasons. First, there is no statistical basis for the "match" assertion. Second, there is also no logical basis for prefunding possible future salary increases. Liability increases arising from salary increases should be funded in the year they occur, thus leaving it to new funding rather than investment policy to hedge these liability increases.

What about the impact of pension funding on economic activity argument? Again irrelevant, according to Exley. His argument here follows that of the irrelevance of asset allocation argument made earlier. Companies can retain their earnings, pay them out as dividends, or contribute them to their pension plans. Whatever they do, individuals determine their own life cycle consumption-savings plans. Whether they execute these plans by establishing their own retirement savings plans, or whether they do it by participating in employer-sponsored pension schemes is irrelevant.

SO WHAT IS RELEVANT?

Having slain some of the most sacred cows in pensiondom with his four irrelevance propositions, what does Exley think are relevant pension funding and investing considerations? He discusses six "second-order" considerations. Each of these considerations increases economic costs without offsetting benefits:

1. **Tax costs.** Certainly complicated, possibly irrelevant. However, to the degree that taxes on bond returns are higher than taxes on equity returns, bonds should generally be held inside tax-deferred vehicles and equities outside them.

2. **Agency monitoring costs.** Complex organizations are managed by agents, not the principals. This introduces agency costs, which are a drag on the economy and should be minimized. Higher financial leverage in companies reduces such costs. If mismatched pension schemes move the optimal amount of leverage downward, agency monitoring costs in the economy will increase.

3. **Signalling costs.** If insiders signal success or failure in a firm to outsiders through changes in dividend policy, a mismatched pension plan balance sheet could short-circuit this signalling process. A rising pension surplus could hide bad news in inefficient firms, while a rising pension deficit could hide good news in efficient firms.

4. **Specialization costs.** Modern organizations have specific core competencies. These should not be wasted on attempting to manage pension balance-sheet risks.

5. **Portfolio construction costs.** In building their own portfolios, individual investors want "pure plays." If companies have risky pension balance sheets, investors need to spend time understanding these additional risks, and will want to offset some of them in their own portfolios. Corporate employees face a related but different risk management challenge, as their jobs and pensions are linked to the default risk of the same firm.

6. **Direct pension fund management costs.** A typical pension fund pays 0.3 percent of assets per annum to a group of advisers and investment managers to trade portfolios of outstanding securities. Where is the economic value associated with these costs, when compared to the lower-cost alternative of simply matching accrued pension liabilities with a portfolio of default risk-free bonds?

And so Exley rests his case. Mismatching by pension funds adds significant costs to economic development through raising the cost of capital. Conversely, matching pension liabilities with assets with similar cash-flow characteristics would free the developed economies of a significant drag, reduce the costs of capital, and foster a higher rate of economic growth.

RESPONDING TO EXLEY

So what should we do with Exley and his "unreasonable" and inconvenient message? Get mad? Or simply dismiss him as misguided and irrelevant? We are reminded of the O'Barr and Conley experience. In their 1992 book *Fortune and Folly: The Wealth and Power of Institutional Investing* (New York: Irwin Professional) these two anthropologists thoroughly trashed the behavior of the professional pension fund management community of the day as pseudoscientific, culture bound, blame deflecting, and fawning in their relationships with outside service suppliers.

The pension industry's response to O'Barr and Conley was interesting. Initial anger quickly gave way to dismissal: "Who are these people anyway?" "What do they know about our business?" However, with the passage of time, there was also a more constructive response in which we had some personal involvement. A pension industry leadership summit built around the question "Pension Fund Excellence: What Is It?" drew many industry leaders to New York in December 1994. One eventual outcome was the 1998 book titled *Pension Fund Excellence: Creating Value for Stakeholders* by Ambachtsheer and Ezra (New York: John Wiley & Sons), which turned out to be a best seller in its day. We believe that Mr. Exley's "unreasonable" message deserves a similar constructive response.

RELEVANT PENSION FUNDS: BUILDING THE CASE

So how do we construct pension funds that are relevant rather than irrelevant? Funds that enhance economic welfare, rather than detract from it? We start with Exley's observation that the real issue here is about meeting the retirement income needs of real people in an economically efficient manner. It is not about protecting the status quo for today's institutions that attempt to do that.

This "real needs of real people" focus immediately raises three key questions:

1. What risks do individuals face as they attempt to articulate and meet their retirement income needs?
2. What potential barriers stand in the way of meeting these needs, and how might they be best overcome?
3. What are the macroeconomic consequences of the "correct" answers to questions one and two?

We show below that following these questions to their logical conclusions does indeed lead to pension arrangements that are both relevant to individuals and contribute positively to economic welfare.

MANAGING RETIREMENT INCOME RISKS

In addition to the fundamental question of lifetime earnings itself, individuals face two further uncertainties in articulating and meeting their retirement income needs. First, no one knows what the return on their retirement savings will be. Second, no one knows how long they are going to live.

How can we help the people who want to manage the risks of (a) an uncertain return on their retirement savings, and (b) possibly outliving these savings? The simple answer is: "By creating special-purpose financial institutions capable of pooling investment risks and mortality risks." Let us be clear that, at best, such institutions can only pool and manage these risks. They cannot eliminate them.

Are we not simply describing financial services firms with investment management and life annuity management capabilities? In a general sense, that is correct. In a more specific sense, that is not the whole story. There is another shoe to drop, and that other shoe is "informational asymmetry." The Nobel Prize for Economics this year went to three economists closely associated with the development of "the economics of information," and of the consequences of buyers and sellers of a good or service possessing unequal information about its attributes and/or quality. They show that in such situations, the party with the superior knowledge comes out on top, unless the other party is aware of the asymmetry and takes defensive steps to eliminate it.

Why are we very pleased with the choice of the Nobel Prize for Economics Committee this year? Because we have long held the view that "real-world" investment and annuity management markets have serious informational asymmetry problems. When these asymmetry problems combine with the joint duties of the leadership of "for-profit" investment and annuity management firms to their customers on one hand, and to their owners on the other, a fundamental conflict arises. Research strongly supports the notion that it is very difficult for the leadership not to use their informational edge to increase profitability for the firm's owners, at the expense of the customers. The result is that most customers of for-profit investment and annuity management firms end up paying too much for too little.

LEVELING THE INFORMATIONAL PLAYING FIELD

Regulators have toiled mightily over the years to level the informational playing field between the buyers and sellers of investment and annuity management services, with only limited success. Fortunately, a far more powerful weapon is at hand. It is institutions that will use any informational asymmetries to be found in the financial markets to the benefit of the customers rather than the owners. There is, of course, only one way that this can happen. The customers and the owners of such institutions must be the same people.

With the exception of Jack Bogle's investment fund Vanguard Group in the United States, the only "live" example of this kind of institution is pension schemes dedicated to serve the investment and life annuity risk-pooling needs of prespecified groups of private- and public-sector employees. This is not to say that all such existing institutions are perfect. Indeed, many suffer from the afflictions Exley has so painfully laid out for us. The point is that the idea is right, even if its execution leaves something to be desired.

GETTING THE EXECUTION OF THE IDEA RIGHT

So how do we get the execution of the idea right? As part of our review of the Myners Review this past summer, we proposed an eight-point "legitimacy" test for pension schemes. That test addresses the key issues Exley raises, including the question of who bears the scheme's balance-sheet risks. Logically, there are only three choices: wholly by the employer, jointly by the employer and the employees, or wholly by the employees. Exley finds the first of these three choices problematic. He may well be right.

Regardless of how the risk-bearing question is sorted out, research shows that we have learned how to create "best-practice" investment organizations capable of generating superior investment results within predetermined risk budgets in a transparent manner. Such organizations have the proper scale and scope, have effective governance and executive structures, and have properly aligned the economic interests of the pension fund executive, and those of the pension balance-sheet stakeholders. As a bonus, they will do this for half of the 0.3 percent of direct assets–related operating costs cited by Exley. By contrast, individuals trying to assemble these services through the for-profit sector often pay 1 to 2 percent of assets or even more for the privilege.

One final thing: The kind of institutions we describe will make excellent long-term investors. They will hold the managements of investee corporations accountable for results in ways that individual share "punters" have not even dreamed of. Thus, these institutions will not only serve their own stakeholders well, they will in the process also reduce (rather than increase) many of the "second-order" costs cited by Exley. Thus, rather than being irrelevant or worse, such pension arrangements in fact represent the next stage in the evolution of democratic capitalism. All that is left for us to do is to build them.

CHAPTER 2

The Pension Revolution — Are You a Believer Yet?

"When you possess great treasures within you, and try to tell others about them, you are seldom believed."
Paulo Coelho, in the *The Alchemist*

"There is a body of work emerging that questions the generation-old assumptions that underlie modern investment theory.... Keith Ambachtsheer observes that the perceived 'truth' of the CAPM is based on three so-called 'proofs,' but, he asks rhetorically, 'What is wrong with these three proofs? In short, everything.'"
From the May 2003 Editorial in *PLANSPONSOR* magazine

"As Keith Ambachtsheer has said, investment management is becoming a risk management business. Out-performance in relative returns is no salve when traditional strategies' absolute returns are negative, as they have been since 2000..."
From the May 26, 2003 Editorial in *Pensions & Investments*

"Many of the worst errors in investment management can be traced to an industry-wide focus on maverick risk. Most of us work as agents, not principals... making it more acceptable to fail conventionally, than to succeed unconventionally. Keith Ambachtsheer, using the CEM database, reports that the typical U.S. pension fund carries six times as much policy risk as active management risk relative to its liabilities. Apart from the perils of maverick risk, there is no business justification for this...."
From the May/June 2003 Editorial in the *Financial Analysts Journal*

A REVOLUTIONARY REORDERING OF THE PENSIONS FIRMAMENT

Professional truth-sayers can identify with Paulo Coelho's observation that their seeds of truth seem to fall largely on barren ground. It is the nature of the business. This makes concurrent citations of one's "truth-saying" work in the editorials of three major industry publications a rare "3-sigma" event. In this chapter, we explore the meaning of this highly unusual occurrence. More importantly, we integrate the "truths" of the three editorial messages into a larger whole, which adds up to nothing less than a revolutionary reordering of the pensions firmament. Are you a believer yet? Read on.

Why is such a revolutionary reordering called for? For three reasons:

1. Many "pension deals" as currently defined (though often not clearly) are unsustainable.
2. The "business models" that guide the management of most pension plans are built on conceptual quicksand.
3. The governance and organization design structures that implement most "pension deals" are ineffective, if not downright dysfunctional.

We elaborate below.

FROM FUZZY PENSION DEALS TO "RISK-SHARING CO-OPS"

Though often not fully aware of it, people attempt to create income streams that maximize personal or family "utility" over their full life spans. This involves the accumulation of intellectual capital (i.e., education) first and financial capital later. For many, this financial capital involves a "portfolio" of future income streams from a social security scheme, from a workplace pension plan, and from individual savings. Thus, when we speak of a "pension deal," we mean the "contract" (whether implicit or explicit) between employers and employees that sets out the nature of the workplace pension plan.

A fully transparent "pension deal" would state a target income replace-ment rate the plan is expected to produce, and the expected cost required to produce it. As importantly, it would also describe the uncertainties that lie behind the expectations, and how (and by whom) those uncertainties are to be borne. All this is quite clear in pure defined contribution (DC) "deals." Plan participants are the risk bearers in these arrangements (although some argue that DC plan participants own an implicit "put option" on the employer for a minimum pension if the amount of capital accumulated at retirement is deemed insufficient).

In theory, all this is equally clear in pure defined benefit (DB) plans. Now the employer is the risk bearer, with the employees 100 percent certain to receive a predefined target pension that is fully inflation indexed over the remaining life of the employee. In practice, things are hardly ever this clear. While employers do indeed shoulder "additional contributions risk" in DB plans, employees are usually risk bearers, too. The employer may go broke or choose to discontinue the plan. Poor vesting and portability arrangements may disenfranchise all but long-term employees. Employees may also be subject to "additional contributions risk"—if not directly, then indirectly through "total compensation risk" (i.e., the employer offsets larger pension contributions with smaller wage increases). Finally, most DB "deals" saddle employees rather than the employer with the bulk of postretirement inflation risk.

Thus, in practice, DB plans are in fact risk-sharing arrangements between the employer and the employees. Unfortunately, this reality is seldom made explicit in the articulation of the "pension deal." Instead, plan text language typically fosters the fiction that DB plans are risk-free, at least from the employees' perspective. This "risk-free" fiction is a highly unstable foundation on which to build sustainable DB pension arrangements. It is an important source of the critical flaws in how DB plans are managed and regulated.

Examples of these flaws include incomplete and potentially misleading plan communications with stakeholders, faulty risk management and measurement practices inside DB plans, and pension regulations that assume DB plans are quasi-captive insurance companies, that can be quasi-regulated with a series of ad hoc rules of thumb. The net result of the fuzziness in most DB pension "deals" is that they are unsustainable in their current form. They must be recast into the only legal and operational structure that has any hope of providing long-term DB plan sustainability: the "risk-sharing co-op" model that we will describe in this book.

TOWARD PENSION "BUSINESS MODELS" THAT WORK: THE RISK ISSUE

Sustainable DB pension "business models" are capable of defining, monitoring, and dynamically managing stakeholder risk exposures over time. We noted above that most "real-world" DB plans are still incapable of doing this. Why? For four reasons:

1. Pension deals are still not fully defined in terms of either types of risk exposures embedded in the "deal" or which stakeholder groups bear them.
2. Balance-sheet risk exposures are still not monitored regularly through time. Instead, true economic exposures continue to be obfuscated by arcane accounting and actuarial rules and practices.
3. Optimistic equity risk premium projections continue to lead to happy outcomes for all "in the long run." So why worry about risk in the shorter run?
4. Nobody else is defining, monitoring, and managing DB plan risk exposures, so why should we?

However, change may finally be in the air. It is one thing to be fighting about the ownership of surpluses (i.e., the situation in the 1990s); it is quite another to allocate the "ownership" of the gaping holes that have appeared on most pension balance sheets in the past three years. Deficits raise far more pressing questions than surpluses.

At the same time, the analytical framework provided by financial economics (including its behavioral finance and contingent claims valuation branches) is beginning to offer far more powerful, transparent tools to measure and allocate embedded DB plan risks than the seriously flawed historical offerings of the accounting and actuarial professions. Also, DB plan "best management practices" are actually beginning to reflect the reality of the risk-sharing co-op model, and are beginning to adopt the new risk monitoring and management tools offered by financial economics. Thus, the "maverick risk" associated with doing "the right thing" is beginning to decrease.

TOWARD PENSION "BUSINESS MODELS" THAT WORK: THE SCALE ISSUE

In addition to a capability to define, monitor, and manage embedded risks, another "sine qua non" characteristic of pension plan sustainability is scale. Simply put, without significant scale economies, pension plans cannot deliver "value for dollars" to its stakeholders. Why? For two related reasons:

1. The unit costs of the plan's investment and pension administration "businesses" will be too high to be "competitive."
2. The plan cannot afford to assemble the necessary nucleus of internal expertise to effectively manage the investment and pension administration "businesses." Such internal expertise is needed even in cases in

which operational investment and administration outsourcing strategies are employed.

Despite these realities, there are still far too many pension plans in existence today that are far too small to ever create "value for dollars" for their stakeholders. This is a serious problem that should be correctable through good governance practices. Specifically, good governance practices would recognize that the plan is uneconomic and either merge it with a larger plan or outsource the entire management of the plan to a "value for dollars" provider. Unfortunately, good governance practices continue to be in short supply in the pension "industry."

THE PENSION GOVERNANCE ISSUE

It has been over a decade since anthropologists O'Barr and Conley published their infamous book *Fortune and Folly,* which pronounced the governance of major U.S. pension funds culture-bound, fawning, blame deflecting, and generally ineffective. Unfortunately, despite some notable exceptions, we hold the view that not very much has changed in the past 10 years. Using more polite language, this is how we would characterize the pension governance scene today:

- Too many people continue to be appointed to pension governance positions not for the skills and experience they bring to the governance body, but for the interests they represent (e.g., the union, the employer, the pensioners, the state governor, their own).
- The result is too many boards that still do not understand their role in the management of the pension plan. A classic example of this is the recent public debate in *Pensions and Investments* (P&I) between Gary Findlay (executive director, Missouri State Employees' Retirement System [MOSERS]) and Matthew Potter (chairman, board of trustees, Wyoming Retirement System), where Potter argues that it is the board of trustees that should hire and fire external investment managers. Unfortunately, the breathtaking lack of understanding of the meaning of good governance displayed by Potter in his arguments is by no means unique. His view continues to be the majority view.
- The corporate variant for this misplaced pension governance focus is the management pension committee, usually chaired by the chief financial officer (CFO) or treasurer. Now the primary issue often becomes how changes in investment policy play out on the financial statements. For example, many CFOs refused to reduce their pension balance-sheet risk exposure over the course of the past few years because such

a decision would also require lowering their ROA (return on pension assets) assumption, which, under Financial Accounting Standards Board Statement 87, would negatively impact earnings per share. This is "fiduciary" thinking?

The result of these poor governance practices is that while their pension balance-sheet stakeholders have been burning, most pension governance bodies have been fiddling with operational and accounting details. The sad thing is that poor governance usually begets more poor governance. Thus, ironically in such situations, only utter disaster will ultimately lead to change for the better.

TWO ROLE MODELS

All this is not to say that there is no innovation in the pensions world. There is. Two good examples with which we have had recent personal involvement are the Dutch health care–sector pension fund PGGM, and the Australian collective corporate-sector pension fund for the state of Queensland, SunSuper.

PGGM

PGGM has initiated a balance-sheet "fair value" research project that aims to not only measure total balance-sheet risk over time using a contingent claims valuation framework, but to also allocate that risk among its various stakeholder groups. So, for example, it estimates its current balance sheet to be 32 billion euros in deficit on a fully indexed, marked-to-market basis if only "normal" contributions are made over the next 40 years. With a balanced asset mix policy, the 32 billion euro deficit becomes a 36 billion euro put option (the cost of insurance against future deficits) partially offset by a 4 billion euro call option (the present value of possible future surpluses). If this 36 billion euro deficit risk is to be insured internally, dynamic contribution rate and conditional inflation indexation regimes will have to be introduced to reduce the 36 billion euro put option value to zero. One possible solution increased contributions by 25 billion euros and reduced the pension liability by 18 billion euros. The light at the end of the tunnel was an 8 billion euro increase in the value of the call option representing the present value of possible future surpluses. How should the ownership to this 8 billion euro option value increase be allocated among various plan stakeholders? Logically, in proportion to the contribution they made to extinguishing the 36 billion euro put option representing the cost of insurance against future deficits. This kind of arithmetic will become essential in the sustainable management of DB pension plans structured as risk-sharing co-ops.

SunSuper

SunSuper demonstrates what can be done when the private-sector employers of a particular geographic area band together to create their own DC plan "co-op." This banding together creates scale measured in the hundreds of thousand of participants. Because it is a co-op, the interests of the plan's owners, its board, its management team, and its participants are naturally aligned. The plan has a board of trustees that clearly understands its governance responsibilities. Thus, it has empowered a carefully selected chief executive officer (CEO) to present a strategic plan for their approval, and to implement it. This currently involves an investment and participant education program built around three investment options (low, medium, and higher risk), each carefully optimized and rebalanced over time. Individual investment mandates, as well as most administrative functions, are outsourced to "value for dollars" providers. However, it is the internal executive "brain trust" that calls the operational shots. The SunSuper model is the answer to the thousands of underscaled, undermanaged plans that continue to litter the global pension landscape.

GREAT TREASURES?

We started this chapter by sympathizing with Paulo Coelho's observation that those who share with others the great treasures within them are seldom believed. The treasures we share here add up to nothing less than a revolutionary reordering of the pensions firmament. Do you believe it?

CHAPTER 3

After the Perfect Pension Storm: What Now?

"Friends who set forth at our side,
Falter, are lost in the storm,
We, we only, are left!"

Excerpt from *Rugby Chapel*, Matthew Arnold

FROM VEGAS TO OXFORD: IN SEARCH OF ANSWERS

A recent odyssey took us to the lights of Las Vegas, the beaches of Santa Monica and then those of Zuid-Holland, a meeting room at Schiphol, and, finally, the ancient splendors of Oxford University. While the locations could not have been more different, there was a common discussion theme. It was the perfect pension storm of March 2000 to March 2003 and its possible consequences.

You do remember the perfect pension storm, don't you? It was the three-year period that took the mark-to-market funded ratios of defined benefit (DB) pension plans around the world down by 25 to 50 percentage points, depending on the plan's characteristics, location, and investment policy. How did this happen? Through extended, parallel declines in equity prices and bond yields. The former action depressed asset values; the latter pushed up the present value of future pension promises. Nor did this painful double whammy create havoc only in DB pension plans. While maybe less visible, the parallel drop in equity values and bond yields also hurt the financial condition of defined contribution (DC) plans and endowment funds. Why? Because while asset values were falling, the cost of buying risk-free future cash flows was going up.

Recently rising equity values and bond yields have reversed some of the financial damage caused by the perfect pension storm. Thus, the financial markets have provided fund fiduciaries with some breathing room. So what to do now? Breathe a sigh of relief and carry on as before? Or is this a window of opportunity through which to ask some fundamental questions about pension "deals," about pension delivery mechanisms, and about national pension policies? These are the questions this chapter addresses.

DO NOTHING OR SOMETHING?

Let's deal with the easy question first. Do fiduciaries just celebrate that their pension plan survived the perfect storm and carry on as before? They could, but they should be aware that if they carry on as before, they face two possible outcomes: Either things really will be okay, or the plan may falter and be lost in the next pension storm. If the latter outcome unfolds, fiduciaries may be postponing decisions on issues that are better assessed and dealt with now, rather than later. Thus, the "do nothing" strategy carries significant risk with it. Indeed, the current calm offers fiduciaries an excellent opportunity to at least pose some fundamental questions about their pension arrangements and delivery mechanisms.

There are two fundamentally different contexts in which such questioning could take place:

1. **The corporate pension context.** Many corporations have long histories of sponsoring one or more pension plans for their employees. We have noted in other chapters that with the passage of time, neither the pension "deals" nor the mechanisms through which they are delivered have kept up with changing circumstances. Specifically, pension "deals" have become riskier for both plan members and shareholders over time as the size of these plans has grown in relation to the rest of the corporation's balance sheet and other operations. At the same time, the ability to respond to adverse financial developments has decreased in many cases, and there has been little or no evolution in the way the increasing pension-related risk exposures have been measured and managed. Meanwhile, new pension accounting rules will likely soon make these economic realities far more transparent to investors than they were in the past.

2. **The industry/public-sector pension context.** An important difference here is that there is usually now an organization structure that looks at both plan assets and liabilities in a more or less integrated manner. While pension promises here are not subject to the same kind of default risk that can exist in a corporate context, there are still some important

risk-related issues to be addressed. For example, how do asset shortfalls get resolved? Through higher contributions? If so, who pays? Through lower benefits? If so, by what formula? How much balance sheet mismatch risk should be taken? Who decides? Clear answers to these questions have often been hard to come by. This is especially so in cases where there is an organizational separation between asset management and the management of the rest of the pension plan.

We examine each of the two contexts in turn, identifying choices that should be made, and issues that should be addressed.

THE CORPORATE CONTEXT: TWO BASIC CHOICES

The perfect pension storm had at least one positive effect. It moved pension issues onto the radar screens of many corporate boards and chief executive officers (CEOs). Those corporations that are not prepared to carry on with their DB pension plans on a "business as usual" basis have two choices:

1. **Keep the DB plan,** but explicitly manage it as a financial subsidiary of the corporation. Such a move would have three positive consequences: (1) a decision to gear maximum pension mismatch risk exposure to overall corporate sustainability and willingness to bear this kind of risk, (2) the establishment of a minimum acceptable cost of risk capital target for DB balance-sheet management consistent with corporate return on equity (ROE) requirements, and (3) the creation of an organizational structure capable of dynamically managing the DB balance sheet in this integrated "new paradigm" reward/risk framework.
2. **Close the DB plan.** This raises two further questions. First, should the accrued liabilities be immunized, or should mismatch risk be permitted on the closed DB balance sheet? In the latter case, the same financial subsidiary issues arise as described in option 1 above. The second question relates to whether new pension-related benefits are to accrue under an existing or new DC or DB/DC hybrid arrangement. This latter question in turn raises further important questions about how any new corporate pension arrangement should be governed and managed.

So keep the DB plan or close it? Which is the better choice? We doubt that the same answer is right for all corporations. However, there are still some things we can say with conviction. Under either choice, the DB balance sheet should be either immunized or dynamically managed under "new paradigm" principles. In the latter case, the new business model should incorporate an explicit maximum balance sheet risk budget and an explicit minimum cost of capital target. Further, someone must be held accountable for dynamically managing this integrative process over time.

NEW DC PLAN "BUSINESS MODEL" ALSO NEEDED

What about managing DC pension plans? What can we say about that? Other chapters in this book (see Part Two) make it clear that we are not happy with the way most DC pension plans are being managed, especially in North America. Too many choices at too high cost with too little oversight that has the best interests of plan participants foremost in mind. These are the characteristics of the typical "supplier-driven DC business model." This model currently prevails, and will continue to prevail unless we consciously think through what a "participant-driven DC business model" would look like. We suggest that this latter model would offer few investment choices at low cost with skilled oversight that works in the best interest of participants. As importantly, it would also offer an annuitization option for those participants who want to start buying future lifelong cash flows now.

Why are there so few participant-driven DC business models in action in North America and the United Kingdom? Because there is no profit incentive to create such models. Take the Teachers Insurance and Annuity Association–College Retirement Equities Fund (TIAA-CREF), for example. It was created by the Carnegie Foundation in 1918. Take Commonfund, TIAA-CREF's equivalent in the endowment world, for example. It was created in 1971 through a grant from The Ford Foundation. There are also a few employers who have consciously created exemplary DC structures for their employees. However, these are still anomalies in a sea of supplier-driven DC and endowment fund structures in North America. Is there some way to bridge the supplier-driven versus participant-driven gap in North America and the United Kingdom? This is a major public policy issue not on any public policy screens today that we know of. It should be.

THE INDUSTRY/PUBLIC-SECTOR PENSION CONTEXT

Just as the perfect pension storm played an important educational role in the corporate sector, it also did so in the industry-wide/public sector. The material financial deterioration of DB balance sheets in this sector is forcing fiduciaries to consider important questions that had never been fully addressed. We have characterized these questions in other chapters as "pension deal" issues (see Part Two). For example, what kind of risks are embedded in any given "pension deal"? How are these risks shared among various stakeholder groups? As these stakeholder groups should include future generations of plan members and taxpayers, how are their pension deal interests represented?

Such pension deal questions in turn raise important operational questions. How can the embedded risks in a pension deal be quantified? What impact do investment policy choices have on the magnitudes of these risks? What is the best way to integrate risk management with reaching out for higher returns? What role should "investment beliefs" play in all this? Whose investment beliefs? How do all these elements get translated into a viable strategic plan for the pension fund? Again, these kinds of questions move pension fiduciaries irrevocably toward "new paradigm" territory.

Addressing so many profound questions all at once can seem an overwhelming task. So where to start? Is there a logical first question with which to begin the journey toward adopting a new paradigm business model for industry-wide/public-sector pension plans? We think there is.

THE "FAIR VALUE" QUESTION

All of the questions posed above lead to possible new destinations. However, arriving at any new (and presumably better) destination requires knowing where you are today. Shockingly, this is not the case in many industry-wide/public-sector pension plans. One of the meetings we attended in our recent "perfect storm" odyssey focused on the current poor funded status of many DB balance sheets. A member of the board of trustees of a municipal pension plan stood up and proudly announced that they had solved their funded status problem. How? By discounting their accrued pension promises at 8 percent. Indeed, he proudly announced, with an 8 percent discount rate, their balance sheet was not in deficit at all. They have a nice surplus!

Admittedly, most fiduciaries know better than to get up in a public forum and share this kind of "information." Still, there is a broad perception that taking on balance-sheet mismatch risk somehow lowers pension liabilities. Why does this perception exist? Not because it is true (indeed, the "law of one price" says it is fundamentally untrue), but because it is useful. How is it useful? Because it hides bad news about the true financial status of the DB balance sheet by understating pension liabilities. And why is this a bad thing? For two reasons—one obvious, the other more subtle.

The obvious reason that using a return assumption with a risk premium embedded in it to value pension promises is a bad thing is that it understates the true cost (value) of issuing these promises (i.e., it makes something that is really worth \$1 apparently available for 80 cents). The more subtle reason is that it is not clear who in fact bears the burden of the difference between the apparent cost of the pension promise (80 cents) and its true cost (\$1). Why?

Because the difference between the apparent cost and the true cost reflects an embedded "put" option held by the current generation of plan members and taxpayers on the next generation. Specifically, if taking on investment risk works out, the current generation gets its $1 pensions for 80 cents, and the next generation is in a position to do the same thing. However, if taking on investment risk does not work out, the current generation will still insist on drawing its $1 pension down the road, and try to "put" to the next generation the bill for the financial shortfall.

The point is this: We can't run fair pension plans without a transparent "fair value" framework for disclosure. This fundamental reality continues to be lost on not just members of industry-wide/public-sector DB plans, but also on 99 percent of the people responsible for governing, managing, and valuing these plans. The reality is that serious change in this sector is impossible without a broad-based move toward a "fair-value" framework for financial disclosure.

BETTER PUBLIC PENSIONS POLICY

It would be nice to conclude by observing that governments understand the importance of reforming the rules governing employment-based (i.e., Pillar 2) pension plans, and that they are playing a positive role in bringing it about. For example, governments could be actively facilitating the creation of what we called *participant-driven DC business models*. They could be actively facilitating the introduction of a "fair value" disclosure framework for DB plans. Unfortunately, we see little evidence that this is the case. Indeed, as large employers themselves, governments are often part of the problem, rather than part of the solution.

So where are the political champions of genuine Pillar 2 pension reform? The search continues.

CHAPTER 4

Beyond Portfolio Theory:
The Next Frontier

"...investment managers and advisors have a much richer set of tools available to them than they traditionally use with clients.... I see this as a tough engineering problem, not one of new science..."

Professor Robert Merton, Harvard University

"One of the most interesting challenges of the 21st century will be the development of systems to help investors carry out the task of strategic asset allocation..."

Professors John Campbell and Luis Viceira,
Harvard University

INVESTMENT THEORY'S NEXT FRONTIER:
THE ACADEMIC VIEW

Notwithstanding the origin of the two kickoff quotes above, this chapter will not offer a survey of the current Harvard University thoughts on investment theory and its implementation. Instead, we offer these quotes as examples of a widely held view by the finance and investment academic community at large as to where investment theory's next frontier lies. The key words in the two quotes are *engineering* in the one case, and *systems* in the other. They reflect a perception that today's challenge lies in figuring out how to place the incredibly powerful tool kit of financial decision-making processes and products invented by the academic community over the course of the past 50 years in the hands of individuals and their advisers.

The academic community can be justifiably proud of its intellectual achievements since the 1952 publication of Harry Markowitz's Nobel Prize–winning treatise on portfolio selection. The Merton quote comes from his recent award-winning "Perspectives" piece in the *Financial Analysts Journal* ("Thoughts on the Future: Theory and Practice in Investment Management," Jan–Feb 2003). Campbell and Viceira's comes from their 2002 award-winning book *Strategic Asset Allocation: Portfolio Choice for Long-Term Investors*" (Oxford: Oxford University Press). Both offerings focus on the implications of important recent advances in investment theory and research findings.

For example:

- Most investment contexts require the consideration of multiple horizons rather than just a single horizon. In some cases, short-horizon considerations dominate, in others, the primary focus should be on assessing long-horizon outcomes.
- Prospective future cash flows (and their purchasing power) typically offer a more useful perspective for assessing the reward and risk of long-horizon investment strategies than future wealth prospects. This makes long inflation-linked bonds the natural reference portfolio for assessing the reward and risk of alternative investment strategies in most cases.
- For individuals, investment-related rewards and risks should be integrated with other considerations such as human capital–related rewards and risks, longevity/mortality, real property, and education. Corporations also need to adapt this broader integrative approach to managing investment-related reward and risk (e.g., in their pension funds). The same is true for endowments and foundations.
- Long-horizon equity and bond return prospects have time-variant, predictive components. This makes strategic asset allocation a dynamic rather than a static process.

There can be little argument that these four extensions of "old" portfolio theory represent major advances in investment theory, broadly defined. However, does that reality logically make the "engineering" of "systems" to incorporate these extensions into actual practice the next frontier for investment theory and its implementation?

INVESTMENT THEORY'S NEXT FRONTIER: TWO FURTHER CONSIDERATIONS

We believe there are two other (related) factors to be considered before we settle on what investment theory's next frontier really is. They are:

1. **Information theory** asks whether economic actors (e.g., buyers and sellers of investment-related services) are in equivalent positions from an information perspective as they make decisions. It also addresses the economic consequences of informational asymmetry.
2. **Principal-agent theory** asks whether the economic interests of principals (e.g., individuals) and agents making decisions on their behalf (e.g., investment managers) are aligned. It also addresses the economic consequences of misalignment.

Both of these factors have rich academic histories of their own. For example, 2001 Nobel Prize winner George Akerlof's classic "The Market for Lemons" goes back 30 years. The article asks why the prices of new cars plummet once their owners drive them off the lot. Ackerlof's answer is informational asymmetry between the owner of the (now used) car and any future buyer. The sellers of used cars know whether their cars are lemons. The buyers do not. Used car pricing reflects this reality.

What about the market for investment management services? This too is a market where the sellers typically know more about what they are selling than the buyers know about what they are buying. Using John Maynard Keynes's famous 1936 "beauty contest" analogy, the sellers' challenge is to persuade buyers that they are better than their competitors at forecasting which securities the participants in securities markets will find beautiful tomorrow. The buyers' challenge is to figure out whose claims to believe (a practically impossible challenge for nonexperts!). In such a market, it is not pricing (i.e., fee structures) that determines market share. Instead, it is the persuasiveness of a seller's message.

The acute informational asymmetry characteristics of the financial services marketplace lead logically to principal-agent considerations. The classic treatise here is "The Modern Corporation and Private Property" by Adolf Berle and Gardiner Means in 1932. They examine the implications of the separation of corporate ownership and control at a time when the "robber baron" era of capitalism personified by Carnegie, Ford, Morgan, and Rockefeller had clearly come to an end. In a world where owners are millions of remote, faceless shareholders rather than powerful individual owner-managers, Berle and Means asked: Would boards and managements continue to serve the financial interests of shareholders? Or would they use their power to serve their own interests?

There is a clear parallel to these questions in the financial services arena today. Now we ask: "In a world where the beneficiaries of various types of financial services organizations (e.g., pension funds, mutual funds, endowment funds) are millions of remote, faceless individuals, will the boards and managements of these organizations serve the financial interests of these beneficiaries? Or will they use their power to serve their own interests?

THE NEXT FRONTIER: "INTEGRATIVE INVESTMENT THEORY"

So, yes, "old" portfolio theory should be extended to incorporate the cornucopia of conceptual and empirical jewels the academic finance and investment community has bestowed on us over the course of the past 50 years. But that is not enough. We need more than just the "reengineering" of investment decision "systems." We must also integrate the profound issues raised by the highly asymmetric distribution of information that exists in the financial services marketplace, and by the fact that millions of ultimate beneficiaries at the bottom of the financial food chain depend on a mosaic of intermediary "agent" organizations to provide products and services that truly serve their financial interests.

What would an investment theory that integrated "old" portfolio theory with not only the post-1952 technical offerings of academia, but also the highly relevant economic concepts of "asymmetric information" and "principal-agent theory" look like? It would recognize that beneficiary value creation is a function of the successful integration of five value drivers. In Figure 4.1, these drivers are designated as A, G, R, IB, and FE:

1. **Agency issues** (A). Agency issues can hinder beneficiary value creation in a number of ways. In one way or another, all these ways lead

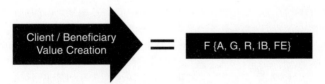

FIGURE 4.1 Integrative Investment Theory from Better Theory to Better Outcomes

to beneficiaries' being financially disadvantaged by agents working on their behalf. Thinking through what can be done to minimize agency problems can pay large dividends for the clients/beneficiaries of financial services organizations.

2. **Governance** (G). Good organizational governance goes beyond simply aligning the economic interests of a financial services organization's clients/beneficiaries and its management. It also sets the context for the organization's mission, delegates planning and implementation to a competent executive team, and regularly monitors progress toward mission achievement.

3. **Risk issues** (R). "Old" portfolio theory dealt with investment risk and risk tolerance in a creative but very limited way. We noted that academia has moved the yardsticks of relevant, practical risk definitions and measurement considerably since the early days. As importantly, the governors of pension and endowment funds must insist that specific risk definitions and risk management are relevant to the context of their clients/beneficiaries.

4. **Investment beliefs** (IB). The degree to which an investment organization believes prospective return components to be predictable over multiple horizons should be an important determinant of how its investment processes are structured.

5. **Financial engineering** (FE). Integrating properly specified client/beneficiary risk tolerances with time-varying return expectations in a noisy, complex investment arena full of fees and transaction costs is no mean task. Here is where well-engineered, integrative investment systems can add significant value.

Will a better investment theory produce better outcomes for the clients/beneficiaries of financial services organizations? We have no doubt that it would. For example:

1. **Agency issues.** In our judgment, the premier agency issue in the financial services industry today is the inherent conflict that results from "for-profit" organizations providing management services to millions of mutual fund investors. The combined forces of acute informational asymmetry and pronounced principal-agent problems logically lead to many clients paying too much for too little. This is a major public policy issue that is not being addressed in the fundamental manner it deserves. Variants on this same broad theme can play out when "for-profit" organizations sponsor defined benefit (DB) or defined contribution (DC) pension plans. Why? Because in such situations it becomes impossible to sort out whose financial interests should be

maximized. "Not-for-profit" co-ops with the necessary scale and scope offer the best hope of addressing "the too little value at too high a cost" outcomes that combinations of informational asymmetry and economic interest nonalignment lead to.

2. **Governance.** Addressing agency issues is a necessary but not sufficient condition for enhancing client/beneficiary value creation. There is no guarantee that a "not-for-profit" co-op will be well managed. Just as there is a body of thought that constitutes financial theory today, so is there a body of thought that constitutes governance and organization design theory. Our 1998 article (with Ronald Capelle and Tom Scheibelhut), "Improving Pension Fund Performance (*Financial Analysts Journal*, Vol. 54, No. 6), showed that pension funds with strong governance and organization design characteristics outperformed those with poor characteristics by statistically significant magnitudes. Yet even today, governance and organization design issues receive only sporadic attention in organizations active in the financial services arena.

3. **Risk issues.** Academia has played a major role in extending the conceptual framework in which we can frame and discuss risk-related issues. The challenge now is to move these new risk concepts into practice. For example, DB pension plans represent a complex web of contingent claims that various stakeholder groups have "issued" to/on each other. Yet, there is no hint of this reality in either the articulation of stakeholder risk tolerances, or in how DB balance sheet assets and liabilities are valued or disclosed.

4. **Investment beliefs.** If the expected equity risk premium is always equal to its historical 5 percent realization, "investing" for most pension and endowment funds boils down to taking on lots of equity market exposure to generate return, and some bond market exposure to create a modest risk buffer. Attempting to produce a bit of net alpha by taking on a bit of additional risk becomes a justifiable sideshow. This simple investment paradigm becomes dysfunctional if the expected equity risk premium in fact varies materially over time in a predictable manner. What is *your* belief? Similarly, what are your beliefs about what is predictable within the securities markets? Answers to these questions should materially impact how investment processes are structured.

5. **Financial engineering.** The array of investment tools in the implementation tool kit continues to grow faster than institutions can devise ways to use them. For example, it takes a 626-page book for Bob Litterman and Goldman Sachs Asset Management (GSAM) colleagues to describe the tools in their current kit (*Modern Investment Management*, Hoboken, NJ: John Wiley & Sons, 2003). Selecting the right tools out of the tool kit requires context, and that is where the prior, effective

integration of risk issues and investment beliefs is essential. But such effective integration in turns requires organizations that have mission clarity and good governance. The integrative investment theory (IIT) circle is complete.

Despite its logic, IIT will not change the world tomorrow. After all, it took "old" portfolio theory 20 years to get traction. Yet, the advent of IIT is inevitable. Why? Because it produces better financial outcomes for millions of "ordinary" people. They will not be denied.

CHAPTER 5

The United Airlines Case: Tipping Point for U.S. Pension System?

"The company's investment strategy emphasizes diversification among asset classes, among investment strategies, and among investment managers..."

Rich Nelson, UAL
As quoted in the *New York Times*, August 13, 2004

THE UNITED AIRLINES CASE

The unfolding United Airlines (UAL) pensions story is rapidly becoming a cause celebre for the U.S. workplace pensions system. In this chapter, we suggest the case has the makings of a "tipping point"—that marginal element in a heretofore apparently steady-state system that tips the balance toward disequilibrium and material change. Why? Because the UAL story is ruthlessly unmasking the fiction that the mere existence of the Employee Retirement Income Security Act of 1974 (ERISA) automatically aligns the financial interests of such disparate stakeholder groups in corporate defined benefit (DB) plans as retirees, active employees, shareholders, corporate management, and the Pension Benefit Guaranty Corporation (PBGC). The case is laying bare for all to see the reality that the financial interests of these stakeholder groups are in fact potentially conflicting. It is also painting a clear picture of the conditions required to turn potential conflict into actual pitched battle. What are we to make of all this from a strategic perspective? What are the strategic lessons to be learned from the UAL case, and what actions do they imply? Those are the questions this part of the book addresses.

The key elements of the UAL case can be summarized:

- UAL has been operating under chapter 11 since December 2002.
- The company's four pension plans have assets of about $7 billion and liabilities of $13 billion. These plans have been exposed to material asset-liability mismatch risk over time, and (as far as we know) continue to have this risk exposure.
- UAL management has negotiated business continuity financing on the condition that it makes no further contributions to its pension plans.
- The UAL board of directors has eliminated the pension management committee and has named the company as sole fiduciary.
- UAL unions have sued the corporation's top three officers for breach of fiduciary duties. Management in turn is seeking an injunction to stop these "baseless" suits.
- The PBGC has taken UAL to court over nonpayment of pension contributions.
- The U.S. Department of Labor has intervened, and announced that the company has agreed to the appointment of an independent fiduciary to represent the interests of 120,000 employees and retirees who are pension plan members.

No wonder the case has caught the media's attention. It has all the makings of a Greek tragedy, with the question of who lives and who dies still unresolved. But what does it all mean from a strategic perspective? That is what the *New York Times* article cited above tried to get at by asking a very specific question about UAL's investment policy for its pension funds.

A GOOD QUESTION AND TWO VERY DIFFERENT ANSWERS

The *New York Times* article first observed that the investment policy for UAL's $7 billion of pension assets seemed to be no different from that of other corporate pension funds: about 60 percent in stocks, 10 percent in alternatives, and 30 percent in bonds. Then the writer's very specific question was this: "Given its obviously precarious financial condition, why did UAL choose to continue to invest its $7 billion of pension assets in a manner that created material mismatch risk against its accrued pension promises?"

We quoted from UAL's specific response in the epigraph of this chapter. The company argued that its pension funds followed a prudent investment policy that was diversified by asset classes, investment styles, and investment managers. Further, the company said, its pension assets were invested for the long run. Why did this make sense? Because its pension obligations also stretched into the long run. By inference, UAL's current precarious financial situation was not a consideration in the determination of the investment policy for its pension funds. We might call this the *silo* approach to pension fund investing.

Almost 30 years ago, Jack Treynor laid the foundation for a very different answer to the *New York Times* question. In his little book, *The Financial Reality of Funding Under ERISA* (with Patrick Regan and William Priest, New York: Dow Jones-Irwin, 1976), he explained succinctly why, from a corporate finance perspective, this "silo" approach to pension fund investing makes no sense. Ultimately, he and his coauthors demonstrated, pension obligations are corporate obligations and pension assets are corporate assets, with one important difference. If the corporation runs into financial trouble, it can "put" its pension plan to the PBGC. The value of this "put" increases as the size of a plan's unfunded liabilities increases, and as the degree of mismatch risk between pension assets and pension liabilities increases. This "corporate finance" approach to pension fund investing suggests that what UAL was really doing by underfunding its pension plans and choosing a risky investment policy for pension assets was to maximize the value of its PBGC "put."

So which of the two answers offers the more plausible explanation for UAL's choice of pension investment policy? Its own "silo"-based answer? Or Treynor et al.'s "corporate finance"–based answer? It is entirely possible that this critical question will become the basis of a major court case. If this happens, we have no doubt that the "corporate-finance"–based explanation will win the day. Why? Because it is self-evidently the correct one in UAL's case.

ERISA'S "SOLE INTEREST" RULE

ERISA requires that the fiduciaries of corporate pension plans "act in the sole best interest of plan beneficiaries." The UAL case makes it abundantly clear that the "sole interest" standard is an impossible one for the management of corporations to live up to. Why? Because DB pension plans are inherently risk-sharing arrangements among the various stakeholder groups party to the "pension deal." Pensioners bear one set of risks, active employees another set, shareholders yet another set, and, finally, corporate management has its own set of exposures to the potential rewards and risks of various possible future pension balance-sheet outcomes. In short, DB plans represent a complex web of contingent claims among these stakeholder groups.

To demonstrate its impossibility, we might ask what UAL management should have done if they deemed upholding ERISA's "sole interest" standard their number one priority over the course of the past few years. Clearly, as the company's operating risks increased and its operating performance declined, it was in the financial interest of retiree plan members, and of active long-service plan members to increase funding and decrease asset-liability mismatch risk (for most plan members, their pension claims under the PBCG would be significantly lower than their accrued benefits under the UAL plans). However, such actions would have been inimical to the financial interests of shareholders and corporate management. Why? Because with the passage of time, the PBGC "put" became increasingly critical to the ongoing financial viability of the airline. In such a situation, is anyone surprised that management chose to maximize the value of the PBGC's "put," rather than choose the course that would maximize the value of the pension claims of its retiree and long-service active plan members?

Let's try another thought experiment and imagine under what circumstances the financial interests of all stakeholder groups in a corporate DB plan might be fully aligned. A significantly overfunded plan sponsored by an AAA-credit employer comes to mind. In such a rare situation, the PBGC "put" value would be tiny, as would the probability that the employer would ever have to make unanticipated pension contributions. However, even in this rare situation, some interesting questions related to future inflation protection and surplus ownership remain. The point of all this is that ERISA's "sole interest" rule is a legal oxymoron, a corporate impossibility. The best that can be hoped for is that corporate managements are reasonably even-handed in assessing the reward/risk implications for all DB plan stakeholders as they make their funding and investment policy decisions.

LESSONS FROM ABROAD

Is this "best hope" something to be counted on? Not if the U.K. pensions scene offers a window on the future of corporate DB plans in North America. A recent article by Martin Wolfe titled "Lessons from Britain's Pensions Dilemma" (*Financial Times*, August 20, 2004) states that 60 percent of corporate DB plans are now closed to new members, with 10 percent also closed to new accruals. The article foresees "a huge shift in risk-bearing from institutions to individuals" in the private sector. Why is this happening? The article suggests that five factors have been at work:

1. Differing stakeholder groups have competing financial interests.
2. The corporate goal is employee retention, not security of postretirement income streams.
3. Informational asymmetry between DB plan agents and principals.
4. Fuzzy, incomplete pension "deals."

5. Individual corporations are inherently unstable over the extended time horizons that pension plans must operate in.

Wolfe argues that these five dysfunctional elements have always been there. They have recently been crystallized by a confluence of events in the United Kingdom, including volatile equity prices, a decline in long-term interest rates, a move toward "fair value" accounting for pension assets and liabilities, the 1997 Gordon Brown raid on dividends, and heavy-handed government intervention in workplace pension arrangements.

The problem with the *Financial Times* piece is that it offers no hope. Doom and gloom everywhere. A recent judgment in a corporate pensions case by the Supreme Court of Canada provides a more constructive perspective. The specifics of the case (a dispute about distribution of surplus in a partial plan wind-up) matter less then the context the court articulated in explaining its decision:

- Pensions have evolved over time from employer gratuities to enforceable legal claims.
- The intent of pension legislation is to "strike a fair and delicate balance" between employer and employee rights and obligations.
- Pension plans represent risk-sharing arrangements between employers and current and former employees. There should be a fair distribution of both risks and rewards between various stakeholder groups in any pension arrangement.

Surely, this is a far more realistic and useful perspective from which to assess where we are with corporate pension plans than ERISA's oxymoronic "sole interest" perspective. The judgment also points to the direction we must take corporate pension arrangements in, if we want them to be sustainable. Specifically, it points to the "supreme" pension design question that was not addressed in the judgment: "What are the necessary and sufficient conditions for creating and maintaining sustainable risk-sharing pension arrangements between employers and employees?"

SEARCHING FOR "SUPREME" ANSWERS

If that is the supreme pension design question, what is the answer? Remarkably, it is a question we seldom see posed and debated. Our own efforts in this area, represented by the chapters in this book, have received little feedback. Our approach has been to argue that all workplace pension arrangements should be governed by the application of three principles: (1) clarity in pension "deals" and legislation, (2) balanced consideration of stakeholder interests, and (3) good governance and administration. Some chapters identified the characteristics of ideal pension "deals" and of ideal pension-delivery institutions, and then scored the effectiveness of today's traditional DB and DC plan models against those ideal characteristics. Neither of the current models scored particularly well by "ideal" standards.

Other chapters suggested that the current calm (after the March 2000 to March 2003 "perfect pension storm") should be a time for action, rather than inaction, by pension fiduciaries. For the fiduciaries of corporate DB plans, we suggested the time had come to decide whether to continue to sponsor a DB plan, or to close it. In either case, the time had come to cease being "brain-dead" to the very material asset-liability mismatch risk embedded in virtually all of these plans. The choices are stark. This risk should either be placed in its proper context and properly managed, or eliminated.

For fiduciaries of most corporate DC plans, the choices are equally stark. Either continue with the current "supplier-driven DC business model" that offers plan participants too many choices at too high cost with too little oversight, or consciously think through what a "participant-driven DC business model" would look like. We suggested that the latter model would offer far fewer investment choices at low cost with skilled oversight that works in the best interest of participants. It would also offer an annuitization option for those participants who want to start buying lifelong future cash flows now. The public policy challenge is to figure out how to create DC plans that conform to this latter participant-oriented model. There is no profit motive to create institutions that would adhere to such a business model.

THE UAL CASE IN CONTEXT

So what are the strategic lessons to be learned from the UAL case, and what actions do they imply? First of all, it so clearly exposes the impossibility of ERISA's "sole interest" rule that it should be taken out of the law. Instead, the law should recognize the reality that all DB arrangements are inherently risk-sharing arrangements among various stakeholder groups. The only reasonable standard of conduct for fiduciaries in such situations is to be consciously even-handed among all these groups in making funding and investment policy decisions.

This logic raises further fundamental questions, however. Can corporate executives ever be truly even-handed in making such decisions? The UAL case makes it abundantly clear that there are situations where this becomes a practical impossibility. Indeed, the Department of Labor has recognized this by causing an independent fiduciary to be appointed. So if "even-handedness" is not a reasonable expectation, what then? The answer is move to arm's-length pension arrangements that in fact can be governed in an even-handed manner. Australia and the Netherlands have already acted on this logical conclusion. North America and the United Kingdom may yet follow. If they do, the UAL case may well have been the tipping point.

CHAPTER 6

Peter Drucker's Pension Revolution After 30 Years: Not Over Yet

"No book of mine was ever more on target when it was published in 1976. And no book of mine has been ever more totally ignored."
Peter Drucker, writing in 1996 about his pensions book, *The Unseen Revolution,* first published in 1976

TWO UNFASHIONABLE THEMES

Thirty years ago, Peter Drucker's "on target, but totally ignored" book on pensions, *The Unseen Revolution: How Pension Fund Socialism Came to America* (New York: HarperCollins, 1976), explored two related themes. Both themes were, at the time, deemed unfashionable or even irrelevant in a society dominated by young Baby Boomers just beginning to enter the workforce:

1. **Aging and longevity would become dominant socioeconomic issues** as the outsized Boomer cohort begins to retire 30 years hence.
2. **Pension funds would become dominant owners of the means of production** as the massive cash flows going into these funds over the coming decades would increasingly be invested in equities rather than debt securities.

The Unseen Revolution was not intended as a prescriptive book, offering specific solutions to lists of coming challenges facing an aging society and the challenges of the "socialization" of capitalism taking place through pension fund ownership. Instead, it was a prescient book, clearly describing the nature of the challenges lying ahead and identifying the issues that would have to be addressed along the way.

The goals of this chapter are twofold. Its first is to list the pension politics, design, and management issues that Drucker identified 30 years ago as needing our attention. His issues fit neatly into some of the "pension issue categories" of this book: Specifically, these categories are:

- Politico-agency issues.
- Pension contract and risk issues.
- Investment beliefs issues.
- Pension governance and management issues.

The second goal of this chapter is to develop a scorecard to assess how well we have actually handled these issues over the course of the last 30 years. It turns out that Drucker was far better at identifying the critical pensions-related issues that we would be facing than we have thus far been at addressing them. In short, 30 years later, the pension revolution is far from over.

POLITICO-AGENCY ISSUES

Drucker identified Charles Wilson, president of General Motors for much of the 1940s and 1950s, as the father of the typical post–World War II corporate defined benefit (DB) plan. Wilson believed that his corporate pension plan design would forge a direct, strong bond between the corporation and its workforce. Further, by investing pension contributions through a segregated pension fund in equity positions in Corporate America, workers would have a direct incentive to enhance the financial health and productivity of their employers. When the new DB pension plan was introduced at GM in 1950, union leaders at the United Auto Workers (UAW) were less than enthusiastic. They (correctly) viewed Wilson's initiative as an attempt to undermine union power to impact the future affairs of the corporation. So, ironically, the GM pension plan was implemented over the objections of the UAW at the time. The Wilson pension formula was subsequently adopted by many other large corporations in the early 1950s. The essence of the Wilson formula would later be codified as the Employee Retirement Income Security Act of 1974 (ERISA).

Drucker recognized that the politics and dynamics of public-sector and multiemployer-industry pension plans were quite different from those of the corporate sector. While he saw nothing wrong with such arrangements in principle, Drucker saw much wrong in practice. State and local governments seemed to just make up "rules" for their pension plans as they went along, with little apparent fiscal discipline or consistency. The same seemed to be generally true for union-run industry plans, even though these plans fall under the ERISA code. As a counterpoint, the evolution of the Teachers Insurance and Annuity Association–College Retirement Equities Fund (TIAA-CREF) proves that it doesn't have to be that way, with TIAA-CREF's "enviable record of performance and innovation" starting in 1918.

So what does Drucker make of all this? He concludes:

- Pension plans can maximize their legitimacy and accountability by operating as single purpose, arm's-length agencies.
- By their very nature, pension plans represent multiple-stakeholder interests, and their governance processes should recognize this fundamental reality.
- Special-interest groups, whether they are unions, business groups, or government agencies, must not "use" pension funds to further their own agendas.

How much progress have we made in the politico-agency arena of pensions over the course of the last 30 years?

We offer the following three observations:

1. The private-sector labor market has "atomized" making corporate DB plans now irrelevant to a significant part of this market. Ironically, the growth of DC/401(k) plans has given rise to a whole new class of agency issues driven by the vast informational asymmetry between plan members and for-profit financial service providers. The result is that many plan members are paying too much for too little.
2. In the part of the private-sector labor market where DB plans are still potentially relevant, such plans have become significantly less attractive as a compensation component for many corporate employers. This is due to the evolving complexity of the collective, shared risk–bearing element in DB plans, and the advent of "fair value" accounting principles. More on this below.
3. There is still a serious shortage of single-purpose, arm's-length pension agencies around the world. A positive development has been the emergence of such agencies investing the national Pillar 1 pension reserves in Canada, Sweden, Norway, Ireland, New Zealand, and, very recently, in Australia and France. And, certainly, there are good examples of such agencies investing Pillar 2 workplace-based pension assets in all the major pension reserve countries, including not just the list above, but also the United States, the United Kingdom, the Netherlands, and Switzerland. Yet, unfortunately, for every good example, there are still far too many bad examples of pension agencies rife with potential

and real unresolved conflicts of interest. The legitimacy, and hence the sustainability, of such agencies is still very much in doubt.

In short, the politico-agency issues of the pension arena that Drucker identified in 1976 are still very much with us today.

PENSION CONTRACT AND RISK ISSUES

As one would expect, Drucker was fascinated with the "property rights" questions associated with DB plan–based pension claims and the reserves backing them. Can these claims and associated reserves be individualized? Or are they the "social property of the plan member community"? He also understood the contingent nature of DB pension claims. In other words, he understood that the value of a pension claim is not absolute, but dependent on such factors as the funded status of the pension plan balance sheet and the financial strength of the plan sponsor, if there was one.

Specifically, Drucker concludes:

- If a pension plan involves risk bearing (and it is hard to imagine situations with no risk bearing at all), the risks should be made transparent with respect to both magnitude and who is actually doing the risk bearing.
- Collective, shared risk bearing is a highly complex concept, both in theory and in practice. Thus, we should favor pension contracts that have both individual capital accumulation and annuitization elements. For example, this combination has served TIAA-CREF participants well for many decades.

How much progress have we made on pension contract/risk issues over the course of the past 30 years? We offer the following observations:

- Traditional actuarial and accounting techniques have arrested the evolution of correctly defining, measuring, managing, and allocating risks in DB (i.e., shared-risk) pension plans. Only recently have the principles of modern finance theory (e.g., contingent claims valuation and risk-based capital reserving) begun to be applied to pension claims and obligations. This shift may well become an important "tipping point" in pension finance.
- The continued absence of clear, dynamic rules regarding funding and benefit adjustments in collective public-sector and industry pension plans has made them subject to game theory–driven outcomes. So we have seen balance-sheet surpluses "spent" by current generations in the 1990s, and are seeing balance-sheet deficits being pushed on to future generations in this new decade.

In short, the pension contract and risk issues that Drucker identified 30 years ago are only now beginning to be addressed.

INVESTMENT BELIEFS

We have sung the praises of Chapter 12, "The State of Long-Term Expectation," in John Maynard Keynes's *General Theory of Employment, Interest, and Money* (New York: Harcourt, Brace & World, 1935) many times in the past. In this chapter, Keynes makes a clear distinction between two radically different styles of investing. On the one hand, genuine long-horizon, value-creating investing embodies new technology and innovation, fosters new jobs, and creates new wealth. On the other hand, short-horizon "beauty contest" investing merely transfers some of the already existing wealth from the pockets of an unsuspecting public into the pockets of the for-profit financial services industry in the form of too high fees. Forty years after Keynes, Drucker covered the same investment ground in *The Unseen Revolution,* expressing views very similar to those of Keynes.

Fast-forwarding another 30 years to today, it is a reflection of the reach and marketing power of the for-profit financial services industry that "beauty contest" investing is as alive and well as it was 30 or even 70 years ago. While, on the one hand, its market share of the institutional (e.g., pension fund) market has declined somewhat, the phenomenal growth of the retail (e.g., mutual fund) market over the course of the last 30 years has ensured that traditional zero-sum "active" management services continue to be well compensated. On the long-horizon, value-creating investing front, there are hopeful signs. A still small number of large, arm's-length, well-governed pension funds around the world have become increasingly active in this arena. They are not only embodying new technology and innovation, fostering new jobs, and creating new wealth with their investment programs; they are also increasingly holding the boards and managements of corporations in which they are investors accountable for measurable results.

PENSION FUND GOVERNANCE

Drucker was predictably direct on the matter of pension fund governance. Pension fund "socialism" would be a legitimate, functional form of social organization only if pension funds could act as genuine, arm's-length, wealth-creating agents for workers and retirees. We noted above that meant these funds had to be free of conflicts with specific union, business, or government agencies. But that would not be enough. Pension funds would also have to be well governed and managed, subject to the same competency standards as the boards and managements of the companies they invest in. That meant professional rather than lay (amateur) boards with relevant composite skill and experience sets. It meant engaging a competent chief executive officer to whom a board could entrust the development and implementation of a relevant, effective strategic plan. It meant an organization design subject to the best thinking on effective delegation and personal incentives. All this in turn meant that pension funds would have to operate at a large enough scale to be able to afford these competencies and operate at low unit costs at the same time.

So we pose the "How have things turned out?" question one more time. The short answer is: "Well in some cases, and not so well in others." Things have turned out well in the sense that we can today point to a number of large pension fund organizations around the world that can comfortably meet any reasonable "well-governed, well-managed" standard. The "not so well" part of the answer relates to the fact that there are still far too few pension fund organizations today that can meet that standard. Maybe not surprisingly, much of the remaining governance and management troubles reside in pension organizations that were already around when Drucker wrote *The Unseen Revolution* 30 years ago. Bad habits seem to die hard.

STILL MUCH WORK TO DO

With the benefit of hindsight, we now know that Drucker batted 1.000 in 1976 in identifying the key politico-agency, contractual-property, investment, and governance issues confronting the successful evolution of pension fund "socialism" at that time. Thirty years later, we can wish that we had been as good at heeding as Drucker was at warning. That has not been the case. None of this means that the pension revolution has been lost. Instead, it means that it has not yet been won.

We still have much work to do.

CHAPTER 7

Winning the Pension Revolution: Why the Dutch Are Leading the Way

"Revolution: a dramatic and far-reaching change."
The Oxford Dictionary

THE GLOBE'S NUMBER ONE PENSIONS COUNTRY

The previous chapter noted that Peter Drucker's 1976 pensions book *The Unseen Revolution: How Pension Fund Socialism Came to America* was remarkably prescient. Decades ahead of his time, Drucker identified four factors that would determine the outcome of the "dramatic and far-reaching change" facing global pensions:

1. Politico-agency issues
2. Pension contract and risk issues
3. Investment beliefs issues
4. Pension governance issues

Although Drucker cautioned that his book was precautionary rather than prescriptive, he offered wise advice in each of these four dimensions nevertheless. Specifically, he suggested:

- Pension plans should operate as single-purpose, arm's-length agencies, not tied to any special-interest group.
- Risk bearing should be made transparent, with respect to both magnitude and who is actually doing the risk bearing.

- Collective risk bearing is a highly complex concept, both in theory and in practice, and is *not* essential to good pension contract design.
- Pension investing should engage the real world through direct investing in such areas as venture capital, as well as play the role of knowledgeable, assertive "owners" of publicly traded corporations.
- Pension funds themselves need knowledgeable, assertive governance mechanisms. Without such mechanisms, pension funds will not acquire the internal management and investment expertise necessary to properly run pension funds as cost-effective financial "businesses." In short, without good governance, pension funds will not achieve "legitimacy" in the eyes of the stakeholder groups they are meant to serve.

We had occasion recently to offer an assessment of how well the world has heeded Drucker's advice on winning the pension revolution. The event was the recent Jean Frijns "farewell seminar," organized in his honor by his colleagues in Amsterdam, with the entire leadership of the Dutch pension community in attendance. Jean had a 17-year career with Algemeen Burgerlijk Pensioenfonds (ABP), playing a major role in transforming the giant Dutch public-sector pension fund from a sleepy bureaucracy into one of the world's most dynamic, influential, expert pension organizations.

So what have we done with Drucker's advice? Generally speaking, Drucker was far better at identifying the critical pension issues we would be facing and how they should be addressed than we have thus far been at heeding his advice. Having said that, we also offered the opinion that the Dutch currently come closest to meeting Drucker's winning conditions, and as a result, Holland currently is the number one pensions country in the world. We offered four pieces of evidence to support this opinion:

1. Pension plan membership is compulsory, and all Dutch pension funds are separate legal entities by law. As important, the leading Dutch funds also have increasingly become arm's-length, single-purpose agencies in action. This has increased their "legitimacy" in the eyes of the employer-employee-pensioner stakeholder groups they serve.
2. Dutch pension contracts are in the process of being clarified and reengineered. Contract clarification has centered on the nature of the pension promise and who the pension promise underwriters are. Reengineering efforts have focused on introducing modern financial economics principles into the definition and valuation of contingent pension claims. These developments in turn enhance the prospects that the redefined pension arrangements will be transparent, fair, and sustainable. While many of the new pension arrangements continue to contain elements of collective risk sharing, they can no longer be described as traditional defined

benefit (DB) plans. Predetermined policy protocols now automatically adjust benefits, contributions, and even investment policy to changing circumstances.

3. Dutch pension funds are leaders in the global hunt for new investment opportunities—and in raising global corporate governance standards. Dutch investors are now seen as "smart money" in such divergent fields as infrastructure investing, "green" investing, shareholder activism, and absolute-return strategies.

4. The once-taboo subject of pension fund governance itself is beginning to get significant airtime. While there is no consensus yet on the ideal organization design of a Dutch pension fund, the debate is on. If the pension governance debate is engaged with the same vigor as the now almost three-year-old pension contract debate, we should begin to see measurable positive results as early as 2007.

All this raises an interesting question. Why is it the Dutch who are leading the pension revolution today? The answer turns out to be equally interesting. In our view, the Dutch pension revolution has emerged from the confluence of three unique elements: culture, compactness, and leadership.

CULTURE, COMPACTNESS, AND LEADERSHIP

From personal experience we know that the Dutch have always taken financial matters seriously. They are probably the only nationality that could teach the Scots a few things about money. The Dutch are also integrative thinkers. For example, many of the leaders in the pension industry also hold university appointments. A recent effort to fund an ambitious academic-government-industry research/teaching effort on the financial implications of aging raised an astounding 36 million euros from multiple sources, to be disbursed over a six-year period.

Their integrative philosophy extends into a willingness and ability to combine insights from multiple disciplines. So macroeconomic perspectives are naturally tied to microeconomic perspectives. Actuarial perspectives are tied to modern finance perspectives. Labor market perspectives are tied to pension contract design perspectives, and so on. You get the idea.

Continuous efforts toward pension consensus-building also pervade the country. In my 10 years of actively observing the Dutch pensions scene, there has been a continuous stream of formal stakeholder group debates, conferences, and seminars, supplemented by never-ending informal discussions by phone, by e-mail, and in person. Everything is geared to building a better pension system.

"Compactness" greatly facilitates these efforts. The country is physically small and has only a single national government that deals with all pension matters, from both legislative and regulatory perspectives. Taken together, these conditions make Holland a country where pension "tipping points" should occur more frequently than in most other countries. And they do. One such "tipping point" in the 1990s was the decision that an element of competitiveness should be inserted into the pension arena. This decision was a key factor in the transformation of ABP from a local, sleepy, public-sector pension monopoly into a globally competitive pension powerhouse.

Which logically brings us to the leadership element. Good revolutions need good leaders. Without them, revolutions either fizzle out—or worse—turn into chaos. The Dutch pension community has been blessed with its share of strong leaders—people who are integrative thinkers, not afraid to speak their own minds, willing to lead by example, and patient enough to build strong organizations of talented professionals. Jean Frijns, of course, has personified all of these qualities on the institutional side of the Dutch pensions "industry."

REGULATORY LEADERSHIP

September 2002 saw the emergence of Dutch pension industry leadership from a surprising source. The pension regulator (the PVK, which has since been integrated into De Nederlandsche Bank) issued a letter to the pension fund community stating that, in its view, Dutch pension plans had become materially underfunded. The PVK outlined a series of tough capital adequacy measures designed to deal with the situation. The bottom line of these "fair value"–based measures was that contribution rates would have to rise considerably, benefit promises would have to be scaled back considerably, or some combination of the two would have to occur.

The initial reaction of pension fund managers was shock and anger. However, eventually (and predictably!), the PVK letter triggered a public debate on the future of the Dutch pension system, focusing especially on the characteristics of pension contracts with the joint characteristics of transparency, fairness, and sustainability. Now it was the turn of organized labor to lead. Its leaders acknowledged that, while final earnings-based, inflation-indexed pensions were still the goal, it was no longer realistic to demand that employers or future generations guarantee this outcome. As a compromise, it was agreed that a modest guarantee would be maintained: a floor pension based on career-average compensation—with no indexation. This collective recontracting process has inserted sufficient flexibility into the Dutch pension system to buy it sustainability for some years to come.

RESEARCH LEADERSHIP

Meanwhile, a serious, innovative research effort into the economics of pension contracting was already well under way by the time the PVK issued its famous letter. This effort followed the standard Dutch formula of involving both the academic and practitioner communities. An important question this research was designed to address focused on the potential welfare/utility gains of collective, risk-sharing pension contracts versus pension accumulation arrangements without this characteristic. Or, stated in plain English, under what conditions do collective pension schemes "beat" individual pensions in providing the most good (i.e., stable lifetime consumption patterns) for the most people?

A working paper by Jiajia Cui, Frank de Jong, and Eduard Ponds entitled "Intergenerational Risk Sharing within Funded Pension Schemes" (July 14, 2006) offers important insights into this question. First, the standard DB arrangement "beats" the standard defined contribution (DC) arrangement according to a welfare/utility gain metric they developed. However, that is not the end of the story. A more sophisticated individual "life cycle" pension arrangement involving a target pension, dynamic contribution rate adjustments, and an annuitization option in turn "beats" the standard DB arrangement. Even more sophisticated hybrid DC/DB arrangements in turn "beat" the individual "life cycle" arrangement, but not by much. These findings confirm Peter Drucker's intuition from 30 years ago that collective risk bearing is *not* essential to good pension contract design. Drucker's conclusion becomes even more telling when the difficulties of actually enforcing collective, shared-risk pension contracts in practice are factored into the calculation.

A REMAINING CHALLENGE: SOLVING THE ORGANIZATION DESIGN PUZZLE

So do any challenges remain for a country that has almost 100 percent workplace pension coverage; that has arm's-length, single-purpose pension agencies; that has pension contracts that score high in terms of transparency, fairness, and sustainability; and that has competitive investment capabilities? Yes, in our view, there is still one major challenge to be addressed. It is to build a web of pension organizations that score high on a global effectiveness scale. Thirty years ago, Drucker saw organization effectiveness as a "sine qua non" for winning the pension revolution. Organization effectiveness in pension funds starts with good governance practices, which in turn lead to these funds being effectively managed as "financial businesses" in the sole interest of the stakeholder groups they were created to serve.

Why do we say that improving organization effectiveness is a remaining challenge for Dutch pension funds? Because, like in other pension fund countries, organizational structures here have evolved over time in response to specific circumstances, rather than as the result of following some optimal design blueprint. We know this to be the case because we have actually spent some time tracing the organizational evolution of a number of large Dutch pension funds. Each seems to have its own creation story that starts with (like all creation stories): In the beginning there was ... and then this happened ... and then that happened ... and that's how we got here.

Does good organization design matter? Absolutely. A 1997 international study found that pension funds with strong organization design characteristics at the governance, management, and operations levels outperformed those with weak characteristics by an average risk- and cost-adjusted 1 percent per annum. An update of this study in 2005 confirmed that these findings continue to hold. In today's low-return environment, earning, say, 6 percent rather than 5 percent is easily equivalent to a 20 percent increase in ultimate pension payments. With this knowledge, pension fiduciaries would not be meeting their moral and legal obligations to their stakeholders if they failed to take measures to raise organization effectiveness. This is not the place to detail what those measures might be. Suffice it to say that research into what constitutes good organization design has a long, honorable history. The time has come to apply the findings of this research to the pension fund sector. This is done in Part Three of this book.

WHAT ABOUT THE OTHER PENSIONS COUNTRIES?

So much for the Dutch. What about the other pensions countries? Are they prepared to follow the Dutch (and Australian) example and legislate compulsory (or at least automatically enrolled) membership in workplace-based pension plans? To foster the creation of strong, single-purpose, arm's-length pension agencies? To reengineer pension contracts so that they become transparent, fair, and sustainable? To encourage innovation in pension investing? And to keep up with the Dutch as they tackle the challenge of building more effective pension organizations?

Only time will tell.[1,2]

---

[1] See the chapter in Part 7 on the Turner Commission Report for a recent U.K. initiative in this direction.

[2] It seems appropriate to disclose that this chapter's author is Dutch by birth and inclination.

CHAPTER 8

Pension Reform: Evolution or Revolution?

"Congress, regulators, lobbyists, and the news media are all scrambling to find out what has gone wrong with the pension system ..."

New York Times, July 31, 2005

A PENSION "TIPPING POINT" INDEED

In an earlier chapter written in 2004, we noted that the United Airlines (UAL) pensions case had "all the makings of a 'tipping point': that marginal element in a heretofore apparently steady-state system that tips the balance toward disequilibrium and material change." The observation seems even more on the mark today. For example, yet another UAL pensions article appeared on July 31, 2005, in the *New York Times* titled "How Wall Street Wrecked United's Pension" by Mary Williams Walsh.

Strangely, the article misdirects its aim by blaming UAL's money managers and other financial advisers for the airline's pension troubles. In contrast, we have been arguing for years that at the heart of UAL's (and many other employers') pension troubles lie only partially defined, complex risk-sharing "deals." Under financial stress, such "deals" invite game theory–driven bargaining between such strange adversaries or bedfellows as retirees, older workers, younger workers, corporate boards, corporate managements, bondholders, shareholders, and the Pension Benefit Guaranty Corporation (PBGC). Pension regulators, securities regulators, actuaries, accountants, and the courts all play supporting roles in the scripts of these bargaining dramas. Given these realities, it seems disingenuous for the

Times to blame Wall Street for legally generating fees out of such potentially chaotic situations.

Where the *Times* is right is in its observation that finding out, and fixing, what is wrong with the workplace-based pension system is now on everybody's radar screen. There are already reform proposals in circulation from governments and various professional bodies. Rather than recite in detail what these proposals have to say, the goal of this chapter is to develop a broader perspective on pension reform, now that the winds of change are in the air. What, in an ideal world, *should* happen? Will the measures actually being proposed narrow the gap between where we are and where we ideally should be? These are the questions to be addressed below.

WHAT SHOULD HAPPEN?

Prior chapters have already set out our answer to the "What should happen?" question. The pension revolution has five key elements. Some of these elements build on ideas first expressed by Peter Drucker in his book *The Unseen Revolution* 30 years ago:

1. **Increase pension plan participation.** The Dutch and the Australians have made workplace pension plan participation mandatory. This not only smooths out lifetime income and consumption for workers, but also takes considerable pressure off their national, unfunded Pillar 1 social security systems. In addition, mandatory participation creates a strong incentive to innovate and increase productivity in funded Pillar 2 workplace-based pension plans. As icing on the cake, diverse widespread Pillar 2 pension plan membership promotes the idea of "an ownership society" far more effectively than partial funding under a remote Pillar 1 social security system, with or without the optional individual pension accounts proposed by the Bush administration.
2. **Foster pension plan autonomy.** Pension delivery organizations should operate as single-purpose, arm's-length agencies, not beholden to any special-interest groups in the labor, corporate, or government sectors. This will minimize the potential for "agency" factors hijacking what should be the only mission of pension plans: to produce adequate, reliable pensions at a reasonable cost.
3. **Make risk bearing transparent.** The inevitable risks embedded in pension arrangements should be made transparent, with respect to both magnitude and who is actually doing the risk bearing. This is especially important in defined benefit (DB) schemes, where risks are borne collectively in complex ways by multiple-stakeholder groups.

4. **Refocus pension investments.** Investment strategies should clearly be assigned one of three possible goals. Risk-minimization strategies focus on risk control. Adversarial trading strategies focus on generating net trading profits within preestablished risk budgets. Long-horizon investing strategies focus on purchasing uncertain future cash flows at reasonable prices. This third strategy makes pension funds important investors in society's means of production, which in turn implies a necessity on their part to act as responsible, knowledgeable, and assertive long-term business owners.

5. **Improve pension plan governance.** Pension plans themselves must act as responsible, knowledgeable organizations. This implies a need for strong internal governance mechanisms. Without such mechanisms, it will not be possible to refocus pension investment programs and create needed risk transparency along the lines set out above. In short, without good governance, pension plans will not achieve the required "legitimacy" in the eyes of the stakeholder groups they are meant to serve.

If this is what *should* happen, will the pension reform proposals actually being floated move the Pillar 2 pension system in the right direction? That is the question we address next.

PENSION REFORM IN THE UNITED STATES

While Social Security reform has stalled in the United States, the UAL saga has created enough momentum to result in the floating of a series of measures to stabilize the finances of corporate DB plans. Congress's Pension Protection Act sponsored by John Boehner (R-Ohio) seems to be the best candidate to be passed into law at this point. The legislation has seven goals:

1. **Tighten funding rules.** For corporate DB plans, this means a standardized market-based yield curve to discount accrued pension promises, raising the minimum solvency funding target from 90 percent to 100 percent, shortening the amortization period for solvency deficits to seven years, and prohibiting the use of credit balances in lieu of cash contributions if the funded ratio is under 80 percent. Multiemployer plans have similar measures.

2. **Increase contribution room.** Corporations can continue to contribute to DB plans up to a new ceiling of 150 percent of the accrued liability.

3. **Prevent "gaming."** Pension benefits cannot be increased and lump-sum distributions cannot be made if a plan is less than 80 percent funded. Executives cannot be given "generous deferred compensation arrangements if the corporation has a severely underfunded pension plan."

4. **Improve the financial condition of the PBGC.** While tighter funding rules should improve the future financial prospects of the PBCG, the Act also proposes modest PBCG premium increases.
5. **Strengthen the legal status of cash balance plans.** Details to be announced.
6. **Improve disclosure.** More detailed and timely information to be included on Form 5500 and 4010 filings.
7. **Improve financial advice to DC plan participants.** The bill is to clarify that employers do not incur legal liability for individual advice given by professional financial advisers to plan members, and to require that financial advisers are "fully qualified to offer quality advice solely in the interests of plan members."

While these measures are deemed to be quite radical in some quarters, others think they don't go nearly far enough. For example, seasoned Washington-based pension attorney Steve Saxon recently called the Boehner bill a *stopgap measure,* which does little to address the fundamental flaws of the American corporate DB system. Unfortunately, he correctly points out, wholesale conversion to DC plans does not solve United States' looming retirement income crisis either. In his words, "It is time (and perhaps long overdue) for us in Washington to develop better opportunities for Americans to save for retirement" (see the July 2005 issue of *PLANSPONSOR*, p. 86). We heartily agree with Saxon.[1]

PENSION REFORM ELSEWHERE

Thus far, legislators and pension regulators in the United Kingdom and English-speaking Canada have not been any more insightful or creative than those in the United States in reforming their respective pension systems. The United Kingdom's situation changed dramatically with the release of the Turner Commission Report in November 2005 and the subsequent Treasury White Paper on pension reform. See the Turner Commission chapter in Part Seven. The Québec pension regulator Régie des rentes offers a refreshing contrast to these uninspiring records. In a consultation paper issued earlier this year, the Régie makes the following telling observations (our words):

- A combination of factors have turned *DB* plans into serious financial burdens for many employers. The five-year amortization period for solvency deficits can be especially troublesome.

---

[1] The final version of the U.S. Pension Protection Act became law in August 2006. As expected, it tightens the funding requirements of corporate DB plans. The Act also facilitates auto-enrollment of workers in employer 401(k) plans.

- The asymmetrical treatment of pension balance-sheet surpluses and deficits in tax, accounting, and legal contexts creates strong incentives for employers to underfund and adopt aggressive investment policies.
- Actuarial methods are generally imprecise, lacking in theoretical rigor regarding the measurement and management of risk. For that matter, none of the other pension fiduciaries seem to be able and/or willing to measure and manage balance sheet risk either.

These observations led the Régie to make a series of reform proposals, including:

- Funding targets should include a buffer for adverse experience. Preliminary research indicates "15 percent of the value of solvency liabilities would be sufficient for most plans."
- Increase the amortization period for solvency deficits to 10 years.
- Allow financial instruments (e.g., letters of credit from a qualifying financial institution) to be used to guarantee amortization payments for solvency deficits.
- Limit contribution holidays to the year immediately following an actuarial valuation.
- Permit agreement in advance on the allocation of balance-sheet surpluses in excess of the required target buffer for adverse experience. Such an agreement would be negotiated between representatives of the employer, the employees, and pensioners.

Implementation of these Régie proposals would move the regulatory framework for Québec-registered DB plans significantly toward the new Dutch framework with its tough capital adequacy requirements in relation to pension guarantees, and its underlying philosophy of explicit risk sharing. We noted in the prior chapter that the net result of these measures in the Netherlands has been a move toward reducing the level at which pensions are guaranteed in collective pension schemes, making the actual level of pensions paid (subject to a nominal floor guarantee) conditional on the financial status of the pension plan balance sheet.

PENSION REFORM: EVOLUTION OR REVOLUTION?

The measures enacted in Washington's Pension Protection Act offer a classic example of the evolutionary approach to pension reform. Tighten up the funding standards a bit, raise the surplus ceiling a bit, increase PBGC premiums a bit, reduce opportunities for gaming a bit, say some nice things about cash-balance and DC plans, and maybe everything will turn out okay. Maybe, but not likely.

Québec's Régie des rentes proposals go much further. First, its consultation paper is far more blunt in opinionating that there continues to be a serious lack of transparency in DB plan risk measurement and management protocols. Second, its reform proposals are far more ambitious, starting with the concept of a balance-sheet buffer against adverse experience, through to the facilitation of contribution payment guarantees by qualified commercial third parties (rather than guarantees through a noncommercial, hamstrung government agency), and offering encouragement to DB balance-sheet stakeholders to fully articulate their "pension deal," including claims on potential future surpluses. The Régie's attitude and proposals begin to approach those of the Dutch pension regulator with its new revolutionary "fair-value"-based capital adequacy approach to risk management in shared-risk pension plans.

It should by now be clear where we stand on the pension reform "evolution or revolution?" question. The time for evolution has come and gone. The time for revolution has arrived. That means making workplace-based pensions available to the entire workforce. It means delivering pensions through expert, single-purpose, arm's-length pension organizations. It means making risk bearing transparent, with respect to both how much and who is doing the risk bearing. It means integrating risk management with asset-return generation. Finally, it means fostering governance processes in pension organizations that have legitimacy in the eyes of all stakeholder groups. Thus, these processes must be, and must seen to be, both expert and even-handed with respect to the financial interests of all stakeholder groups.

While the implementation of such a package of reforms would be revolutionary rather than evolutionary, its elements are by no means "pie-in-the-sky" abstractions. Each element already has a concrete counterpart somewhere in the real world. What has been missing is the leadership to turn all the pieces into one coherent whole. Through its proposals, Québec's Régie des rentes has made the prospect of a genuine pension revolution in North America just a little brighter.

Building Better Pension Plans

"Science has made little progress dealing with whole systems. It tends to become arrested in the stage of singling out isolated bits, with little grasp of how these interact with other bits of integrated systems."

Jane Jacobs from *Dark Age Ahead*

CHAPTER 9

Can Game Theory Help Build Better Pension Plans?

*"Von Neumann's approach to game theory had been
co-operative, involving collaboration and win-win situations.
Nash came from the opposite direction. To him, collaborative
games were a mere convenience. Players will co-operate with each
other for their own gain, but are liable to break off their
arrangement when it is to their advantage to do so..."*
Paul Strathern, from his book *Dr. Strangelove's Game*

PENSION GAMES

By the time we saw the John Nash movie *A Beautiful Mind* and read
Paul Strathern's book *Dr. Strangelove's Game* over the Christmas holidays,
the seed for this chapter had already been planted. It came at the end of
a strategic discussion with the board of trustees of a major public-sector
defined benefit (DB) retirement system earlier last fall. There had been a
somewhat fractious debate among board members and senior management
about funding policy. Some wanted to forgo making new contributions
to the fund, others wanted to improve member benefits, and still others
wanted to just raise the contribution rate. At the end of the meeting,
the chief investment officer leaned over and whispered: "Game theory in
action!"

Which brings us to the theme of this chapter: Is the application of
game theory useful in thinking about how to build better pension plans?
For example, is it useful to think of both DB and defined contribution
(DC) pension plans starting out as cooperative win-win arrangements

between plan stakeholders? Then, as Nash points out, depending on how the cooperative win-win "game" unfolds, may it at some point become in the interest of some of the stakeholders to switch to an adversarial win-lose framework?

Are such "game" switches inevitable? Do they matter? If cooperative win-win pension games produce generally preferred outcomes in a broader social context, can we devise game rules that would prevent some plan stakeholders from jumping to the adversarial win-lose ship as the game progresses? If we can identify such rules, would they help us build better pension plans? How would we know? These are the question we explore below.

WHY DO PENSION GAME SWITCHES OCCUR?

Why do pension games switch from collaborative to adversarial in the real world? As Nash pointed out, the simple answer is "when one or more stakeholder groups judge it to be in their financial interest to switch." For example, the unanticipated high inflation rates of the 1970 s created win-lose conflicts in DB plans. Pensioners argued loudly that they hadn't signed up for 10 percent per annum declines in the real value of their pensions. Many plan sponsors on the other hand, argued they hadn't signed up for underwriting open-ended inflation risk either.

The 1980s and 1990s saw the emergence of a very different source of win-lose conflict in DB plans: the buildup of significant balance-sheet surpluses. Who should benefit from these unanticipated surpluses? Well, again, that depended on which stakeholder group you asked. Each thought the surplus was theirs. Likely, this first decade of the twenty-first century will see yet another theme switch as the surpluses turn to deficits. How are these emerging deficits going to be managed? Through increased contributions? Through benefit reductions? Once again, each stakeholder group has the predictable right answer. That is the new win-lose conflict lying before us now.

For a while, it looked like there was simple solution to all these DB conflicts: The DC plan surely was the ultimate win-win pension game! The wonderful bundle of visibility, portability, investor choice, high returns, and low contribution rates all made for happy employees and employers alike. That is, until the equity markets started to tank (compounded in some cases by large own-company stock positions that tanked even more). The class-action lawyers always knew it would be only a matter of time.

Even today, after two years of stock market turbulence, the arithmetic of the stock market still doesn't work very well. The prospective equity risk premium is still not very generous. And there is worse DC plan news yet to come. Many people are destined to outlive their DC asset accumulations during their retirement years. So they will go after someone when the money runs out. Their DC plan sponsor employers will be obvious targets, as will taxpayers at large through recourse to the public purse. Thus, a potentially large adversarial win-lose DC pension endgame still lies ahead of us.

WHO ARE THE STAKEHOLDERS AND WHAT DO THEY WANT?

So where do we start our search for collaborative pension schemes that stay collaborative? Table 9.1 identifies the three key pension scheme stakeholder groups and itemizes their preferences and motives. Note the apparent commonality of interests among the three groups: competitive compensation, adequate pensions, and no surprises. How can these apparent common interests deteriorate into adversarial win-lose games? Simply put, when the "no surprises" condition fails to hold. Indeed, we have already noted that unanticipated inflation leads to conflict. Unanticipated surpluses or deficits lead to conflict. Lower than anticipated pension payments (or none at all) lead to conflict.

Thus, the game theory perspective on pension scheme design has already yielded an important insight. A necessary condition for a collaborative pension scheme to stay collaborative is that it must meet the "no surprises" test as well as the adequacy and competitiveness tests. Of course that raises a rather important question: is it possible to design pension schemes that meet all three of these tests simultaneously? Probably not: too expensive. Yet, we're on to something important here. Even if we can't design the "perfect" scheme by these three criteria, how close can we come?

The game theory perspective tells us where to look. As we are not consciously going to build pension plans that are uncompetitive and produce

TABLE 9.1 Three Key Stakeholder Groups in Employment-Based Pension Schemes: Motives and Preferences

Group	Motives and Preferences
Active employees	Adequate target pensions, portability, no surprises
Pensioners	Continuity of pension payments in real terms, no surprises
Employers	Competitive compensation, manageable cost, no surprises

too little pension income, our focus should be on searching for the best way to relax the "no surprises" condition. Stated differently, the key is to clearly identify the sources of risk in pension schemes, to assess how to best control these risks through win-win risk pooling strategies, and to assess how to best load the remaining un-diversifiable risks on the various pension plan stakeholder groups in a transparent manner.

SOURCES OF RISK IN PENSION SCHEMES

So what are the potential sources of risk in pension schemes from the perspectives of the three key stakeholder groups? In other words, what forces could prevent pensioners from receiving their expected pension check tomorrow, active employees from eventually achieving their target pension income, and employers from sponsoring pension schemes that are competitive and cost effective? Well, there are micro risks and macro risks.

Micro risks are specific to individuals or small groups. For example, DC plan participants with undiversified individual retirement savings accounts are exposed to two material micro risks: first, their investments might fail, and second, even if they don't, plan members may still outlive their retirement savings. Similarly, individuals that move from DB plan to DB plan every five years during their working lives may end up with a very low income-replacement rate upon retirement. Also, private-sector workers are always exposed to the financial failure of their employers.

Macro risks impact entire generations of employees, pensioners, and employers. The unanticipated high-inflation experience of the 1970s impacted most pension scheme stakeholders negatively at the time. Similarly, the unanticipated high-equity-returns experience of the 1990s impacted most stakeholders positively at the time. Now, the unanticipated (by most) low-equity-returns experience of this new decade will once again have a negative impact on pension scheme stakeholders living through it. Meanwhile, we know that the economy's retiree-to-worker ratio will climb significantly over the next few decades, introducing a new macro risk element into our collective future.

MITIGATING MICRO RISKS

We know how to mitigate micro risks. On the investment side, the key is diversification. An interesting question for debate is how far to take the diversification idea. Starting at one extreme, it is arguably an "adversarial" act by employers to force employees to hold own company stock in their DC plans. Even in a voluntary context, a strong case can be made for a 10 percent ceiling on own company stock exposure in DC plans. Then there is the question of how far employees should be left to their own devices to build their own retirement funds, and what tools (in terms of education, advice, and investment options) they should be provided with. Once again, a strong case can be made that individual investment programs should be placed on an "expert automatic pilot" path, unless individual participants pass at least a basic "financial literacy" test and consciously choose to make their own investment decisions.

Regarding the risk of "outliving your money," the obvious answer is to create cost-effective mortality risk-pooling mechanisms for DC plans. This is not rocket science. We know how to do this. It is just that most DC schemes haven't yet got around to connecting mortality risk pooling mechanisms to capital accumulations at the point of retirement. Thus, even pre-retirement, a strong case can be made for a life annuity-based "automatic pilot" acquisition path, unless the individual participant passes yet another "financial literacy" test at that point.

CAN WE MITIGATE MACRO RISKS?

DB plans are designed to mitigate the DC plan-related micro risks just described. Yet, we have already noted that the DB form of retirement income scheme too can easily deteriorate into an adversarial win-lose contest. Why? Because there are still macro risks (e.g., unanticipated demographic, economic, and capital markets experiences) that must be borne by DB plan stakeholders. Because these kinds of risks are difficult to anticipate, and because they tend to be longer-term phenomena, they lead plan stakeholders into situations that neither they, nor the original plan architects may have anticipated.

Can such risks be mitigated? Yes, to the degree macro risk exposures can be shifted to third parties. For example, if governments issue inflation-linked bonds, then inflation risk can be shifted off DB plan balance sheets unto those of future taxpayers. More generally, to the degree pension promises can be hedged by default risk-free financial instruments issued by third parties, macro risks can be mitigated. Having said that, the record shows that DB plan sponsors have thus far generally chosen not to go the risk-minimizing route in managing their pension plan balance sheets.

IS INVESTMENT RISK WORTH TAKING IN DB PLANS?

Instead, DB plan sponsors have generally taken on investment-related mismatch risk on their plan balance sheets in the hope of earning a "spread" between the return on plan assets, and the asset return that could be earned through simply "immunizing" the plan liabilities. Indeed, the record shows that over the last 25 years, that "bet" has paid off in the form of emerging balance sheet surpluses. Or has it? Not if the fruits of this risk-taking must be shared with other balance sheet stakeholders (e.g., with active employees and/or pensioners in the form of improved pensions or other side-payments, or with the government in the form of additional taxes). This has indeed been the rule rather than the exception in the 1980s and 1990s.

What about the other side of the DB plan risk-bearing equation? Now that the surpluses are turning into deficits, will these same "other balance sheet stakeholders" volunteer to share the pain? The game theory framework provides the obvious answer: not on your life! And this is a fundamental flaw in the traditional *DB* plan: its politics make it an easily "gameable" proposition against the risk-bearing plan sponsor. No wonder an increasing number of sponsors want "out" as the sole risk bearers in these arrangements!

CAN GAME THEORY BUILD BETTER PENSION PLANS?

So now we come back to the question we started with: Can the "game theory" framework developed here help us build better pension plans? We think it can. The framework clearly shows the deficiencies of both DB and DC pension plans as they have traditionally designed. Simply put, they offer too many opportunities to switch from collaborative to adversarial games. We invite you to use the framework set out in this chapter to build your own version of the collaborative pension plan design most likely to stay collaborative. We promise to do the same. Let's compare notes and see if together we can design better pension plans!

CHAPTER 10

If DB and DC Plans Are Not the Answers, What Are the Questions?

"It is not the answer that enlightens, but the question."

Eugene Ionesco

FROM ANSWERS TO QUESTIONS

We are struck by people's willingness to assume that traditional defined benefit (DB) and defined contribution (DC) plans are the only possible answers to the pension question, and that our only challenge is to figure out which of these two pension plan options is "better." What if we started with the ultimate pension questions behind the answers? Would those questions logically lead to DB or DC plans as they currently operate as the only possible answers? The message of this chapter is "We think not."

We start below by first finding the ultimate pension questions behind the traditional answers. The best answer to the first of such questions in turn leads to another question, and so on it goes. Eventually, this "answer-and-question" process leads to some powerful benchmarks against which to evaluate the effectiveness of traditional DB and DC plans. The bad news is that neither of the traditional pension plan formulas scores particularly well on the resulting pension delivery effectiveness scale. The good news is that our "answer-and-question" logic gives direction to the search for better pension models.

ULTIMATE PENSION QUESTIONS AND THEIR CONSEQUENCES

So what are the ultimate pension questions and answers with which to launch our quest for better answers? We think the first sequence goes something like this:

> Q: *What can we do now to ensure the eventual delivery of adequate postretirement income streams that deal effectively with default risk, multiple employer risk, inflation risk, and longevity risk?*

> A: *By saving the necessary proportion of current income, and investing the proceeds in portable securities that promise default risk-free, life annuities upon retirement with payment streams tied to productivity growth and inflation.*

This answer leads directly to the next ultimate Q&A sequence:

> Q: *Do such securities exist?*

> A: *No.*

So very quickly, our Q&A quest has led to a very important consideration in building better pension delivery models. It is this: There is no market-based security that will deliver a portable, certain pension for life, adjusted for productivity growth and inflation. This conclusion leads to an important corollary: Either some intermediary underwrites the mismatch risk between the securities that financial markets offer and the ideal pensions people want, or people are going to have to underwrite that mismatch risk themselves.

UNDERWRITING PENSION MISMATCH RISK: ANY VOLUNTEERS?

So we have logically arrived at our next Q&A sequence:

> Q: *Are there logical third parties who would willingly underwrite the pension mismatch risk as defined above?*

> A: *Not obviously.*

In national Pillar 1 pay-go pension systems (e.g., the U.S. Social Security system), prior generations decided that pension mismatch risk would be borne by successor generations. Such systems are sustainable as long as contribution rates stay within "affordable" bounds, and deliver "reasonable" pensions. Such pay-go systems become unsustainable when the "affordable contribution rate/reasonable pensions" conditions can no longer be met. In such situations, the intergenerational mismatch risk underwriting process breaks down. As a result, the risks of higher contributions rates and/or lower pensions are crystallized, and pushed back from future to current generations. Specifically, the current generation is forced to either pay more, receive less, or work longer (thus far, the United States has only pushed back the retirement age a few years over an extended period of time).

What about Pillar 2 workplace pension plans? Are there natural pension mismatch risk underwriters here? What about current employers? Maybe, maybe not. On one end of the spectrum, we could visualize broad taxpayer groups having considerable pension mismatch risk underwriting capacity in their role as public-sector employers. On the other hand, we could visualize small corporate employers not having any such capacity at all. Of course, there is a difference between having pension mismatch risk underwriting capacity and actually putting that capacity "in play." Putting it in play implies an employer should ensure that its use of pension risk underwriting capacity is properly valued as a component of total compensation, and that this value is understood/appreciated by employees.

What about future employers (e.g., ultimately future taxpayers or shareholders), and for that matter, future employee/pension plan members themselves as pension mismatch risk underwriters? These future groups are tempting targets for today's employers and plan members, as these future groups are not at the table today to defend their economic interests. Not surprisingly, "real-world" pension deals often push pension mismatch risk bearing ahead to these future groups. Fairness and plan sustainability both argue for, once again, the need to value the use of pension risk underwriting capacity, even if it is on behalf of people not at the table today. In other words, tomorrow's risk bearers should not be put in a position where they are bearing risk in a way where they can only lose, or at best only break even. If they are being put in a position where they can lose, they should also have equal potential to win. Further, their risk exposure should be bounded so as not to be so large as to incent them to break the contract if potential risks turn into reality and become too financially burdensome to bear.

So again, our Q&A quest leads to an important conclusion: The most obvious third-party candidates for bearing pension mismatch risk are future generations of employers and employees. However, if intergenerational risk transfer "deals" are to be sustainable, they must be transparent, properly valued, symmetrical, and bounded.

SHOULD PENSION MISMATCH RISK BE MINIMIZED?

Let's go back for a moment to the "perfect pension" formula (i.e., a portable, adequate postretirement income stream with zero default, inflation, and longevity risk). We noted that the financial markets do not offer securities that are perfect hedges against such "perfect pension" promises. This raises yet another ultimate question:

Q: *What could be done to minimize "perfect pension" mismatch risk?*

A: *Two steps would go along way toward achieving a pension risk minimization objective.*

These two steps are:

1. Pool longevity/mortality risk among large groups of participants, making self-insurance a practical alternative, as the longevity/mortality risk characteristics of large participant groups are highly predictable (although actuaries have been underestimating improvements in longevity for decades).
2. Use long-term, default risk-free, inflation-linked financial securities (e.g., real return bonds issued by the U.S. Treasury) to lay off the default and inflation risk elements of the "perfect pension" contract.

The problem with this "solution" is that the cost of delivering the "perfect pension" today works out to about 25 percent of pay or even more. This is too expensive! Thus, the next Q&A sequence becomes:

Q: *What can be done to make the "perfect pension" more affordable?*

A: *Take investment risk, earn a "risk premium" and use the extra return to reduce the required contribution rate.*

With long investment horizons and the magic of compounding, it is true that 25 percent of pay contribution rates can be magically shrunk to 15 percent or even 10 percent of pay, if a 2 to 3 percent excess return over inflation-linked bond returns is in fact earned over the long run.

Now we are getting into familiar territory. By the late 1990s, it had become an article of faith that such excess returns were indeed available to long term investors, and that hence "perfect pensions at bargain prices" were available to all who subscribed to this long term view. The last three years have reminded all of us that the long run is made up of a successive series of shorter runs, each of which must be survived in order to get to that nirvana-like "long run."

So with this new knowledge painfully acquired over the last three years, where do we stand on the pension mismatch risk question now? It seems to us that we have learned that risk minimization is not a strategy that should be automatically dismissed, even if it implies scaling down pension promises to more affordable levels. If, however, decisions are taken to continue to reach for excess returns, surely the experience of the last three years has taught us that such decisions should not be taken casually. Further, we'd better be sure we understand which parties are going to be underwriting what "pension deal" risks, that we can measure the amounts of risk being taken, that risk and reward potentials are symmetrical, and that the financial consequences of potential risk exposure becoming reality are bounded, and hence sustainable.

PENSION-DELIVERY INSTITUTIONS

All this leads to yet another Q&A sequence about pension-delivery institutions:

Q: *Are there effective pension-delivery institutions that can sort out these pension risk measurement and management issues, and that can cost-effectively deliver pension streams that meet the criteria of adequacy and risk transparency developed above?*

A: *No, but a few are working on it.*

The sad truth is that much of the pension "industry" suffers from serious silo problems. In other words, most pension people are so focused on their own pension tree that they cannot even see the pension forest within their own organization, let alone in a broader context. The silo problem is especially serious in the corporate sector, where human resources does benefits, Treasury does investments, and nobody manages enterprise-wide pension risks. With such widespread organizational dysfunction, we should not be surprised that few are asking the ultimate pension questions behind the traditional DB and DC plan answers.

BENCHMARKING TRADITIONAL DB AND DC PLANS

The time has come to use the sequence of ultimate pension Q&As in this chapter as benchmarks to measure the effectiveness of traditional DB and DC plans as pension delivery vehicles. Specifically, relative to the

TABLE 10.1 Benchmarking Traditional DB and DC Plan Effectiveness

Criteria	DB Plans	DC Plans
Pension adequacy	Good to moderate	Moderate to poor[1]
Contribution rate risk	High to moderate	High to low[2]
Default risk	Moderate to low	Low
Inflation risk	Moderate to low	High
Longevity/mortality risk	Low	High
Multiple-employer risk	High to moderate	Low
Transparency	Poor	Good/poor[3]
Organizational effectiveness	Moderate to poor	Poor

[1]Investment regime risk, choice overload, and high cost burdens are all problematic.
[2]In some corporate DC plans, employer contributions depend on profitability.
[3]Transparency in DC plan is generally good regarding account balance values and poor regarding what pension those account balances will ultimately buy.

"perfect pension" standard and its associated costs, risks, disclosure, and organizational requirements developed above, how do traditional DB and DC plans fare? Specifically, how effectively do current pension-delivery mechanisms deal with pension adequacy, default risk, multiple employer risk, inflation risk, longevity/mortality risk, contribution rate risk, and the broader questions of transparency, sustainability, and organizational effectiveness? Table 10.1 tells the tale, at least the way we see it. The bottom line is that neither of the traditional pension plan formulas scores particularly well when all eight benchmarking criteria are considered.

THE WAY AHEAD

Can we design pension formulas and organizations that are more effective than those of the traditional DB and DC plans? Absolutely. The eight criteria listed in Table 10.1 show the way. Clearly, pension adequacy and portability are two important considerations. However, we believe that it is in the measurement, management, and disclosure of the various kinds of risks embedded in "pension deals" that the greatest scope for improvement lies. There is an important caveat, of course. Material improvements in the measurement, management, and disclosure of pension risks cannot occur without organizational structures willing and able to perform these tasks. That is why traditional DB and DC plans are not the answers.

CHAPTER 11

Human Foibles and Agency Dysfunction: Building Pension Plans for the Real World

"Underlying this global movement towards participant choice is an implicit assumption about behavior: That the employee-citizen is a well-informed economic agent who acts rationally to maximize self-interest."

Olivia Mitchell and Stephen Utkus, quoted from their book
Pension Design and Structure

SOME FUNDAMENTAL QUESTIONS FIRST

Much has been spoken and written about pension design. Discussions usually revolve around the relative merits of "defined contribution (DC) versus defined benefit (DB)." In other words, is it somehow better to define a contribution rate, invest the money, and see what pension it ends up buying 35 years later? Or is it better to define a target pension level 35 years hence, estimate what target contribution rate is needed to finance it, and then continue to adjust actual contributions over time until the target pension is eventually financed? Of course, anybody who knows pensions knows the answer to these questions: it depends.

Our goal in this chapter is to take this question-and-answer approach about pension design to a much more fundamental level. Thus, we intend to go well beyond such standard DC versus DB juxtapositioning as:

- DB helps retain key long-service employees.
- DC offers employees better portability.

- DB offers greater pension benefit certainty.
- DC is less risky for employers.
- DB can be run as a profit center by employers.
- DC benefits are more tangible, and hence valued more by employees.

While these are all valid observations, they don't really go to the heart of the matter. A much more fundamental approach must start with questions such as: What should a pension arrangement attempt to accomplish? What critical considerations need to be taken into account in the design of an ideal pension arrangement? What does the resulting ideal design look like? How does this ideal design compare with the designs of today's "real-world" DC and DB pension plans? What barriers stand between "actual" and moving to the "ideal"? Can they be overcome? How?

Just as these questions go to the heart of the pension design matter, we believe that you will find the answers to them that follow do so as well. The result is TOPS—"The Optimal Pension System."

BACK TO FIRST PRINCIPLES

A genuine new look at pension design requires going back to first principles. What should a pension design attempt to accomplish? Classical economic theory offers a good starting answer. The life-cycle model of individual economic behavior suggests that people should try to optimize consumption over their lifetimes. For most, this means going into debt to acquire an education, shelter, and consumer durables in early adulthood; paying down that debt and building up financial assets in midlife; and turning those financial assets into a stable stream of consumption expenditures during the retirement years.

This sensible life-cycle savings/consumption theory pioneered by Robert Merton and Zvi Bodie would be the end of it, except for the problem that real-world people are generally not very good at turning this life-cycle savings/consumption theory into practice. Research suggests that there are two fundamental problems:

1. People have trouble living up to the rational lifetime utility maximizer standard that economists and their theories have set for them.
2. Principal-agent and informational asymmetry problems combine to create a large potential intermediation wedge between individual savers and their money.

Taken together, research convincingly suggests that these two problems are serious enough to make a mockery of the proposition that classical life-cycle savings/consumption theory offers the complete answer to the pension design question.

HUMAN FOIBLES

The fact is that most people are not very good at solving the retirement savings problem on their own. People have difficulty keeping track of too many moving parts. Even rational experts have difficulty estimating their actual pattern of lifetime earnings, asset returns, taxes, longevity, and then deriving the optimal savings rate and investment policy from these projections. In addition, beyond these complex computational challenges lie important behavioral issues.

In their book *Pension Design and Structure,* Olivia Mitchell and Stephen Utkus (Oxford: Oxford University Press, 2004) list six such issues:

1. **Lack of self-control.** Many people rationally understand the need to save for retirement, but are incapable of following through on their intention. So they constantly overconsume today and undersave for tomorrow. Why is this? One theory is that proactive decision making for most adults requires both cerebral and emotional elements, and that for most people a far-off event like retirement lacks the necessary emotional stimulus for immediate action.
2. **Lack of firm preferences.** Research shows that many people will answer the same question differently, depending on how it is asked. For example, enrollment in voluntary DC plans is much higher if employees are automatically enrolled with the choice to opt out than if they have to make a positive election to opt in.
3. **Inertia and procrastination.** People tend to follow the path of least resistance in their decision making. For example, after investment education seminars, a high proportion of participants say they are going to change their fund and asset allocations, but only a small proportion actually do.
4. **Choice overload.** Research suggests that there is a negative relationship between the number of investment choices offered in DC plans and the plan participation rate. So, ironically, plans that offer 10, 20, or even more investment choices do not serve their members as well as those that offer three clearly articulated, optimized choices.
5. **Improper inferences and/or overconfidence.** People tend to see patterns in random data or simply rely on readily available data rather than the right data. For example, fund or asset mix shifts are often made based on just a few years of good or bad historical performance.
6. **Loss Aversion.** Faced with the realization of a certain loss, many people will double up in an attempt to recoup their investment. This aversion to realizing losses may explain why life annuities are so unpopular with many DC plan participants: they may die early and lose their bet with the insurer!

Clearly, many people are not the rational utility maximizers that classic economic theory assumes them to be.

AGENCY ISSUES

Adolph Berle and Gardiner Means set out the principal-agent problem clearly in their classic 1933 book *The Modern Corporation and Private Property*. Their fundamental question was: What happens to capitalism when you interpose a small group of agents (i.e., management) between the corporation and its owners (i.e., a large group of diverse, remote shareholders)? Their answer was that these agents have the potential to extract significant rents from shareholders. Media reports tell us that what was true in 1933 continues to be true today. Without the active, countervailing force of good governance, that is, a strong, knowledgeable, independent board of directors, many corporate managements continue to extract significant rents from their shareholders to this day.

Organizations that collect and invest the public's retirement savings are not immune from the potential misalignment of interests between the managements of such organizations and their customers/beneficiaries. The mutual fund industry offers a classic example. It is largely made up of for-profit organizations selling the hope of good performance, packaged in many imaginative ways, to millions of individual investors around the world. These individual investors do not realize, nor are they told by the mutual fund industry, that there is an adding-up problem—namely, that collectively, they will only earn market returns less costs. Unfortunately, these costs can easily add up to 2.5 percent of assets annually (i.e., sales costs, management costs, excess trading costs). Research shows that −2.5 percent is also a good estimate of the average annual amount by which mutual funds underperform their benchmarks. Prospectively, a 2.5 percent cost level probably exceeds any risk premium mutual fund investors could reasonably expect to earn in the future. So, while individual investors take the risk, the mutual fund industry gets the reward.

The client-adverse economics in the for-profit sector of organizations managing retirement savings contrast sharply with the client economics in the buyers co-op sector. For example, the benchmarking firm CEM Benchmarking Inc. (CEM) has been collecting return and cost data on a large sample of DC pension plans of large American corporations (80 funds, median size $2 billion). The database shows a median total cost of 0.4 percent (i.e., including both management and administrative fees/cost allocations). Further, the median benchmark-relative five-year gross excess return for the sample was a positive 0.5 percent. Thus, in fact, plan participants as a whole in this group of DC plans attained their benchmark performance for free over the 1999 to 2003 period.

Why do participants in the DC plans of large American corporations do so much better than the customers of the mutual fund industry? Because the executives managing DC plans and those managing mutual fund management companies have different objectives. There is a natural alignment between the interests of DC plan executives (i.e., the agents) and DC plan members (i.e., the principals): Both the principals and the agents value good DC plan cost effectiveness. This is not so in the mutual fund case. Here, the managers have a (legal) option to extract wealth from their clients for their own benefit due to the informational asymmetry between them. In other words, mutual fund managers know more about what they are selling than their clients know about what they are buying. Mutual fund performance results suggest that many for-profit retirement savings managers choose to exercise this wealth-extraction option.

COUNTERACTING HUMAN FOIBLES

Can something be done to counteract this listing of human financial foibles and agency-related dysfunction? Of course! The observed human foibles can be counteracted by the following three actions. The process of building TOPS has begun.

1. **Exploit inertia, procrastination, and lack of decision-making will-power.** Automatically enroll all employees in the pension plan, and automatically set contribution rates at high enough levels to produce reasonable income replacement rates on retirement. People need to know that, assuming a realistic net return, it can take a 20 percent of pay contribution rate over a full working life to replace 70 percent of final earnings on an inflation-indexed basis. Of course, for lower-income earners, Social Security contributions (with or without a personal investment account component) can make up a significant part of the 20 percent contribution rate. The point is that the setting of the automatic pension plan contribution rate should be explicitly tied to a consciously decided target income replacement rate, and a realistic target net return on assets.

2. **Design a simple auto-pilot investment program.** A complex menu of investment choices creates choice overload, leading to choice paralysis. Research suggests that choices should be severely limited, and possibly not provided at all. The simplest auto-pilot investment policy design would see the pension provider offer only one optimally managed risky portfolio option, and one risk-minimizing deferred annuity option.

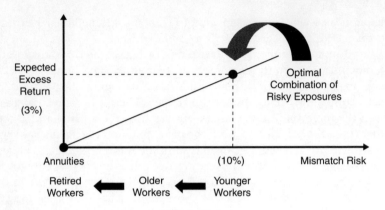

FIGURE 11.1   Auto-Pilot Investment Program

Participants' exposures to these two options would automatically be adjusted based on age. Figure 11.1 shows the key program elements we have in mind. Younger people with lots of human capital and little financial capital logically start out 100 percent in the risky investment option. Over their working lives, workers automatically move down the risk scale (i.e., to the left on the horizontal axis), eventually ending up with a life annuity on retirement.

3. **Emphasize the reality of longevity risk after retirement.** Make annuitization the default choice upon retirement, rather than the lump-sum withdrawal of the accumulated assets in the retirement savings account, as is currently usually the case. The auto-pilot default investment option should begin to acquire deferred annuities well before the target retirement date in order to control the risk of buying the entire annuity at a point in time when interest rates are at cyclical lows. The concept of pooling mortality/longevity risk has been around a long time. It is automatically embedded in traditional DB pension plans. It should also be embedded in the TOPS design.

With this pension design in mind, we now turn to the question of TOPS organization design.

MINIMIZING AGENCY COSTS

Minimizing agency costs also involves the implementation of three strategies:

1. **Create single–purpose pension co-ops.** We have already provided evidence of an annualized net excess return gap of 2.5 percent between a broad sample of U.S. mutual funds and the 80 large employer-sponsored

DC pension plans that provide return and cost data to the CEM Benchmarking Inc. (CEM) database. We attribute this performance gap (in favor of the DC plans) largely to the agency costs associated with for-profit mutual fund companies managing the financial assets of a clientele that is in the main financially unsophisticated. Such companies have two conflicting goals: to produce good returns for the clients and to produce good profits for the owners of the mutual fund company. In contrast, most large employer-sponsored DC plans have only a single purpose: to facilitate the accumulation of pension wealth as cost effectively as possible.

2. **Foster good governance and organization design.** Minimizing the potential for conflicting interests that can materially reduce the returns of TOPS participants is not enough. Steps must also be taken to ensure that the TOPS organization is well governed and managed. Research has found an excess return gap of 1 percent per annum between well- and poorly governed pension funds. Key is the composition of the board of trustees. The board should have the requisite collective skills/experience set. Each of its members should value the work, be collegial, and be capable of thinking strategically. A board with these characteristics will create the context for the organization to successfully carry out its mission.

3. **Build economies of scale.** The most certain path to enhanced financial wealth creation is to reduce unit costs, as long as such reductions do not impair the ability of the organization to operate effectively. Research from the CEM database suggests that every 10-fold increase in asset size reduces unit costs (and increases net returns) by 0.2 percent per annum. So, for example, the findings imply that all other things equal, $5 billion pension funds enjoy an average 0.4 percent per annum return advantage over $50 million pension funds. Of course, all other things are typically not equal between $5 billion and $50 million pension funds. Most importantly, the board of trustees of the $5 billion fund can afford to hire a qualified CEO to whom it can delegate the development and implementation of a fund strategic plan. The board of the $50 million fund, however, can't afford that luxury. Thus, large funds do not only enjoy a cost advantage, but a management advantage, too.

This TOPS blueprint has major implications for the employer community, for public policy, and for the future of DB plans. Some thoughts on each topic follow.

TOPS, EMPLOYERS, AND PUBLIC POLICY

We start with the premise that employees who participate in clearly understood retirement income arrangements are more productive than those who don't. (There is an interesting causality question here: Do these arrangements increase productivity, or do more productive people seek out employers that offer such arrangements?). An important related factor is that effective retirement income arrangements facilitate the transition of older workers out of employment into retirement. We also note that about 40 percent of the private-sector North American workforce is currently covered by some form of a workplace-based pension arrangement. Of those covered in the United States, 58 percent had a DC plan only, 19 percent had a DB plan only, and the remaining 23 percent participated in both a DC and DB plan.

Given the above, it follows that being able to offer membership in a TOPS arrangement would be a "good thing" for employers that currently do not offer any kind of retirement income arrangement to their employees. An important caveat is that these employers would not incur material additional financial or legal obligations. What about employers already providing employees access to a pension arrangement? What would shifting to a TOPS arrangement do for them? We see two advantages: (1) TOPS will generate materially higher, more predictable pensions than most current DC pension plans for the reasons set out above, and (2) there is no need for an employer to be the direct legal sponsor of the TOPS arrangement, thus eliminating current legal concerns surrounding the sponsorship of DC plans.

Do the merits we attach to TOPS arrangements play out in practice? In the United States, we can point to the venerable national pension plan for college and research workers: Teachers Insurance and Annuity Association–College Retirement Equities Fund (TIAA-CREF). Founded through an initiative by Andrew Carnegie, it has operated successfully since 1918. It currently covers about three million workers and pensioners in 15,000 separate pension plans with collective assets of over $370 billion. In Australia, the entire workplace pension system has been moving toward TOPS structures since membership in a workplace pension plan was made mandatory in 1992.

We see two major socioeconomic benefits arising out of broad workforce coverage in TOPS pension arrangements. First, raising workplace pension coverage well above the current 40 percent level offers the possibility of material productivity gains and reduces future dependence on the public purse to provide income support for people with inadequate levels of retirement income. Second, TOPS structures are ideally suited to facilitate the dispassionate investment of long-horizon retirement savings. Investment processes based on such a foundation offer the prospect of more effective corporate ownership behavior. This in turn leads to the prospect of reducing agency costs at the corporate level and increasing the productive allocation of financial capital across the global economy.

TOPS AND DB PLANS

TOPS are neither DC plans nor DB plans as these arrangements are currently operated. They are clearly superior retirement income–generation vehicles to most current DC plans for the reasons set out above. What about versus DB plans? Are TOPS superior to current DB plans, too? That depends on the value we attach to intergenerational risk sharing. While intergenerational risk sharing would seem to be a welfare-enhancing feature in principle, can it be implemented fairly in practice? That is the ultimate question defenders of DB plans must successfully address if DB plans are to have a future. We address this question in the next chapter.

CHAPTER 12

DB Plans and Bad Science

"Science has made little progress dealing with whole systems. It tends to become arrested in the stage of singling out isolated bits, with little grasp of how these interact with other bits of integrated systems . . ."

Jane Jacobs from *Dark Age Ahead*

SCIENCE AND THE DESIGN OF PENSION CONTRACTS

In her book *Dark Age Ahead,* Jane Jacobs reminds us that bad science leads to bad outcomes. Specifically, the legendary chronicler of the life and death of North American cities shows how bad research in the fields of traffic engineering, public health practices, and the economics of urban development has led to bad policy and design decisions in each of these fields.

What about policy and design decisions in the pensions field? Are they grounded on good science-based research? Or are they based on bad science, too? And if they are, what are the consequences? As it pursues the answers to these questions, this chapter ends up concluding that defined benefit (DB)-based pension contracts contain a serious, potentially fatal, design flaw. This design flaw poses a serious, potentially fatal, threat to the sustainability of DB plans. Can the flaw be fixed? We invite you to reach your own conclusion after you study the logic presented below.

THE TOPS CONTRACT

The prior chapter developed The Optimal Pension System (TOPS) from first principles. Its design is based on sound theory and sound research.

It starts with the premise that rational individuals wish to devise lifetime consumption plans that maximize lifetime utility or satisfaction. Two types of barriers stand in the way of individuals' achieving this goal on their own. First, devising such a plan is a highly complex undertaking, leading most people left to their own devices to either make highly suboptimal decisions or simply ignore the problem altogether. Second, getting expert help with pensions-related planning, investing, and administration brings its own set of agency-related problems, leading to the prospect that people will end up "paying too much for too little."

The TOPS arrangement addresses both types of barriers. The knowledge/behavioral problems are addressed by an "auto-pilot" savings, investment, and annuitization protocol. This protocol aligns income replacement targets with target savings rates and optimal investment/annuitization policies. The agency problems are addressed through the establishment of single-purpose pension "co-ops" of sufficient scale to be able to operate these "auto-pilot" savings/investment protocols at low unit costs.

TAKING ON INVESTMENT RISK: IMPLICATIONS

The life-cycle savings/investment theory underlying TOPS does not require the undertaking of investment risk during the capital accumulation phase. In other words, the theory is valid even with all retirement savers choosing risk-free investment policies. Justification for undertaking investment risk requires two conditions:

1. The TOPS participant has the requisite tolerance for risk taking.
2. The TOPS organization's investment team is able to construct a series of investment portfolios with the requisite net reward/risk ratios through time.

Unfortunately, these two conditions do not guarantee that all TOPS participants undertaking investment risk will end up with higher pensions than those who do not. Some might still end up with lower pensions than could have been generated by adopting the risk-free investment policy. This would be the case even if all TOPS participants stayed with the same set of auto-pilot savings/investment rules. Why? Because capital market returns are not constant over time. There will be extended high-real-return periods, and there will also be low-return periods. Thus, even the most expert TOPS investment team in the world would be challenged to provide the same real returns for the plan participants who happen to retire near the end of a high-return regime and those retiring near the end of a low-return regime. This reality raises an important question: Is there a way for TOPS participants to insure against this type of investment regime risk?

IS INVESTMENT REGIME RISK INSURABLE?

In principle, TOPS participants could band together and agree that at least some of the high-return-regime gains be used to supplement the pensions of TOPS participants retiring in low-return regimes. The assumption of risk aversion suggests that in principle this type of insurance is a good idea for everybody. How could this intergenerational insurance concept be put into practice? This question is best answered through a thought experiment. Imagine the following series of events:

1. Knowledgeable representatives of the current and future generations of participants of a TOPS-based plan meet to negotiate an intergenerational pension insurance deal deemed to be fair for all.
2. They agree on the economy's long term wealth-creating potential, the expected term structure of risk-free investment returns, and the expected long-term cost of risk capital (i.e., the expected premium for taking on investment risk). They also agree on the potential intergenerational variance around these long-term expectations.
3. Next, using the agreed-on long-term expectations, they calculate the expected normal pension of a TOPS participant who follows the plan's auto-pilot savings/investment rules. They also calculate the potential intergenerational pension variance around the expected auto-pilot pension, as well as what this normal pension would cost if a risk-free investment policy is followed.
4. The expected auto-pilot TOPS pension leads to a 70 percent final earnings replacement with full inflation indexation, with a 35-year contribution rate of 15 percent of pay. The low-return-regime outcome produces only a 40 percent earnings replacement, while the high-return-regime outcome produces a 100 percent replacement. Finally, a 70 percent replacement pension can be earned on a risk-free basis with a 30 percent of pay contribution rate.

These analyses lead to the visualization of three possible outcomes for Generation 1 after a 35-year accumulation period: (1) the accumulated assets are indeed sufficient to buy an inflation-indexed annuity replacing 70 percent of final earnings, (2) the accumulated assets are sufficient to buy 100 percent replacement; and, (3) the accumulated assets can buy only a 40 percent replacement pension. These prospects raise the following critical questions: How much does Generation 2 have to be compensated in order to underwrite the risk that there are insufficient assets at the end of Generation 1's accumulation period to buy the normal 70 percent replacement rate pension? Or, in other words, what kind of insurance premium does Generation 2 have to be paid to underwrite Generation 1's shortfall risk?

INTERGENERATIONAL BARGAINING

Now the bargaining begins. Generation 1's negotiator makes the first offer: Generation 1 will forgo all the upside if Generation 2 underwrites all the downside. Generation 2's negotiator responds that a deal based on this offer would mean that Generation 1 would get the normal pension, which costs 30 percent of pay on a risk-free basis for only 15 percent of pay, but without taking any risk. Generation 2 would have to be risk-neutral rather than risk-averse in order to accept this offer. This is not a defensible stance for Generation 2's negotiator to take, although the specific degree of risk aversion to assume is a very difficult assessment to make. So the offer is turned down.

Generation 1's negotiator now realizes the following: In order for Generation 2 to underwrite any of Generation 1's shortfall risk, Generation 1 has to give up more than just the upside in case of a high-return-regime outcome. In addition, Generation 1 will either have to contribute more than the normal 15 percent of pay during its 35-year accumulation period, accept less than the normal 70 percent replacement rate pension in case of a low-return regime outcome, or do a combination of the two. After a few more rounds of bargaining, the deal is struck. For agreeing to underwrite half of the estimated low-return-regime risk, Generation 2 is promised that Generation 1 will: contribute 20 percent of pay rather than 15 percent, give up all of the upside in case of a high-return-regime outcome; and, accept a 60 percent replacement rate pension in case of a low-return-regime outcome.

This thought experiment has produced four important conclusions:

1. Investment-regime risk is indeed potentially insurable up to a point.
2. If the current generation imposes investment-regime risk on future generations, these future generations should receive fair compensation for undertaking this burden.
3. Deals fair to following generations are unlikely to be struck unless a bargaining agent representing their interests is present at the bargaining table (Woody Brock also makes this point in his February 2005 Strategic Economic Decisions Report).
4. Even if a fair deal is struck, the question of its future enforceability remains.

ROBUST COURSE-CORRECTION MECHANISMS REQUIRED

Seen through the prism of our thought experiment, this shared investment risk pension (i.e., DB plan) is a natural extension of The Optimal Pension System (TOPS) set out in the previous chapter. From the individual participant perspective, the auto-pilot savings/investment approach remains in DB plans in the sense that they are not involved in contribution rate/investment policy decisions. Organizationally, the arm's-length, well-governed pension co-op with sufficient scale to be cost-effective also remains. Even the aggregated investment policy of all the TOPS participants taken together might not be very different from the normal investment policy of the collective DB model.

So what is different in the DB model? Pension co-ops operating DB plans need effective course-correction mechanisms to remain sustainable. This means that when actual investment experience moves plan assets materially above or below their target value, the pension deal must trigger some predetermined, fair combination of changes in contributions, changes in benefits, and changes in investment policy to return the plan to a sustainable trajectory. Research shows course-correction packages must be aggressive in order to maintain plan sustainability, implying simultaneous adjustments may be needed in contribution rates, benefit levels, and risk budgets.

This need for effective and fair course correction mechanisms is the Achilles heel of today's public sector and industry DB pension plans. Most of the mechanisms we see in use today simply cannot pass the predetermined, effective and fair test. Instead, they are usually ad hoc, ineffective, and unfair. Corporate DB plans suffer from the further complication that the finances of the corporation and of the pension plan are intertwined. The existence of pension benefit insurance in case of insolvency creates an additional layer of complexity. Now the financial interests of the current generation of plan members, bond holders, shareholders, corporate managers, and pension guarantors can often not be resolved, let alone those of future generations.

THE FLAWED DB MODEL

The potential welfare/utility gains attached to generating pensions through TOPS arrangements are likely to be highly material for most people. The solid research results on the dysfunctional financial behavioral of individuals, and on material agency costs, offer persuasive evidence that participants in TOPS arrangements will easily end up with twice or three times the pension payments that people might generate if left to their own savings and investment devices.

Relative to this research-based TOPS standard, will moving to a risk-sharing DB arrangement result in further clear welfare/utility gains? The logic of this chapter suggests the answer is, possibly in theory, but not likely in practice. For example, current DB deals have been struck without the involvement of bargaining agents representing the interests of future generations. As a result, DB-based pension contracts unfairly favor current generations at the expense of future generations. Research further suggests that current course-correction mechanisms are not vigorous enough to maintain long-term DB plan sustainability when faced with material adverse experience. Finally, in a corporate context, the potential conflicting interests of current plan members, bond holders, shareholders, management, and pension guarantors add additional sources of game theory-driven moves by bargaining groups to extract wealth from, and shift losses to weaker stakeholder groups.

So we conclude that relative to the TOPS standard, as a practical matter, DB plans do not enhance the aggregate welfare/utility of stakeholder groups, but merely redistribute it from stakeholder groups in the weakest bargaining positions to those in the strongest positions. This is the serious, potentially fatal, flaw in DB plans we spoke of at the beginning of this chapter.

BAD SCIENCE

A final question: Why has it taken us so long to reach so fundamental a conclusion about pension contracts that involve shared risks between various stakeholder groups? Our short answer is: bad science. In other words, many of us have gone along with the proposition that collective risk-sharing in pension arrangements is a "good thing" without examining whether the proposition stands up to the hard, bright light of logic and science. We have permitted the actuarial and accounting professions to tell us how to manage and account for DB arrangements without really thinking through the underlying economics. Rephrasing Jane Jacobs, we have "become arrested in the stage of singling out isolated bits of pension systems, with little grasp of how they interact with the other bits." Mea culpa.

CHAPTER 13

Peter Drucker's Pension Legacy: A Vision of What Could Be

"Mr. Drucker was celebrated for his clear thinking and engaging analysis, rather than any single theory or research. He had a good eye for things to come..."

From Peter Drucker's obituary by Kathryn Harris,
Bloomberg News

November 11, 2005

TWO HANDSHAKES TO REMEMBER

The two of us stood huddled together on a pier overlooking the windy Wellington, New Zealand, harbor a few weeks ago. Suddenly the grizzled old-timer turned to me, shook my hand, and announced that he had been a steward on the Cunard liner *Queen Mary* during World War II, and had personally served Winston Churchill his morning coffee many times. He said: "You have just shaken a hand that shook Churchill's hand 60 years ago." Two months prior, I was one of three visitors to the Drucker household in Claremont, California, where a 96-year old Peter Drucker himself had also greeted me with a handshake. Two handshakes to remember! When I arrived back home from my New Zealand–Australia trip, Drucker's obituary was waiting for me. I read there that Drucker's first book *The End of Economic Man* (1939) had been favorably reviewed in the *Times Literary Supplement* by none other than ... Winston Churchill. The past had miraculously touched the present.

As examples of her observation that he "had a good eye for things to come," Kathryn Harris noted in her obituary that Drucker predicted the coming importance of computers in the 1950s, foresaw the rise of Japan as an economic power in the 1960s, and warned of a coming backlash against executive pay practices in the 1990s. As have most other Drucker-watchers, Harris missed his prescient observations in the 1970s about the coming "pension revolution." About his 1976 book *The Unseen Revolution: How Pension Fund Socialism Came to America,* Drucker himself would write 20 years later: "No book of mine was ever more on target, and no book of mine has been ever more totally ignored." Two earlier chapters revisited the messages of Drucker's 1976 book. Here, we expand on our earlier assessment, and evaluate how some of the globe's major retirement income systems rate today relative to the Drucker pension vision set out 30 years ago.

THE MELBOURNE MESSAGE

The rating project arose out of an invitation to assess the quality of the Australian pension system in front of 1,800 delegates to the 2005 Australian Superannuation Fund Association (ASFA) in Melbourne on November 10. Our presentation, titled "How 'Super' Are Australian Pension Funds?", commenced by constructing The Optimal Pension System. TOPS, of course, is the manifestation of Drucker's pension vision. Admittedly, we have rearranged some details, and filled in some gaps. But the broad strokes of TOPS were already there 30 years ago.

The Drucker vision starts with motivation. Developed economies should foster the adequate, stable consumption of goods and services for all citizens from birth until death. While governments can and should underwrite a basic level of universal income support through the tax system, Drucker believed that workplace pensions should also play an important role in providing adequate, stable postretirement income to workers. To achieve this goal, workplace pension plans should cover most workers, and should address two further important challenges:

1. Pension plans should be designed so that workers are not left to make complex savings and investment decisions on their own.
2. Pension plans should be structured so that decisions are made solely in the best interests of plan participants by arm's-length, "expert" organizations.

We noted that during the last 30 years, a significant body of research has confirmed these two TOPS requirements. Behavioral finance research has documented a long list of human foibles such as lack of self-control, lack of firm preferences, inertia/procrastination, overconfidence, and aversion to realizing losses. At the same time, the underperformance of mutual funds relative to pension funds seems to be largely explained by the much higher costs of mutual fund investing. These much higher costs in turn seem to be related to a fundamental conflict of interest between mutual fund managers who prefer higher compensation to lower compensation, and most of their clients who are not as sensitive to high-fee structures as they should be.

TOPS: NEITHER DC NOR DB

Figure 13.1 lists the six critical characteristics of TOPS. Three address the "human foibles" challenges, and the other three address the "agency" challenges identified by Drucker. The result combines the best features of traditional DC and DB plans, but without their historical baggage. For example, TOPS is an individual-based, rather than a collective scheme, in the sense that individual participants have their own investment accounts. However, there is also an automatic, dynamic, age-based, transparent process of accumulating a portfolio of deferred annuities over time. In this sense, TOPS also has a collective element related to pooling longevity risk. Organizationally, TOPS is managed by an expert single-purpose pension co-op large enough to enjoy significant scale economies.

At the same time, TOPS leaves the historical baggage associated with traditional DC and DB plans behind. Gone are the 20 (or more!) investment choices and high fees still associated with so many DC plans today. Gone are the fuzzy valuations and the game theory-based risk shifting strategies still associated with so many DB plans today. Gone are the amateur, ad-hoc

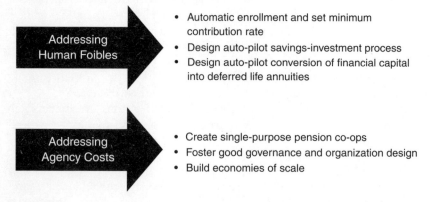

TOPS: THE OPTIMAL PENSION SYSTEM

Addressing Human Foibles
- Automatic enrollment and set minimum contribution rate
- Design auto-pilot savings-investment process
- Design auto-pilot conversion of financial capital into deferred life annuities

Addressing Agency Costs
- Create single-purpose pension co-ops
- Foster good governance and organization design
- Build economies of scale

FIGURE 13.1 The Optimal Pension System (TOPS).

governance and decision-making processes still associated with so many DC and DB plans today.

Peter Drucker would heartily approve!

TOPS AND INVESTING

As Drucker's obit noted, he was a grounded, clear thinker and analyst rather than a theorist. So, like John Maynard Keynes before him, he was profoundly skeptical of the institutional investment processes he observed. While he didn't use Keynes's "beauty contest" metaphor, he also observed the futility of investment managers trying to outperform each other in a giant zero-sum investment game less fees. Yet, Drucker observed that at the same time, workers were becoming the indirect owners of the means of production through their participation in pension plans. It was this observation that inspired his 1976 book title *The Unseen Revolution: How Pension Fund Socialism Came to America.*

All this logically leads to the definition of the three functional "investment styles" we have been writing about. Risk-minimizing (RM) strategies match investment flows from interest and principal maturities to payment obligations. Short-horizon risky (SHR) strategies exploit the behavioral foibles of retail and institutional "beauty contest" investors to generate material returns at modest levels of risk. Long-horizon risky (LHR) strategies acquire or create uncertain long-horizon cash-flows at prices that reflect risk-based required rates of return (hurdle rates). It is these LHR strategies that logically lead to Drucker's conclusion that pension funds must begin to act like the owners of the means of production. Collectively, they increasingly *are* the owners of the means of production.

Another logical extension of this investment framework is that TOPS pension funds need to only manage two portfolios over time. The RM portfolio continually mimics the portfolios of current and deferred annuities already purchased by plan participants. The SHR/LHR portfolio is the combination of SHR and LHR strategies that continually maximizes expected net excess return per unit of risk relative to the RM portfolio, subject to a predetermined risk budget. Younger plan members have largely SHR/LHR portfolio exposure. Older plan members (especially retirees) have largely RM (i.e., current and deferred annuities) exposure.

TOPS AND GOVERNANCE

Drucker stated the obvious when he observed that if pension funds are going to become the dominant owners of society's means of production, they need to be effective owners. But pension funds can only become effective owners if they themselves are effectively governed. That in turn requires that pension fund boards of trustees be effective bodies that collectively understand the meaning of "good governance," and have the mandate and the motivation to implement it. Drucker correctly identified this latter requirement as the potential Achilles heel of his 1976 vision of "pension fund socialism."

Drucker was right to be worried. In the first formal assessment of the quality of pension fund governance that we are aware of (1992), anthropologists William O'Barr and John Conley concluded that the pension fund governance practices they observed were like "looking into an airliner cockpit at 30,000 feet and finding that there is no one in there." Subsequent studies in which we were personally involved confirmed that there were indeed identifiable elements of dysfunction in pension fund governance practices around the world. A new 2005 study sponsored by the Rotman International Centre for Pension Management (ICPM) at the University of Toronto confirms that even today, board of trustee selection and board effectiveness evaluation processes continue to be problematic, including in many of the globe's largest pension funds (this new research is covered in Part Three of this book).

Yet good pension fund governance is not rocket science. It is a matter of being true to the following four principles (from Ronald Capelle, 2004 ICPM Colloquium):

1. Board is accountable for ensuring work to further stakeholder interests is done optimally.
2. Board does *not* do this work itself.
3. Board member selection criteria are (a) appropriate skill/knowledge sets, (b) value the work, (c) constructive behavior, and (d) strategic reasoning capability.
4. Board must establish self-management and self-evaluation capability.

Is your pension fund applying these four governance principles today?

TOPS AND THE REAL WORLD

So, finally, here is the report card evaluating the globe's pension systems against the TOPS standard:

1. **Human foibles**. The Dutch and the Australians lead the way in enforcing high workforce coverage, encouraging high contribution rates, and designing auto-pilot savings-investment processes. DC plans everywhere (with a few notable exceptions) still lack automatic annuity transition mechanisms.

2. **Agency issues**. The Dutch and the Australians also lead in the creation of large, arm's-length, single-purpose co-ops to manage their pension arrangements. North America continues to have material pension components that are politically tainted or company sponsored, and mutual fund managed.

3. **Governance**. Governance processes are improving everywhere, but there are still only a handful of pension funds around the world today that could pass Drucker's "good governance" standard with flying colors.

4. **Investing**. Not surprisingly, it is the globe's large, well-governed, single-purpose pension co-ops that are leading the way in driving "beauty contest" investing out of their investment processes. These institutions are also beginning to behave as the responsible owners of the means of production that Drucker envisaged.

So Drucker might observe today that students of his 1976 pension manifesto around the globe are showing considerable progress in some areas, but that much work remains to be done.

THE DRUCKER VISIT

As our visit with Peter Drucker commenced in late August, it was immediately clear that his health was failing. Yet, he still spoke with passion about the importance of a life-time commitment to learning, and about the importance of effective not-for-profit organizations in sustaining civil society. I asked him how he thought his now 30-year old "pension revolution" was unfolding. He observed that risks were being individualized, and that it would take a major economic setback to assess how strong today's pension systems really were.

I reminded him that he had praised the Teachers Insurance and Annuity Association–College Retirement Equities Fund (TIAA-CREF, the American TOPS poster child) as an effective pension organization in his 1976 book. With a slight smile, he responded: "Yes, and they still send Doris and me our pension check on time every month." A poignant reminder why the pension revolution must go on.

Three

Pension Fund Governance

"The meaning and purpose of a problem seems not to lie in its solution, but in our working on it incessantly."

Carl Jung

CHAPTER 14

Reinventing Pension Fund Management: Easier Said than Done

"A paradigm shift takes place when [our] world is qualitatively transformed and quantitatively enriched by fundamental novelties of either fact or theory..."

Thomas Kuhn

A PARADIGM SHIFT?

Sixty pension fund executives from the United States, Canada, and Europe representing 47 organizations with aggregate assets of about $1 trillion gathered in Toronto recently. Their mission was to participate in a workshop hosted by KPA Advisory Services Ltd. and CEM Benchmarking Inc. (CEM). The workshop goal was to assess whether, by Thomas Kuhn's standard, the pension fund management paradigm has indeed shifted and, if so, how pension funds should respond. The shift conclusion was a somewhat hesitant "yes." Why hesitant? Because while participants agreed that the pensions world has indeed been qualitatively and quantitatively transformed and enriched (impoverished?) by fundamental novelties of both fact and theory, it was not clear to many of the attendees what they or their organizations should, or even could, do about it.

The purpose of this chapter is to sketch out how and why the defined benefit (DB) pension fund management paradigm has shifted, and to explain why it is so difficult for many pension fund organizations to effectively respond to that shift. As the chapter title says, reinventing pension fund management is easier said than done.

NOVELTIES OF FACT

So what has changed? For starters, workshop participants reflected on these four facts:

1. The mark-to-market funded ratio of the typical DB plan has dropped some 40 points (say from 130 percent to 90 percent) in the last three years, as both equity prices and interest rates have fallen.
2. This had made pension regulators nervous, as it has security analysts studying the financial consequences for companies with large and mature DB pension plans. Chief financial officers (CFOs) are searching for the best way to plug the net liability holes.
3. In the public sector, there is no budget room for making additional contributions into now underfunded pension plans. The search for financial resources to shore up sagging funded ratios has begun.
4. At the same time, there is a growing realization that, despite much hoping and even praying, the next equity bull market may not just be around the corner.

This is a very different pensions world from that of the late 1990s.

NOVELTIES OF THEORY

Meanwhile, important new ideas have surfaced, too. Workshop participants discussed these four:

1. The recent prominence of John Nash and his contributions to game theory has made us realize that traditional DB plans are "game-able." Why? Because they offer opportunities for certain pension plan stakeholder groups to cut themselves into balance-sheet gains that they are, from a risk-bearing perspective, not entitled to. On the flip side, other stakeholder groups may be able to shift the financial pain associated with risk bearing to others, when they should really be sharing in that pain. "Game-ability" becomes especially problematic when the DB "pension deal" has not been fully spelled out. Incomplete "pension deals" turn risk management into a quagmire. Whose risks are to be managed? Can the question even be answered?
2. "Good governance" is another idea whose time has finally arrived. It has been 10 years since anthropologists William O'Barr and John Conley dropped their book bomb *Fortune and Folly* on an unsuspecting pension fund management community. Their tales of hide-bound culture, responsibility shifting, and fawning behavior toward service suppliers

by pension trustees and executives rocked the pension community. Subsequent quantitative work by Ambachtsheer and others supported the original O'Barr-Conley conclusions. More recently, the entire corporate world has been rocked by "Enronitis," shorthand for endemic governance failure well beyond the pension fund sector. Thus, "good governance" has finally become more than just a buzzword.

3. While "enterprise risk management" is not a new idea, taking it seriously in the pension fund sector is. Behavioral finance helps explain why. To truly understand risk, you've got to feel the pain. Working through the consequences of a 40-point drop on a pension plan's funded ratio will do that for you. Thus, trustees and pension executives now face an interesting practical risk management question that was once only hypothetical: "Is our plan risk tolerance the same with a 90 percent funded ratio as it was at 130 percent funded?" A question easier asked than answered. What is certain is that without changing balance-sheet risk exposure, a funded ratio in the 60 to 80 percent range now becomes a real possibility for a few years hence. That was not the case three years ago, when the ratio was 130 percent.

4. The current fund management paradigm continues to distinguish between "asset mix policy" and "implementation" decisions. Increasingly, we are beginning to see this split as an artifact created by a capital asset pricing model long on theoretical elegance and short on realism, by a historical constraint on computational power, and by a service-provider industry (consultants, money managers, custodians) with considerable vested interest in maintaining the status quo. However, the number of influential voices questioning the validity of the current fund management paradigm is growing. Its Achilles heel is the 5 percent equity risk premium (ERP), which justified taking the "status quo" view of the pension fund management world in the 1980s and 1990s. However, even today, after a three-year equities bear market, calculations suggest that 2 percent is a more realistic ERP expectation than the historical 5 percent. Thus, loading 95 percent of balance-sheet risk on the traditional 60-40 asset mix policy continues to be problematic. This mix doesn't offer enough excess return over the risk-minimizing asset mix policy to justify the total balance-sheet risk exposure it creates. Thus, today's fund management challenge is all about identifying and implementing investment strategies that do pass some reasonable minimum required price of risk (MRPR) test.

These "novelties of fact and theory" argue strongly for a reinvention of the pension (and endowment) fund management process. So how should the pension (and endowment) fund management community respond?

PENSION INDUSTRY RESPONSES

How did the workshop participants see the implications of the cited "novelties of fact and theory" for them and for their organizations? Well, there was a minority view and a majority view. The minority of the fund management organizations represented at the workshop has developed, or is in the process of developing, proactive integrative responses to the new pensions world. Thus, it is fair to say that they have, or are in the process of, reinventing themselves as fund management organizations. However, for the majority of the organizations represented in the room, it seemed to be, more than not, business as usual. By logical extension, this is the likely mind-set of the vast majority of fund management organizations outside the room as well.

Why is responding proactively to changing circumstances and ideas so difficult for so many pension fund organizations? Here are some of the reasons that surfaced at the workshop:

- **No focus, or the wrong focus "at the top."** In the public and union sectors, this may mean political or personal goals trumping fiduciary goals. In the corporate sector, it may mean accounting requirements trumping economic risk management requirements. In all sectors, the "no/wrong focus" problem may simply reflect an inadequate "at the top" knowledge and understanding of pension economics, finance, and investments. What is the typical response to these inadequacies? A strong belief that there is safety in numbers, so let's just do what everyone else is doing. As John Maynard Keynes observed almost 70 years ago, absent strong convictions, people prefer failing conventionally to succeeding unconventionally.
- **"Silo" organization designs.** An integrative approach to pension plan management requires an integrative approach to organization design. Yet inefficient "silo" approaches continue to dominate. For example, assets continue to be managed without regard for the liabilities and their financial characteristics. The CEM database of DB pension funds provided a shocking example of this reality. The funds in the database were ranked by the inflation sensitivity of the associated liabilities, and then split into "most inflation-sensitive" and "least inflation-sensitive" halves. These material differences in liability inflation sensitivity should have resulted in similar material differences in asset mix policy. Yet the average asset mixes of the two halves were identical!
- **Management by committee.** Additional poor organizational practices inside the silos often compound the problem. Surely, the most fundamental organization design rule of all is to clearly separate the

governance, executive, and operations functions. Yet this rule continues to be blithely ignored by many pension plan sponsors, as they persist in encouraging their pension committees to play the dual roles of both the governors and the manager of the pension fund. This is organizational folly!

- **Poor professional advice.** Problems here often start with actuarial advisers who tell clients only what they want to hear. Economic truths are buried by rosy assumptions. So, for example, pension liabilities are often understated by assuming pension assets will earn a risk premium. The riskier the investment policy, the lower the pension liability. This is not a joke. It really happens. Investment advisers then often move in to foster further dysfunction with static asset liability management studies using unrealistic projections, and with investment management structures that suit their own needs more than their clients'. The combined result of all this is that many pension ships are being navigated by pilots who neither know nor care about the ships' final destinations.

- **Legislative/regulatory instability.** Sometimes the legislative/regulatory yardsticks move in the middle of the game. For example, the Dutch pension regulator has just announced stringent new DB funding requirements in the face of declining funded ratios. Meanwhile, the Ontario government has just withdrawn legislation that would have clarified DB "pension deals" there and, by extension, in the rest of Canada. It's hard to play a game where the rules may change in the middle.

Yet, despite these barriers, some funds do reinvent themselves. How do they do it?

CROSSING THE "INNOVATION CHASM"

In the closing workshop session, CEM partner John McLaughlin drew a parallel between the reinvention challenge facing pension fund leaders today and the implementation challenges facing all visionaries/innovators at all times. Researchers write of an ever-present "innovation chasm" between a tiny band of visionaries/innovators and a much larger group of "pragmatists" who represent the most promising candidates to adopt new ideas and their implications. However, while these "pragmatists" will consider new ideas on the one hand, they are very much "show me" people on the other. Thus, they will not move without a convincing, compelling cost-benefit story.

Workshop participants heard a number of such convincing, compelling stories from members of the tiny visionaries/innovators band in the pension fund management field. What were the common threads in these stories? Not surprisingly, an integrative ability to deal with the barriers to change cited above. Internally, this involves mission clarity and leadership at the top, clarity in organization design, and a capacity for making and implementing strategic decisions consistent with the mission. Externally, it involves confidently employing service providers (whether actuaries, investment consultants, money managers, or custodians) in a "value for money" context defined by the fund organization itself, and not by the outside service providers.

All well and good, you say, but give me concrete examples of actual innovation initiatives discussed in the workshop! Here is a list:

- Fully define the pension contract, including the target benefit and who bears what risks in going-concern and termination contexts.
- Pull together the asset and liability dimensions of the pension plan into one business unit charged with managing both sides of the resulting balance sheet.
- Clearly define the respective accountabilities of the board of governors and the fund's executive in the governance and management of the pension plan.
- Instruct the plan actuary to regularly value the accrued liabilities using the current yield curve of default-risk-free bonds, with and without wage and price inflation "best estimates." Compare the resulting "market value" liability estimates to the market value of plan assets in order to regularly monitor the plan's true funded status. Regularly estimate possible plan cost trajectories based on possible asset-liability trajectories.
- Devise a liability-related risk-minimizing portfolio as the basis for assessing investment policy risk and reward.
- Control balance-sheet risk by establishing a balance-sheet risk budget, which is then monitored regularly over time.
- Establish a hurdle rate (MRPR), which must be surpassed in order to compensate for the balance-sheet risks being undertaken.
- Organize the investment function around three types of strategies: risk-minimizing, long-horizon risky, and short-horizon risky. Drop everything that doesn't clearly fit into one of these three categories.
- Measure only what should be managed. Stop measuring anything that detracts from this fundamental focus.

So where would you like to start reinventing your organization?

CHAPTER 15

Should (Could) You Manage Your Fund Like Harvard or Ontario Teachers'?

"Harvard's investment process looks and feels less like a conventional money management firm, and more like a longer-term version of the proprietary trading operations of the major Wall Street broker/dealers."

Harvard Management Company (2001)
A Harvard Business School Case Study

"We had one of our best return years ever in 2003, yet our risk was lower than it had been during the prior four years. This reflects the fact that we use a disciplined risk management process. We believe that this process sets us apart..."

Bob Bertram, Chief Investment Officer
Ontario Teachers' Pension Plan

FOUR THINGS IN COMMON

Last year in March, our friends at Commonfund asked us to engage Jeremy Siegel in a debate on the equity risk premium. This March, they asked us back to participate in a debate titled "Should (Could) You Look Like Harvard?" Our position was "yes" on both counts, and the goal of this chapter was to explain why. Then the Annual Report of Ontario Teachers' Pension Plan (OTPP) arrived. As the Teachers' Report illustrates many of the "should (could)" points we intended to make about the Harvard

Management Company (HMC) model, the title of this chapter expanded accordingly.

Some of you are thinking: "Wait a minute, Harvard manages endowment assets, Teachers' pension assets. Will that not be like comparing apples and oranges?" An important message of this chapter is that this is not the case. Indeed, we assert that institutional investors creating the kind of measurable value for stakeholders that Harvard and Teachers' have four things in common:

1. A legal foundation that clarifies stakeholder interests and minimizes the potential for agency conflicts.
2. A governance process that crystallizes organization mission and understands the critical elements needed to achieve it.
3. Investment beliefs that can stand the tests of reason, informed debate, and occasional revision when new evidence comes to light.
4. Investment processes that integrate stakeholder risk tolerances and investment beliefs using combinations of seasoned judgment and state-of-the-art financial engineering techniques.

This chapter will show how Harvard and Teachers' pass the stakeholder value-creation test both in principle and in practice. It will also offer reasons why many other institutional investors, whether pension funds, endowment funds, or other, fail on both counts.

LEGAL FOUNDATIONS: SOLID OR NOT?

HMC was founded in 1974 as a wholly owned subsidiary of Harvard University. Its sole purpose is to manage the university's endowment and other (much smaller) financial assets. HMC's board of directors is appointed by the president and fellows of Harvard University. OTPP was founded in 1990 as an independent corporation to manage the assets and administer the benefits of the Ontario Teachers' Pension Plan. OTPP's board of directors is appointed by the pension plan's cosponsors: the government of Ontario and the Ontario Teachers' Federation.

Contrast this clarity of organizational purpose with the fuzziness embodied in the organizational structures of most corporate defined benefit (DB) pension plans. Now there is no separate organization charged with the management of the pension plan, or a separate board of directors to oversee pension plan management. Pension assets are usually managed in one place and the benefits administered in another. This segmentation carries through to the determination of the fund's investment policy. The fiction is that this policy is to be determined "for the sole benefit of the beneficiaries."

The reality is usually driven by some fuzzy mix of corporate and agency objectives.

The mutual fund industry represents an even greater quagmire. Now we have investment funds typically managed by privately or publicly owned "for-profit" management companies. Informational asymmetry between mutual fund unit holders and the professional management companies virtually assures that the former pay too much for too little value, while the latter get overcompensated for doing too little of value. Only the true mutualization of the mutual fund industry can level this very uneven playing field. In contrast, this necessary mutualization was built into the HMC and OTPP charters from their very beginnings.

GOVERNANCE AND MANAGEMENT: UNDERSTANDING THE DIFFERENCE

Boards of directors should govern, not manage. Understanding this may be the critical divide separating effective boards from ineffective boards. Why? Because understanding the difference between governing and managing leads directly to understanding that you can't have a strong organization without a strong leader. Finding and supporting such a leader is a critical board responsibility. This is not the time and place to sing the praises of HMC's CEO Jack Meyer or OTPP's Claude Lamoureux. Instead, we praise the boards of these organizations for clearly delegating the management function to individuals in whom they have complete confidence.

Indeed, there is more praise to come. Attracting and retaining excellent people requires compensation schemes designed with that purpose in mind. That means designing schemes in which people inside the organization share in the value created through their expertise. In the investment business, that means allocating a small percentage of net excess returns relative to appropriate benchmarks to the internal management team. When value creation is high (i.e., in the billions of dollars in the cases of HMC and OTPP), almost any participation formula produces high individual compensation levels (i.e., in the millions of dollars). It takes strong boards to withstand the negative publicity that can follow the public reporting of such "high" compensation levels.

This clarity between what are governance versus management responsibilities at HMC and OTPP contrasts sharply with what we see in many other pension and endowment fund organizations. Many boards (or their equivalent) seem incapable of drawing a clear distinction between governing and managing. Indeed, some boards seem to take pleasure in dabbling in fund management and even operational matters themselves. Many boards also seem to value keeping internal "staff" compensation at measurably low levels. Never mind that organizational performance may suffer as a result.

Ironically, the total unit operating costs of poorly governed pension and endowment funds often end up at the high end of the benchmarking scale. Why? Because funds often pay outside service-provider fees that are high relative to the value these fees actually produce. Of course, these external fees usually don't get directly measured and disclosed. So, apparently, they don't need to be managed either.

INVESTMENT BELIEFS: THEIRS OR YOURS?

Consumer firms have beliefs about how people make purchasing decisions. Technology and health care firms have beliefs about the science behind their production processes. Similarly, investment firms have beliefs about valuation and about how financial markets function. As in other industries, such beliefs should be based on good theory validated by good research. As importantly, investment beliefs should be updated over time as new theories supported by new research findings replace the old. An important caveat for investment firms is that they should "own" their investment beliefs. That is, these beliefs should be debated and developed inside the organization itself, and not blindly imported from the outside.

What might a defensible "investment beliefs" set look like today? Here is our abbreviated offering:

- Investors are generally risk averse and require expected risk premiums before they will hold investments they deem risky.
- Investment risk is contextual, and thus the riskiness of any investment depends in part on the objectives of the investor.
- Investment returns are partially predictable. Predictive processes have either long-horizon or short-horizon orientations.
- Long-horizon processes focus on projecting and valuing uncertain future cash flows and are positive-sum games. Such cash flows can sell at relatively high prices (and offer relatively low prospective returns) in optimistic investment regimes, and at relatively low prices (and offer relatively high prospective returns) in pessimistic investment regimes.
- Short-horizon processes focus on predicting and exploiting temporary securities pricing discrepancies and are zero-sum games before expenses. Someone's positive alpha is always somebody else's negative alpha.
- All other things equal, lower investment costs are always better than higher investment costs.

Do HMC and OTPP subscribe to such a beliefs set? Their organizational structures, their behavior, and their investment results suggest they that they do.

In sharp contrast, most pension and endowment fund organizations import their investment beliefs from the outside, often from the pension investment consulting community. The typical result is continued faith that a 5 percent equity risk premium will eventually carry the day, and that producing some additional return through highly complex external active management structures continues to be worth the time and money spent on it.

INVESTMENT PROCESSES: LIKE WALL STREET?

At the beginning of this chapter, we quoted a Harvard Business School case writer who observed that HMC's investment processes "look and feel less like those of a conventional money management firm, and more like a longer-term version of the proprietary trading operations of a Wall Street broker-dealer." He or she could have said the same thing about OTPP's investment processes. The design of these investment processes is no accident. They follow logically from the kind of "investment beliefs" set just described above.

First, there is a clear distinction between long-horizon and short-horizon processes. The former focus on assessing uncertain future cash flows and how they are being priced. At the Commonfund conference, for example, HMC's Jack Meyer professed to like timber at current prices (he also confessed that HMC already had a material investment in this asset class). North of the border, OTPP has been so successful participating in the creation of new business trusts that strip out a layer of taxation that the recent federal budget contained a measure explicitly designed to limit this value-enhancing strategy. These kinds of activities explain why the "policy portfolio" concept has become a much more fluid, dynamic concept in both organizations.

In contrast, short-horizon processes focus on identifying and exploiting temporary financial market pricing discrepancies. A measure of the importance of this type of activity in a fund is to compare the organization's gross to net assets. If the former are materially greater than the latter, it is a good bet that the organization has considerable exposure to market-neutral, long-short, and other derivatives-based strategies. In their most recent annual reports, HMC's and OTPP's gross-to-net asset ratios were both well above 1.0.

Two final points: First, these approaches to investing do not mean that all investment processes must all be managed internally. If it is more cost effective to outsource, so be it. Second, the investment processes employed by HMC and OTPP (whether managed internally or outsourced) require a major commitment to powerful, real-time risk management processes. Both organizations make it clear that they have made commitments to continuous risk management.

SHOULD YOU MANAGE LIKE HMC OR OTPP?

It is stating the obvious to say that most pension and endowment funds do not manage money or risk in the manner set out above. Should you? Our answer should not surprise you. The "should you?" question is equivalent to asking and answering the following four questions:

Q: *Should your fund have a legal foundation that clarifies stakeholder interests and minimizes the potential for agency conflicts?*

A: *Of course you should!*

Q: *Should your fund have a governance process that crystallizes organization mission and understands the critical elements needed to achieve it?*

A: *Of course you should!*

Q: *Should your fund have a set of investment beliefs that can stand the test of reason, informed debate, and occasional revision when new evidence comes to light?*

A: *Of course you should!*

Q: *Should you employ investment processes that integrate stakeholder risk tolerances and investment beliefs using combinations of seasoned judgement and state-of-the-art financial engineering techniques?*

A: *Of course you should!*

So should you manage like HMC or OTPP? Of course you should!

COULD YOU MANAGE LIKE HMC OR OTPP?

Could you manage like HMC or OTPP today? The answer for most pension and endowment funds today is equally obvious. They cannot. The purpose of this chapter is to provoke a debate on why this is the case. Is it your legal structure? Is it your governance process? Is it because you don't have the internal capability to articulate reasoned, informed investment beliefs? Or is it because you don't have the internal capability to turn those beliefs into sustainable, value-adding investment processes (whether managed internally or outsourced)?

When all is said and done, there is only one legitimate barrier to managing like HMC or OTPP, and that is insufficient scale. There is a critical minimum size requirement to being able to afford the necessary internal core executive capability to get the investment beliefs and the investment processes right. The good news is that this critical minimum size may be smaller than you think. We know some funds in the $2 to $3 billion range that score high on the "best practices" criteria we set out above.

There is even good news for pension and endowment funds below the critical minimum size. There is no reason why a Commonfund (or other large-scale fund of funds organization like it) can't manage like HMC or OTPP. Insist that it does![1]

----

[1] Since this chapter was written, Jack Meyer and some colleagues have left HMC to start up their own investment firm. Can their successors at HMC sustain its "high-performance" culture? Only time will tell.

CHAPTER 16

"Beauty Contest" Investing: Not Dead Yet

"If the whole market became more long-term and was trading on a 10-year outlook, that would be fine, but they're not, so you just have to trade on what they're trading on. . . ."

"If the trust is not in place, you have to make decisions looking over your shoulder, you gravitate towards those decisions which can be most easily defended if you are wrong. . . ."
Both quotes are from a study on institutional investor behavior titled "Meeting Objectives and Resisting Conventions" by Danyelle Guyatt, University of Bath, United Kingdom

(*Corporate Governance*, Vol. 5, No. 3, 2005)

"DÉJÀ VU ALL OVER AGAIN"

Observing active portfolio management from the inside out is quite an eye-opener for the uninitiated. We first had that opportunity 38 years ago when we traded the ivory halls of academia for a "real" job in the financial services industry. Dr. Danyelle Guyatt's opportunity came much more recently, as she studied the relationship between the Statements of Investment Policy & Goals (SIPGs) of three major U.K. financial organizations in the pensions/insurance field, and the behavior of 20 external and internal portfolio managers with investment mandates received from these institutions. The SIPGs and related documentation at the three institutions "amounted to over 250 pages." The 20 portfolio manager interviews, each lasting 1.5 hours, "were recorded and fully transcribed for analysis." The quotes at the beginning of this chapter were just two of many that resulted from these interviews.

Guyatt's findings suggest that little has changed in the institutional money management world since we had our own first look 38 years ago. As Yogi Berra would say, a case of "déjà vu all over again." On the one hand, the three SIPGs of the financial institutions were wonderfully aspirational, including stated intents to be responsible, long-term investors, with due regard for the importance of good corporate governance and other broad, long-horizon drivers of investment value. On the other hand, it was clear from the 20 interviews that most frontline active portfolio managers continue to live in a very different world. In Guyatt's assessment, their world is characterized by:

- **A pull toward short-termism.** While they agreed that it is in the interest of the three financial institutions' stakeholders to focus on longer horizons, the portfolio managers didn't think they could afford to invest that way. The perception is that if you don't beat your benchmark regularly in the shorter term, you won't be around to manage any money at all in the longer term. But that wasn't the only reason for pervasive short-termism among the 20 portfolio managers. There was also a consensus that the short term is where the action is. They relate most three- to six-month price moves to three- to six-month events. If you try to focus on a five- to ten-year horizon, you miss all the action!
- **Gravitation toward the defensible.** Active management involves being wrong. When that happens, you need an explanation that shows you are a "mainstream" investor rather than some flake who went way out on a limb. The easiest way to be "mainstream" is to do conventional things in conventional ways. As John Maynard Keynes once wrote: "Worldly wisdom teaches that it is better for reputation to fail conventionally than to succeed unconventionally."
- **No intellectual integration between institutional aspirations and investment behavior.** There is a genuine intellectual disconnect between the long-horizon institutional aspirations captured in the SIPGs and the implicit or explicit "investment models" being employed by the portfolio managers. There was much talk during the interviews of the need for "tangible evidence" such as changes in various financial ratios to justify portfolio management decisions. The problem with long-horizon investing is that it is based on "intangibles," and these "intangibles" just haven't worked their way into the conventional investment models. In the words of one interviewee: ". . . there is actually no proof that it works."

Guyatt concludes that the best explanation for the portfolio manager behavior she observed last year is rational "herding." Specifically, it is a form of risk management against reputation and career damage. Thirty-five years ago, in a largely pre–modern investment theory world, we observed the same behavior and simply accepted it as the way investment professionals plied their trade. Seventy years ago, Keynes called this type of behavior *beauty contest* investing. In other words, he characterized institutional investing as a giant charade, with the aim being to correctly guess which stocks market participants would find most attractive three to six months from now. Guyatt's contribution is to offer an economic rationale why today, 70 years later, "beauty contest" investing continues to be the dominant "active management" style. This is not just the case in the retail-oriented, unsophisticated world of mutual funds, but also in the supposedly much more sophisticated world of pensions and insurance.

WHY "BEAUTY CONTEST INVESTING" IS UGLY

All this raises two important questions: First, should "beauty contest" investing be eradicated? And second, if the answer is "yes" what is the best way to go about it? The "public interest" answer to the first question is an unambiguous "yes." Even the portfolio management community practicing "beauty contest" investing would agree (remember, they're only doing it because they think they *have* to, not necessarily because they *want* to!). If asked, they will tell you that this style of investing is ugly on both micro and macro levels. At the micro level, "beauty contest" investing is a zero-sum game less fee leakage. As a result, unwitting stakeholders in the mutual fund, pension, and insurance worlds transfer wealth to the suppliers of portfolio management services in the form of too-high active management fees. At the macro level, "beauty contest" investing contributes to dysfunction in the ways society's scarce savings are converted into additions to the stock of wealth-creating capital. By its very nature, this savings-to-productive capital conversion process must deal with long-horizon intangibles. It simply cannot be reduced to three- to six-month decision processes based on changing financial ratios. But, as noted, that's the game most active investment managers think they have to play. And if that is the case, to get their stock price up, corporate managers think they have to play that game, too. And so a self-sustaining, vicious cycle of savings misallocations destruction continues to go round and round....

INTEGRATIVE INVESTMENT THEORY

So how do investing institutions such as pension organizations break this vicious cycle? Two elements are needed. First, society needs a broader normative theory of investing that flushes issues such as "beauty contest investing" out in the open. Second, we need investment decision structures that reward productive forms of investing and punishes unproductive ones. While still in a formative stage, the needed broader normative theory of investing has already begun to emerge. See, for example, our chapter "Beyond Portfolio Theory: the Next Frontier", on what we have called *integrative investment theory* (IIT) in Part One of this book.

IIT identifies five drivers of value for the stakeholders of investing institutions such as pension organizations: (1) agency issues, (2) governance issues, (3) investment beliefs, (4) risk issues, and (5) financial engineering. Where does the "beauty contest investing" problem fit into this theory? Well, it has an agency element in the sense that this kind of investing exposes a misalignment of interests between investing institution stakeholders and the suppliers of investment management services. There is a governance element in the sense that this kind of investing exposes an organization design flaw (i.e., why are these suppliers operating with the wrong incentives?). There is also an investment beliefs element in the sense that if "beauty contest investing" is an unproductive form of investing, what are productive forms, and what is the basis of our beliefs?

INVESTMENT BELIEFS

Addressing the investment beliefs question first, 38 years of observation has led to a personal belief that there are three productive forms of investing: (1) risk-minimizing (RM), (2) long-horizon risky (LHR), and (3) short-horizon risky (SHR). The RM form focuses on covering future payment obligations with as little default and mismatch risk as possible. The LHR form focuses on acquiring or creating uncertain future long-horizon cash flows at prices that produce long-horizon expected returns which embody an adequate risk premium relative to the risk-minimizing strategy. The SHR form focuses on executing adversarial trading strategies that produce expected net returns on risk capital, which embody an adequate risk premium relative to the risk-minimizing strategy.

Not much more needs to be said about RM investing. Today, this is largely a financial engineering challenge, with the goal being to get the best possible match between future payment obligations and future principal and interest cash flows from a financial asset portfolio. Profitable SHR strategies also have large doses of financial engineering embodied in them. Today, they appear as diversified portfolios of 30 to 40 absolute-return strategies, each based on (ideally) independent predictive processes with sufficient accuracy to generate net trading profits. Of course, defining profitable SHR strategies is one thing; successfully implementing them is something else. Separating genuine, sustainable SHR strategies with legitimate excess return prospects from "pretend" ones that are merely repackaged "beauty contest" offerings is no easy task. It requires a high level of expertise not only in investment theory, but also in such areas as organizational stability assessment, incentive compensation structuring, and risk management to successfully separate the wheat from the chaff.

In contrast to successful RM and SHR strategies, financial engineering does not usually play a major role in devising and executing successful LHR strategies. Yes, there is usually a "tangible" element in LHR investing. If there are tangible assets and liabilities, whether physical or financial, they need to be valued. If the prospective LHR investment has a financial history, it should be studied. However, it is often the "intangible" elements that will determine the success or failure of a LHR investment. What are the important assumptions behind the cash-flow projections? What is the right "hurdle rate" for valuation purposes? How strong are the governance and management processes in the prospective LHR investment? Are they committed to long-horizon value creation? If there is a "brand," can it be successfully defended? Are research and development expenditures properly focused? How are environmental and other types of "externality" issues being managed? In short, socioeconomic and business judgments are the critical success drivers in LHR investing.

MANAGING FROM THE INSIDE OUT

So much for theory. What about practice? If a properly specified theory of investing leaves no room for dysfunctional "beauty contest investing," why is there still so much of it around? The question is easy enough to answer in the retail mutual fund world: informational asymmetry. Retail investors generally don't know what they don't know. Many willingly turn over their hard-earned dollars to mutual fund companies that will have great difficulty ever earning back the sales and management fees they charge their unsuspecting customers. But what about the wholesale pension fund world? It still has far too much "beauty contest" exposure as well. What's the explanation here?

Once again, the fault lies squarely on the customer side of the market. Most pension fund decision-making structures are simply not strong enough to place an outright ban on "beauty contest investing" in their investment strategy line-ups. Usually, the weakness starts right at the top, with most members of boards of trustees being scarcely better informed about "integrative investment theory" than their retail market counterparts. So they surround themselves with "expert" investment committees and investment consultants. Unfortunately, while this seems sensible in principle, it seldom works out that way in practice. Why? Because most investment committees and investment consultants are proponents of the "beauty contest" style of investing, too.

In short, "beauty contest investing" can be eradicated in practice only when three conditions exist. First, a board of trustees must understand the difference between the productive RM, SHR, and LHR investment styles and the unproductive "beauty contest" style. Second, they must be prepared to hire a CEO/CIO and give him or her a mandate to create value for stakeholders by maintaining an optimal mix of RM, SHR, and LHR exposures over time. Third, they have to stay the course through thick and thin.

We don't usually name names; however, this three-condition requirement is important enough to make an exception here. The Harvard Management Company, the Yale University Office of Investments, and the Ontario Teachers' Pension Plan have all accumulated outstanding investment records over extended periods of time. Why? Because the boards of these organizations understood the importance of managing "from the inside out." So they hired talented, like-minded "inside" people (specifically, Jack Meyer, David Swenson, and Bob Bertram), and gave them the authority to create value for stakeholders by maintaining optimal mixes of RM, SHR, and LHR exposures over time. Then they stayed the course through thick and thin.

Can your fund meet these three "success" requirements?

CHAPTER 17

Eradicating "Beauty Contest" Investing: What It Will Take

"Companies need to change the nature of their dialogue with stakeholders. That means first identifying investors who will support a company's strategy, and then attracting them."

Ian Davis
McKinsey Quarterly
April 2005

THE UGLINESS OF "BEAUTY CONTEST" INVESTING

John Maynard Keynes penned his famous diatribe against "beauty contest" investing 70 years ago. He characterized the nature of institutional investing as akin to a charade, with the aim being to correctly guess which stocks investors would find most attractive three to six months from now. In the preceding chapter we lamented that, 70 years later, there is little new under the sun. There is still far too much "beauty contest" investing around today, and not only in the retail-oriented, unsophisticated world of mutual fund investing. It continues to be a systemic problem in the supposedly more sophisticated worlds of pensions, insurance, and foundations, too.

"Beauty contest" investing is not just a harmless sport played for the amusement of the people who have situated themselves between millions of individual investors and their money. At a micro level, it is a zero-sum game minus material, value-destroying leakages in the form of intermediary marketing, management, and transaction costs. At a macro level, "beauty contest" investing promotes "short-termism" in decision making, a potentially even greater destroyer of economic value. "Short-termism" leads to the misallocation of society's savings into unproductive short-term uses, rather than into wealth-creating, long-horizon capital formation. For example, in a recent survey of 401 financial executives, the majority indicated that they would sacrifice value-creating projects if it meant falling short of the current quarter's consensus earnings, or break up a smooth progression of reported earnings. (John Graham, Campbell Harvey, and Shivaram Rajgopal, "The Economic Implications of Corporate Financial Reporting," NBER working paper, June 2004).

All this gets us to the goal of this chapter. It is to set out the necessary conditions for finally eradicating "beauty contest" investing from the face of the earth.

A TWO-PRONGED ERADICATION STRATEGY

Eradicating "beauty contest" investing requires two things: First, it requires a normative theory of investing in which "beauty contest" investing can be placed, and shown to be a material barrier to long-horizon wealth accumulation. We have been writing about "integrative investment theory" (IIT) for some time now. The latest version of it appears in Part One of this book under the title of "Beyond Portfolio Theory: The Next Frontier." The basic idea is that a comprehensive normative theory of investing must deal with more than just risk and return. It must also deal with context in the form of agency and governance issues. The agency dimension of IIT involves sorting out conflicts of interest in the financial food chain. It explains why "beauty contest" investing continues to exist from a supply perspective (i.e., suppliers will continue to offer "beauty contest" investment services as long as it is a profitable to do so). The governance dimension involves the building of "buy-side" organizations capable of creating value for stakeholders. Regarding "beauty contest" investing, the governance dimension of IIT explains why it continues to exist from a demand perspective (i.e., supposedly expert "buy-side" organizations continue to incorrectly think it is a wealth-creating activity for their stakeholders).

The second "beauty contest" eradication requirement logically follows from the first. It is not enough to point to required knowledge and behavioral shifts in the financial food chain from an investment theory perspective. There is also the practical "tipping point" question of what can be done to cause such shifts to actually occur. Logically, creating such a "tipping point" will require linking two productive elements in the financial food chain directly together. As McKinsey's Managing Director Ian Davis points out (see quote at the beginning of the chapter), corporations and investing institutions that understand the "win-win" synergy of long-horizon investing need to circumvent the value-destroying "beauty contest" link and begin to deal directly with each other.

WHAT CORPORATIONS MUST DO

Davis observes that to make this direct connection, corporations need to get on message. Shorter-term performance and longer-term corporate health are both important. By delivering on shorter-term commitments, management builds confidence in its longer-term strategies. Despite current concerns about "short-termism," current share prices in relation to earnings imply that investors do recognize that the lion's share of the average corporation's value lies in its earnings prospects beyond those of the next few years. Sound earnings prospects beyond the next few years in turn require a healthy company. That in turn requires a robust, credible strategic plan; productive, well-maintained assets; and innovative products, services, and processes. It means maintaining a fine reputation with customers, regulators, governments, and other stakeholders. Finally, it means being able to attract, retain, and develop high-performance talent. Managing in multiple time frames is difficult. It requires a conscious effort and disciplined organizational processes that support the effort.

Having said all this, Davis offers a final piece of advice. Doing the right things is not enough. A corporation also has to get its message out to its employees and to current and prospective investors. Employees must feel they are "in the loop" and involved in executing a corporate strategy they understand. Similarly, healthy companies should actively seek out investors looking for healthy companies. Such investors appreciate and value strategies that foster sources of sustainable advantage. They also appreciate metrics developed by the corporation to track its performance and health over time. Finally, healthy companies make their operational managers visible to the kind of investors they want to attract. In forming judgments about the sustainability of corporate performance, the caliber of frontline managers is often the determining factor.

WHAT INVESTING INSTITUTIONS MUST DO

Just as corporate behavior must change, so must institutional investor behavior. We don't hold out much hope for the mutual fund sector as it is currently constructed. Turning its informational advantage over its retail clientele into profits for mutual fund management companies is the essence of this sector's business model. Killing the goose laying the golden eggs is simply not on the mutual fund industry agenda. If change is going to come, it will have to come from the pension fund sector, where there is a far better alignment of interests between pension fund management and its stakeholders.

However, potential for positive change is one thing; turning it into reality is something else. Identifying the necessary conditions for change in the pension fund sector is not the problem. Adopting the following four-step discipline at the individual fund level would do it:

1. Embrace IIT and its implications.
2. Articulate a set of defensible investment beliefs.
3. Implement a value-creating investment process within a preestablished risk budget.
4. Monitor, learn, and sustain the process through time.

Adopting such a discipline would lead to an understanding that there are only three legitimate, value-creating investment "styles":

1. Risk-minimizing (RM)
2. Short-horizon risky (SHR)
3. Long-horizon risky (LHR)

RM investing is about covering future payment obligations with as little default and mismatch risk as possible. SHR investing focuses on executing adversarial trading strategies that produce expected net returns on risk capital which embody an adequate risk premium relative to the relevant RM strategy. The domain of LHR investing is acquiring or creating uncertain future cash flows at prices that produce long-horizon expected rates of return that embody an adequate risk premium relative to the relevant RM strategy.

Note that this definition of functional investment styles creates a direct link between corporations that want to create and maintain a sustainable advantage over time (i.e., they want to position themselves as attractive LHR investments), and financial institutions that want to invest in such corporations (i.e., they consciously seek attractive LHR investments).

A DEBILITATING PENSION FUND GOVERNANCE PROBLEM

Given this compelling logic, why does the natural affinity between LHR corporations and LHR investors continue to play out so tenuously in practice? In our view, it is because the pension fund sector continues to suffer from a broadly based, debilitating governance problem. Good governance principles require that boards of pension fund trustees are properly motivated, collegial, can think strategically—and have collective skill/experience sets relevant to carrying out the fiduciary responsibilities they have taken on. Based on personal observation, most boards can easily pass tests 1 and 2. Board members generally want to do the right thing, and want to be collegial about it. It is in passing tests 3 and 4 that the trouble typically lies. While some trustees do come from backgrounds where thinking strategically has been a requirement, many others do not. Trustees with requisite skill/experience sets to understand IIT and its implications for establishing and maintaining functional investment processes are in even shorter supply. Instead, most trustees arrive on the job with the "beauty contest" investment model firmly planted in their minds.

A survey carried out as part of the Rotman International Centre for Pension Management (ICPM) research program into pension fund governance confirms this viewpoint. The survey was first conducted in 1997 (80 responses) and repeated in 2005 (88 responses). The survey asked pension fund CEOs (or their equivalents) to rate 45 statements related to governance (16 statements), management (12 statements), and operations (17 statements) in their organizations on a scale from 6 to 1. A "6" rating indicates total agreement with the statement; a "1" rating total disagreement. The six statements in the Table 17.1 received the lowest ratings in the

TABLE 17.1 The Six Statements with the Lowest Pension Fund CEO Scores in Both 1997 and 2005

Governance-Related

- Our fund has an effective process for selecting, developing, and terminating its governing fiduciaries
- My governing fiduciaries examine and improve their own effectiveness on a regular basis.
- My governing fiduciaries do *not* spend time assessing individual portfolio manager effectiveness or individual investments.

Operations-Related

- I have the authority to retain and terminate investment managers.
- Performance-based compensation is an important component of our organization design.
- Compensation levels in our organization are competitive.

Source: Keith Ambachtsheer, Ronald Capelle, and Hubert Lum. "Pension Fund Governance Today: Strengths, Weaknesses, and Opportunities for Improvement," Working Paper, Rotman International Centre for Pension Management. (rotman.utoronto.ca/icpm).

45-statement universe in both 1997 and 2005 surveys. Collectively, the low CEO scores for these six statements imply that the CEOs of the responding funds continue to believe that trustee selection and evaluation processes are relatively ineffective, resulting in board micro-management and inadequate internal compensation policies.

LIGHT AT THE END OF THE "BEAUTY CONTEST" TUNNEL?

The stated goal of this chapter was to set out the necessary conditions for eradicating "beauty contest" investing. Both the logic and the empirical evidence presented suggest that the key lies in fostering more effective governance processes in the pension fund sector. This implies attracting board of trustees candidates who understand what good governance is, and who are able and willing to apply that knowledge in the context of overseeing the management of pension organizations. Effective oversight will in turn attract executives able and willing to reduce "investing" to the strict allocation of plan assets to the legitimate RM, SHR, and LHR styles. Increasing demand for LHR investments can now be met directly by corporations actively seeking LHR investors as partners. As this virtuous LHR circle between pension funds and the corporate sector grows stronger, "beauty contest" investing's hold on the pension sector will weaken—until it is eventually eradicated.

Can this virtuous circle ever become reality? The cited Rotman ICPM pension fund governance study also measured perceived improvement in governance and management practices from 1997 to 2005. The statements with the largest *increases* in CEO scores related to (1) self-evaluation of board of trustee effectiveness, (2) adoption of formal strategic planning processes, and (3) giving management authority to retain and terminate investment managers. These improvements are hopeful signs. May they really represent light at the end of the "beauty contest" investing tunnel.

CHAPTER 18

High-Performance Cultures: Impossible Dream for Pension Funds?

"Goldman Sachs is a hard place to be hired, a hard place to be promoted, and a hard place to stay."

Henry Paulson
CEO, Goldman Sachs

THINKING AND ACTING LIKE GOLDMAN SACHS

The quote above comes from an article on Goldman Sachs (GS) in the April 29, 2006, issue of *The Economist*. After marveling about GS's financial performance in such disparate areas as trading, asset management, principal investments, and investment banking, the article poses the question of the common thread to it all. In the end, the writer decides the common thread is GS's relentless high-performance culture. The foundations of this culture are highly demanding hiring and promotion processes, which in turn breed intense levels of energy and loyalty among high-performing GS employees. While the article doesn't explicitly say so, we would go further and say that this kind of culture can be sustained only by a senior management team that itself has a high-performance mind-set, and by a board of directors that creates an environment in which it can thrive.

So what do these observations have to do with pension funds? Well, aren't trading, asset management, principal investments, and arguably even investment banking the primary activity areas of pension funds as well? And if GS can make a great deal of money in each of these four areas, why can't pension funds, too? The paragraph above provides what we believe to be the answer. It is because the vast majority of pension funds have not consciously set out to build a high-performance culture. Most senior management teams have not themselves lived it. Most boards of trustees have not created the environment in which it could thrive.

What difference would it make if pension fund boards of trustees and senior managements did choose to adopt and develop high-performance cultures inside their own organizations? We firmly believe that it would make a fundamental difference in two ways. First, it would directly improve the financial performance of pension funds themselves. Second, because of their sheer size, most of pension funds' available risk capital would be allocated to the "principal investments" category (we have used the term *long-horizon risky* or LHR investing in previous chapters). This in turn would lead to increased pressure from pension funds on the boards and managements of these LHR "principal investments" to create sustainable competitive advantage and long-term wealth. As we observed in earlier chapters, such a win-win "upstream" development would close the virtuous "pension fund socialism" circle Peter Drucker foresaw 30 years ago.

Can pension funds in fact choose to adopt and develop a GS style of high-performance culture? Or is this an impossible dream? These are the questions this chapter addresses.

NEW RESEARCH RESULTS

During the 1990s, we participated in a number of efforts to provide objective assessments of the quality and mind-set of pension fund governance and management. The previous chapter noted that efforts were renewed recently under the banner of the Rotman International Centre for Pension Management (ICPM) at the University of Toronto. The senior executive officers (i.e., chief executive officer, executive director, VP pensions, etc.) of 88 major pension funds around the world with an aggregate value of $1.7 trillion have just completed a survey of their views on the quality and mindset of governance and management inside their own organizations. The survey, designed by Dr. Ronald Capelle (Capelle Associates Inc.), Hubert Lum (CEM Benchmarking Inc.), and this author, asked these senior executives to rank 45 statements about governance and management of their pension fund organizations. It also asked them two open-ended questions, to which 63 executives responded:

- *What do you see as the more important governance issues facing your governing fiduciaries (i.e., trustees, directors, board members, etc.) at this time?*
- *What do you see as the more important organizational issues facing you at this time?*

Their responses to these two open-ended questions are summarized in Table 18.1.

TABLE 18.1 Pension Fund Governance and Management: What Really Matters

*What are the more important **governance** issues?*
1. Agency/context issues (44%)*
2. Governance effectiveness issues (36%)*
3. Investment beliefs/risk management issues (20%)*

*What are the more important **management** issues?*
1. Strategic planning/management effectiveness (73%)*
2. Agency/context issues (15%)*
3. Investment beliefs/risk management issues (12%)*

*Proportion of responses.
Source: Keith Ambachtsheer, Ronald Capelle, and Hubert Lum. "Pension Fund Governance Today: Strengths, Weaknesses, and Opportunities for Improvement," Working Paper, Rotman International Centre for Pension Management. (rotman.utoronto.ca/icpm).

Given that the two questions were open-ended, it required some effort to create broad response categories, and to fit the individual responses into these broad categories. In the end, four broad response categories were created. Table 18.1 shows that two of the four were relevant to both the governance and executive functions (i.e., agency/context and investment beliefs/risk management issues). Of the other two, one was relevant only to the governance function (i.e., governance effectiveness issues), the other only to the executive function (i.e., strategic planning/management effectiveness issues). The proportions of responses falling into the four categories tell an interesting story:

- Responding pension fund executives think their governing fiduciaries face important issues in three areas: agency/context issues (44 percent of responses), governance effectiveness issues (36 percent), and investment beliefs/risk management issues (20 percent). We think this represents an astute collective assessment by these executives. Without governance context, there is no legitimacy. Without governance effectiveness, there can be no common vision. Without a basic understanding of how capital markets function and how risk should be defined and managed, the governance function cannot provide effective oversight.

- While a number of the responding pension fund executives believe they themselves have a role to play in resolving agency/context (15 percent) and investment beliefs/risk management (12 percent) issues, they see their major challenges lying in the strategic planning/management effectiveness area (73 percent). Again, we think this to be an astute collective assessment, which bodes well for the future of pension fund management. If the fund's chief executive is not prepared to be accountable for results in the strategic planning/management effectiveness area, no clear organization vision will ever be articulated or actualized.

So what were some of the specific governance and management challenges mentioned in the survey? That is the question we address next.

SPECIFIC GOVERNANCE AND MANAGEMENT CHALLENGES

To repeat, the open-ended nature of the governance and management questions led to 63 responses requiring categorization. Table 18.1 listed the four broad response categories. Table 18.2 continues that process on a more disaggregated level for the governance-related and management-related responses.

In Table 18.2, under "agency/context issues," pension fund executives exhibit a clear awareness of the (sometimes impossible) balancing act defined benefit (DB) pension plans typically force on boards of governors. The reality is that the financial interests of various stakeholder groups in DB plans do not always line up in a nice "win-win" manner. So instead of providing oversight to the pension organization, boards (and to a lesser degree, management) often get involved in sorting out the respective financial interests of retirees,

TABLE 18.2 Pension Fund Governance and Management: Specific Challenges

1. Agency/context issues
   - Balancing stakeholder interests
   - Understanding the legal/regulatory environment
2. Governance effectiveness issues
   - Appropriate skill/knowledge set for board
   - Clear delegation to management
3. Investment beliefs/risk management issues
   - Understanding context-based risk and its management
   - Informed "investment beliefs" and their relevance
   - Shift to risk budget–based investment process
4. Strategic planning/management effectiveness issues
   - Resource planning, organization design, and compensation
   - Clear delegation from board
   - Effective information technology–based implementation systems

Source: Keith Ambachtsheer, Ronald Capelle, and Hubert Lum. "Pension Fund Governance Today: Strengths, Weaknesses, and Opportunities for Improvement", Working Paper, Rotman International Centre for Pension Management. (rotman.utoronto.ca/icpm).

active workers, future workers, bond holders, and shareholders, as well as current and future taxpayers. There is also the related question of trying to understand what light (if any) past, current, and future laws and regulations may throw on these matters.

Under "governance effectiveness issues," the responding pension fund executives point to two fundamental, related challenges that remain unresolved in large swaths of the pensions forest. The first is board competency. The second is the critical requirement for boards to understand the difference between governing and managing. The board competency issue results directly from the often-haphazard methods through which trustees are elected/selected for pension boards. Because there often is a board competency issue, there is often also a board delegation issue. Boards that do not clearly delegate fund managing to fund management doom the organization to mediocrity at best, with the possibility for something far worse.

The board competency issue is often also the source of problems in the "investment beliefs/risk management" area. It is not a question of board members becoming experts in this area. That is not a realistic expectation. However, board members must be capable of strategic thinking. That means they should insist on clear linkages among the pension contract; how the organization defines, measures, and manages risk; and how outcomes are measured and rewarded. It is up to management to show the board how this is best accomplished through a liability-anchored, risk budget–based investment process.

We have already expressed the opinion that assignment by the pension fund executives of a high priority to "strategic planning/management effectiveness issues" bodes well for the future. This view is reinforced by the specific executive focus on resource planning, organization design, compensation, and information technology (IT)-based implementation systems. These are indeed the critical elements required to build a high-performance culture.

IN CONCLUSION

In ending, we return to our original questions: Can pension funds choose to adopt and develop a high-performance culture like Goldman Sachs? Or is that an impossible dream? Now we can also ask: What light do the survey responses of the 63 pension fund executives throw on these questions?

Our answers to the original questions are: "Yes, it can be done; no, it is not an impossible dream." However, the survey responses provide four material caveats:

1. The context in which the pension fund operates (especially "the pension deal") must be clearly understood and supported by all stakeholders.

2. The board of governors must possess the necessary authority and collective competencies to understand their own role, and to provide management with the encouragement and resources to become a high-performance organization.
3. The board must clearly delegate accountability for the development and implementation of a strategic plan to a high-performance chief executive. Proper resourcing of the organization in terms of both people and IT support are critical success factors.
4. Risk must be defined, measured, and managed in an operationally relevant manner.

The harsh reality is that we know of only a handful of pension fund organizations around the world that can currently meet these four "high-performance" challenges. In the vast majority of pension organizations, a lot of work remains to be done before they become places where, in GS CEO Henry Paulson's words, "it is hard to get hired, hard to get promoted, and hard to stay."

CHAPTER 19

How Much Is Good Governance Worth?

"The emphasis of ABP's new mission statement is on the achievement of a sustainable pension system which is attractive to young and old, and which remains affordable thanks to sound financial management . . . the Board of Governors has opted for good governance based on accepted principles . . ."

ABP Annual Report, 2005

GOVERNANCE QUALITY AND ORGANIZATION PERFORMANCE SHOULD BE RELATED

Imagine two boards of pension fund governors (or trustees, or directors). Board 1 has been carefully selected based on a template that sets out optimal board composition in terms of the relevant collective skill/experience set, positive behavioral characteristics, and an unconflicted passion for the well-being of the organization and its participants. Board 2 was randomly selected out of the telephone book. Which of these two boards do you think will provide more effective oversight in the creation and maintenance of pension arrangements that are, in the words of the 2005 Annual Report of the €200B Dutch public-sector pension fund ABP "sustainable, equally attractive to young and old, and affordable thanks due to sound financial management"?

If you answered "Board 1," we are in agreement. This same answer was also given by an international group of 63 senior pension executives, who responded to a survey question: "What do you see as the more important governance issues facing your board of governors at this time?" The executives said that they deemed governance effectiveness issues to be very important, and that they saw effective board selection and evaluation processes as the heart of the matter (see previous chapter for details). Only boards with relevant collective skill/experience sets, appropriate behaviors, and the right motivations can provide the oversight and delegation disciplines necessary for pension fund organizations to offer its participants the sound financial management necessary for sustainability and affordability.

Most of us would probably also agree that with perfect metrics representing governance quality and organization performance, we would be able to statistically "prove" that our hypothesis about the positive relationship between governance quality and pension fund performance was correct. In fact, we will state up front here that we believe that such an exercise would show "high-performance" governance and management to be "worth" as much as 3 percent of additional fund return per annum. However, these perfect metrics do not exist and never will. Does that mean we should never try to test the "positive relationship" hypothesis with less than perfect numbers? No, it does not. There is still great value in attempting the measurement journey. Even if, in the end, the final destination is not reached, much can still be learned along the way.

This chapter describes such a "search for a positive statistical relationship" journey, including what we learned about the measured relationship between governance quality and pension fund performance along the way to the final destination.

A ROAD MAP FOR THE JOURNEY OF DISCOVERY

The previous chapter described a renewed initiative under the auspices of the Rotman International Centre for Pension Management (ICPM) to provide an objective assessment of the quality and mind-set of pension fund governance and management around the world today. The key vehicle is a survey designed by Dr. Ronald Capelle, Hubert Lum, and this author. The prior chapter analyzed the 2005 responses to the open-ended questions part of this survey by 63 North American, European, and Australia/New Zealand pension executives. The two open-ended questions focused on current governance and management issues in pension fund organizations, and the responses provided important insights into the current governance and management challenges facing pension fund organizations.

This same survey also asked pension executives to rank 45 statements related to the governance (16 statements), management (12 statements), and operational practices (17 statements) inside their own organizations on a scale from 6 to 1. A "6" rating indicates total agreement with the statement; a "1" rating total disagreement. The statements were written so that high rankings implied "good" practices, and low rankings "bad" practices. We received 88 completed sets of 45 rankings from pension fund executives representing $1.4 trillion in pension assets. An identical survey conducted in 1997 yielded 80 sets of 45 rankings representing $0.7 trillion in pension assets. In the remainder of the chapter, we will refer to the average of a specific set of 45 rankings as that fund's pension CEO score. So overall, we ended up with 88 pension CEO scores in 2005, compared to 80 in 1997. Again, the higher the score, the higher the CEO's assessment of his or her fund's governance and management practices.

We reported one important finding from an analysis of these pension CEO scores in an earlier chapter entitled "Eradicating 'Beauty Contest' Investmenting: What It Will Take." The six statements that received the lowest rankings in 1997 also received the lowest rankings in 2005! And what did these six statements relate to? Four of the six related to board of governors selection, evaluation, and behavior practices.

The implication is that what senior pension executives saw as relatively poor practices eight years ago, they continue to see as relatively poor practices today. On the brighter side, while still ranked lowest, these governance-related rankings were also among those showing the largest ranking increases over the course of the last eight years.

So if we use the relative pension CEO scores as metrics representing a pension fund's relative governance/management quality, where can we find metrics representing a pension fund's relative organizational performance? CEM Benchmarking Inc. has such metrics for both the investment and pension administration sides of the pension "business" for pension funds from North America, Europe and Australia/New Zealand. This study used an investment performance metric called NVA (net value added is a pension fund's excess return over its asset mix policy benchmark, net of all investment expenses). The NVAs from the CEM database reported below are annualized, based on four years of continuous experience.

THE PENSION CEO SCORE AND NVA METRICS: THE DATA

The mean pension CEO score in the 2005 survey was 4.9, with a standard deviation of 0.7. The comparable statistics for 1997 were 4.8 and 0.6. So the overall rankings in 2005 are slightly higher and slightly more dispersed than they were in 1997. Given that the pension executives were given a scale from 6 to 1, the score averages of a little under 5 in both surveys suggests significant positive ranking bias (i.e., are the overall governance/management practices of these 80+ funds really that good!?). Similarly, we suspect that the actual variance in governance/management quality is greater than that suggested by the modest score standard deviations in the 0.6 to 0.7 range. Despite these likely shortcomings, the 1997 and 2005 sets of pension CEO scores represent unique and valuable additions to our knowledge base about pension fund governance and management.

The mean annual NVA in the CEM database is 0.2 percent with a standard deviation of 3.0 percent. This is based on all 3,513 annual NVAs in the database contributed by 666 different pension funds over the period covering 1992 to 2004. While this data set does not suffer from the same degree of mean and variance biases as we noted is likely the case with the subjective pension CEO scores, all key CEM data is supplied by the participating pension funds, including operating costs and policy asset mix benchmarks. So some level of "noise" is likely introduced in calculating the NVA performance metrics. Further, in theory, the NVAs should be assigned risk-related "haircuts." However, consensus on how to best do this has yet to be reached. As a result of these shortcomings, the NVA metrics are also less than perfect. Nevertheless, once again, this NVA database is unique in the pensions world, and undoubtedly the best available for the task at hand.

PENSION CEO SCORES MEET NVA METRICS

So what happens when the imperfect pension CEO scores meet the imperfect NVA metrics? In other words, does the positive relationship between the pension CEO scores and the NVAs that we would surely find with perfect data come through with our less-than-perfect data? Figure 19.1 tells the tale. The short answer is that, yes, even with imperfect data, the outline of a positive statistical relationship between governance and performance emerges. With the 1997 pension CEO scores, the NVA-CEO coefficient hits +0.4 twice, first for the four-year NVA performance period ending in 1997, and then again for the four-year NVA performance period ending in 1999. With the 2005 scores, the NVA-CEO coefficient hits +0.8 for the four-year NVA performance period ending in 2003, before falling back to +0.4 for the four-year NVA performance period ending in 2004.

What intuitive meaning can we give to the time patterns of these NVA-CEO coefficients? Recall that the pension CEO score range was effectively from 3 to 6. Multiplying this three-point "bad-good" gap by an NVA-CEO coefficient of +0.4 leads to a four-year NVA gap of 1.2 percent per annum. A coefficient of +0.8 doubles the four-year NVA gap to 2.4 percent per annum. The implication is that the "bad-good" governance gap, as assessed by pension fund CEOs (or equivalents) themselves, has been "worth" as much as 1 to 2 percent of additional return per annum, as measured by CEM. In our view, these statistical findings understate the real "value-added" potential of truly high-performance pension fund governance and management. We have already stated that, based on personal observation, we would place that true potential at more like 3 percent per annum.

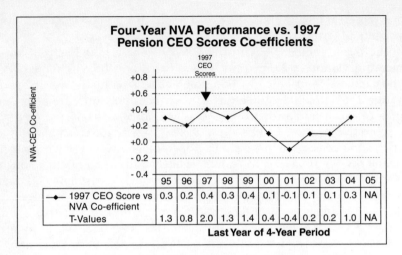

	95	96	97	98	99	00	01	02	03	04	05
1997 CEO Score vs NVA Co-efficient	0.3	0.2	0.4	0.3	0.4	0.1	-0.1	0.1	0.1	0.3	NA
T-Values	1.3	0.8	2.0	1.3	1.4	0.4	-0.4	0.2	0.2	1.0	NA

Last Year of 4-Year Period

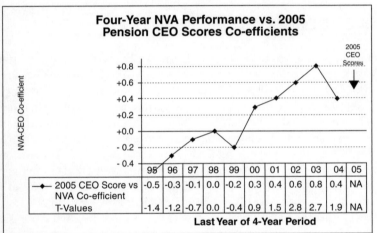

	95	96	97	98	99	00	01	02	03	04	05
2005 CEO Score vs NVA Co-efficient	-0.5	-0.3	-0.1	0.0	-0.2	0.3	0.4	0.6	0.8	0.4	NA
T-Values	-1.4	-1.2	-0.7	0.0	-0.4	0.9	1.5	2.8	2.7	1.9	NA

Last Year of 4-Year Period

FIGURE 19.1 Pension Fund Governance and Performance: Are They Statistically Related?
Source: Keith Ambachtsheer, Ronald Capelle, and Hubert Lum. "Pension Fund Governance Today: Strengths, Weaknesses, and Opportunities for Improvement," Working Paper, Rotman International Centre for Pension Management. (rotman.utoronto.ca/icpm).

FURTHER INSIGHTS

Today, the 1997 pension CEO scores allow us to look at NVA versus pension CEO score experience well after 1997. Note that the statistical significance of the NVA-CEO coefficients based on the 1997 scores peaks at the four-year NVA performance period ending in 1997 (i.e., at a t-value of 2.0), and generally declines after that. In contrast, given the availability of NVA data since 1992, the 2005 scores allow us to look at experience well before 2005. Note that the NVA-CEO coefficients based on 2005 scores are statistically insignificant in the earlier four-year NVA performance periods, and attain statistical significance only when they get closer to 2005, the year the survey was completed. One possible explanation for these patterns is that the quality of pension fund governance has not been not stable over time. There is some statistical support for this hypothesis. For the subset of 28 funds for which there were both 1997 and 2005 pension CEO scores, the correlation coefficient between the two data sets was positive, but a modestly low 0.5.

The statistical tests described above used all of the four-year NVA data available for the funds in the CEM database for which we had pension CEO scores. So in this sense the results do not suffer from "data-mining" problems. Stated differently, while playing with various subsets of the total database produced some additional statistical results that looked interesting, we have resisted the temptation to try and interpret them. Why? Because it is quite possible that any specifically selected subset results, no matter how interesting, simply represent noise rather than signal. Having said that, we make one exception. One of the cost categories in the CEM database is "oversight costs," which captures fund costs allocated to the internal governance, management, and control functions.

A reasonable hypothesis is that funds with higher pension CEO scores would invest more in these functions than funds with low scores. So, statistically, we should find a positive relationship between oversight costs (OC) and pension CEO scores, after adjusting for fund size. The OC-CEO coefficient was in fact 1.4 (t-value 3.0). So again, taking the pension CEO score range to be from 3 to 6, the implication is that high-scoring funds spend as much as 4 basis points (i.e., 3×1.4) more per annum on the internal governance, management, and control functions than low-scoring funds. This is an additional $4 million per year for a $10 billion fund. Clearly, the CEOs and boards of governors of the high-scoring funds are putting their money where their mouth is. This is a very encouraging finding.

THE VALUE OF GOOD GOVERNANCE

Simple logic tells us that good governance must have a positive impact on organizational performance. However, it is also true that "seeing is believing." Actually seeing a positive statistical relationship between performance and governance metrics helps doubters become believers. Using imperfect performance and governance quality metrics, the new study described above allows us to reasonably assign a "good governance" value of 1 percent of additional fund return per year. This author thinks the true value of good governance is significantly higher than that.

PART Four

Investment Beliefs

*"When I was in grade school, I learned that somewhere in india
there is a Hindu tribe whose members believe that the Earth and
the sky above it rest on an elephant and that the elephant rests on
a turtle..."*

Peter Fleck,
Come as You Are
(Boston: Beacon Press, 1993)

CHAPTER 20

The 10 Percent Equity Return Illusion: Possible Consequences

"... there is a risk that investors won't boost stocks back to the high levels of the market's headiest days ... especially if the market continues to disappoint investors accustomed in the late 1990s to annual stock gains of 20% or more. Most stock analysts today think stocks are more likely to return 10% in the future ..."
Wall Street Journal, December 23, 2001

CONSEQUENTIAL MISCALCULATIONS

John Maynard Keynes wrote a scathing critique of the terms of the post–World War I Treaty of Versailles (*The Economic Consequences of the Peace,* New York: Harcourt, Brace, and Howe, 1920) because the arithmetic didn't add up. The Allies were forcing defeated Germany to pay 24 billion pounds in war reparations, when by Keynes's calculations, it could at most afford to pay a tenth of that amount without serious risk of financial ruin and political instability. Though he was ignored at the time, subsequent events would prove his analysis was painfully on the mark.

At a very different time, in a very different context, history seems to be in the process of repeating itself. For a number of years now, a small band of financial analysts have been assessing the economic consequences of a stock market for which, from a valuation perspective, the arithmetic stopped adding up sometime during the 1990s. As was the case with Keynes in 1920, their analyses also continue to be largely ignored.

For proof, we need to look no further than the *Wall Street Journal* article quoted above. It seems the market "pros" now know better than to project the 20 percent gains of the late 1990s into the future. Apparently, they agree that a 10 percent return is now a more realistic number. Unfortunately, the arithmetic of the market doesn't work at 10 percent either. Given the continuing critical importance of prospective long-term stock market returns for all investment fund fiduciaries, we revisit "the 10 percent equity return illusion" question in this first chapter of Part Four of the book.

WHY 10 PERCENT DOESN'T WORK

Why doesn't the arithmetic of the market work at 10 percent either? A recent "live" experiment involving 35 senior pension fund executives showcases the point graphically. The participants were asked for their 20-year "best estimates" (a) for the returns on the Standard and Poor's (S&P) 500 stock portfolio, the 10-year Treasury bond, and the 90-day T-bill; (b) for Consumer Price Index (CPI) inflation; and (c) for real gross domestic product (GDP) growth. Arithmetic was then applied to these projections, focusing especially on what the dividend yield on the S&P 500 would have to be in 2021 for their return projections to be internally consistent.

Table 20.1 tells the tale. First of all, note that the *Wall Street Journal* article has it right. The average of the 35 "best estimate" 20-year S&P 500 return projections is 9.9 percent, very close to the 10 percent return expectation the *Wall Street Journal* reported for its stock market "pros." Given their projections for GDP growth and inflation, and given a current dividend yield of 1.7 percent on the S&P 500, what does the 9.9 percent average S&P 500 return projection imply for the prevailing index dividend yield in 2021? The arithmetic says 0.9 percent.

In other words, given the group's (realistic) average assumptions about economic growth and inflation over the next 20 years, the dividend yield on the stock market would have to almost halve again (i.e., from 1.7 percent today to 0.9 percent) to produce the average 9.9 percent annual return they project. Why? Because a 1.7 percent yield plus projected dividend growth of 4.4 percent (80 percent of nominal GDP growth) only produces a return of 6.1 percent.

To get to 9.9 percent, a further 3.8 percent per annum of capital gains related to further multiple expansion (of dividends and earnings) is needed. It is this required multiple expansion that drives the dividend yield down from an already historically low 1.7 percent today, to an unheard of 0.9 percent in 2021. Therefore, we suggest that this arithmetic does not work, and hence the conclusion that a 10 percent equity return expectation today is an "illusion."

TABLE 20.1   Stock Market Arithmetic

Summary Measures	Max	Q3	Median	Q1	Min	Average
Return S&P 500	18.90%	10.00%	9.00%	7.50%	6.00%	9.90%
Return bonds	12.00	7.00	6.00	5.60	4.00	6.70
Return T-bills	8.50	5.30	4.00	3.60	2.00	4.50
Growth real GDP	4.00	3.00	3.00	2.30	1.00	2.70
Growth CPI	4.50	3.00	2.50	2.30	1.00	2.80
Equity risk premium	10.40	4.00	3.00	2.00	−2.00	3.20
Dividend yield 2021	1.80	1.10	0.90	0.60	0.10	0.90

The first five columns represent the characteristics of the projections gathered from the American, Canadian, and European pension fund executives attending the CEM Benchmarking Inc. client conference on November 28, 2001. In all, 35 sets of projections were submitted. The sixth and seventh columns are calculations based on the projections.

Readers should be careful when they study the data in the Max, Q3, Median, Q1, and Min rows. For example, in the Max row each number is simply the largest of the 35 numbers. There is no comparability across the row in the sense that all of the Max numbers originated from the same forecaster. Indeed it is much more likely that all seven numbers in the row came from different forecasters.

The "equity risk premium" numbers are simply the differences between the stock and bond return projections made by each forecaster. Only two out of the 35 forecasters predicted a negative equity risk premium over the next 20 years.

The "dividend yield 2021" numbers come from a more complex calculation. The key assumptions are (a) that 20-year S&P 500 dividend growth will average 80 percent of projected nominal GDP growth, and (b) that the balancing item between the returns derived from dividends and dividend growth on the one hand, and the total stock return projected by each participant on the other, will be made up by the requisite revaluation of a dollar's worth of dividends. So for example, using the averages calculated above, if nominal GDP growth is 5.5 percent (i.e., real GDP 2.7 percent + CPI 2.8 percent), dividend growth is 4.4 percent (i.e., 80 percent of 5.5 percent). Thus, the implied return from current dividends plus dividend growth only is 6.1 percent (i.e., 1.7 percent + 4.4 percent). However, projected total annual return is 9.9 percent, leaving 3.8 percent per annum (i.e., 9.9 percent −6.1 percent) to come from capital appreciation tied to the upward revaluation of a dollar's worth of dividends. Over a 20-year period, and given a 4.4 percent dividend growth rate, that implies a reduction in the current yield of 1.7 percent down to 0.9 percent by 2021. In only two out of the 35 calculations did the implied 2021 S&P 500 dividend yield end up higher than the current 1.7 percent level.

This experiment was designed and conducted by CEM partner John McLaughlin. The 35 intrepid experiment participants shall remain nameless—at their request.

Source: Based on executive summary from the CEM Benchmarking Inc. client conference on November 28, 2001.

PAINTED INTO AN AWKWARD CORNER?

Is there a way out of the logic trap most investment professionals seem to have fallen into? For example, the 9.9 percent average return projection could be achieved without any further multiple expansion if dividends would grow at 8.2 percent (i.e., 9.9 percent − 1.7 percent) rather than the calculated 4.4 percent. Unfortunately, there is no historical precedent for corporate earnings or dividends growing faster than the economy as a whole for any length of time. Indeed, an article by Robert D. Arnott and Peter L. Bernstein in 2002 suggests that over the past 200 years real dividends have grown only 1 percent per annum versus real GDP growth of 3.7 percent. ("What Equity Risk Premium Is Normal?" *Financial Analysts Journal,* March–April 2002).

What about the fact that corporations have been paying out ever-smaller proportions of their earnings as dividends (e.g., 30 percent on the S&P 500 today versus a historical "norm" of 50 percent)? Could today's unusually large proportion of earnings being retained not lead to unusually high future earnings and dividend growth? Again, history offers no support for this proposition. Indeed, a paper by Robert D. Arnott and Clifford S. Asness shows that exactly the reverse has been the case. ("Surprise! Higher Dividends = Higher Earnings Growth." *Financial Analysts Journal,* January–February 2003).

Their research finds that high retention ratios have historically been associated with slow future earnings growth and high payout ratios with fast future earnings growth. It appears that corporate decisions to retain higher proportions of earnings are associated with management assessments of poor future earnings prospects, with poor corporate investment decisions, or some combination of these two factors.

In short, history offers no long-term scenarios consistent with the very high earnings and dividend growth rates required to support today's 10 percent stock return expectations of investment professionals. Thus, it appears that the only way a 10 percent return will be realized over the next 10 or 20 years is for today's still richly valued stock market to become even more richly valued with the passage of time. Investment professionals appear to have painted themselves into a very awkward corner.

The conclusion that investment professionals have painted themselves into an awkward "10 percent" corner raises an obvious question: Why have they done this? Why do they continue to assume that stocks can earn a 10 percent return going forward from here when the arithmetic doesn't work? Let's return for a moment to those post–World War I negotiations at Versailles. Why were Wilson, George, and Clemenceau determined to impose reparation demands on a defeated Germany for which the arithmetic didn't work, and hence made no economic sense over the long term? Because it suited their short-term political purposes.

Similarly, we note that the "10 percent assumption" suits the short-term purposes of a lot of players in the pension finance and investments game. It means corporations can continue to report pension plan–related "earnings" that no longer exist. It provides justification for further postponement of pension contributions that should be made now to keep pension balance sheets whole. It means "65–35" continues to be a defensible equity-debt asset mix policy. It means investment professionals can continue to focus on the peripheral questions of benchmark-related "alphas" and "tracking errors" rather than on the fundamental question of managing total balance-sheet risk.

And then there is a final irony. When investment professionals are challenged on the "10 percent assumption" they offer an iron-clad rebuttal. Both history and theory are on their side! Haven't stocks historically earned 10 percent over the long term? Why should the future be any different? Further, doesn't the efficient markets hypothesis suggest that stock market prices are set by rational, well-informed, risk-averse investors? Thus, the stock market must offer a risk premium over bonds. How much? History suggests that 4 percent is a defensible equity risk premium. Current long-bond yields are 6 percent, so the expected return on stocks must be 10 percent. See? It all checks out! If there is arithmetic that questions their iron-clad case, there must be something wrong with the arithmetic. (When pressed for an answer on just what precisely might be wrong with the arithmetic, our experience is that the subject is quickly dropped).

CONSEQUENCES

The consequences of the faulty Treaty of Versailles were horrendous. As Keynes predicted, Germany would be unable to meet the reparation demands of the Allies. As a consequence, post–World War I Germany would lurch from hyperinflation, to political instability, to the rise of fascism, with all of its unspeakable consequences.

What about the consequences of a faulty assessment of future stock market returns now? Luckily for us, it is highly unlikely to produce hyper-inflation, political instability, and fascism. However, there could be some nasty consequences, nevertheless. Consider these three possible scenarios:

1. Despite all of the above, the market somehow generates the expected 10 percent return over the next 20 years. In this case, we promise a careful analysis of how this happened 20 years from now.

2. The economy unfolds according to the expectations set out in Table 20.1, including dividend growth of 4.4 percent. However, stocks continue to sell on their current 1.7 percent dividend yield basis. Thus there are no revaluation-related gains, and stocks end up returning about 6 percent, equal to today's bond yields.
3. Investors grow increasingly impatient with the market's inability to generate 20 percent or even 10 percent returns over the next few years. They begin to wonder why they should subject their financial assets to considerable ongoing price volatility without receiving any compensation for it. Stock prices begin to fall, and don't stabilize until a healthy risk premium has returned. This will require a doubling of the current 1.7 percent dividend yield, and hence a further 50 percent drop in stock prices.

Where do good fiduciaries go from here? As a first step, they could decide to put the "10 percent equity return illusion" question on the agenda of their next board meeting. We would be pleased to participate in the resulting discussion and debate.

CHAPTER 21

Stocks for the Long Run?
... or Not?

"Through his classic step-by-step guide Stocks for the Long Run, Prof. Jeremy Siegel invites virtually all investors and savers of every income class to build wealth the historically proven way: in the stock market! When historians record the financial history of the 1990s, this book will be viewed as a seminal event...."

From the dust jacket of *Stocks for the Long Run,*
by Jeremy J. Siegel

A DEBATE WITH JEREMY SIEGEL

When our friends at Commonfund invited us late last fall to debate Wharton School's Professor Jeremy Siegel on whether "stocks for the long run" is really such an obvious proposition, we readily accepted. Why? Well, to a wintry Torontonian, the date and location (Orlando, March 25) made good sense. To the contrary, the "stocks for the long run" proposition does not. Certainly not for "virtually all investors and savers of every income class," or for most pension and endowment funds either. A debate with Siegel would offer good incentive to update the reasons why we continue to hold this view.

This chapter sets out our position on the "stocks for the long run" debate once again. It does so by documenting how over the course of the last 30 years, a few elegant hypotheses and theories about investment behavior and portfolio construction have "morphed" into a hard-wired, incontrovertible dictum about how to amass long-term wealth. Unfortunately, many of the assumptions behind the elegant hypotheses and theories do not square well with real-world behavior and experience. Thus, we should be suspicious of any investment conclusions based on them.

Indeed, a very different investment dictum emerges when we allow real-world behavior and experience to guide the construction of an investment theory for the twenty-first century, or at least for the first decade of it. Now, a Post-Bubble Blues Decade continues to loom large before investors (how did you like the first three years of it?). If history (properly interpreted) is any guide at all, Siegel's promised stock market nirvana will be on hold for some time yet.

HOW INVESTMENT THEORY BECAME INVESTMENT PRACTICE

Some 50 years ago, Harry Markowitz showed how, with forecasts for expected returns and covariances of a universe of investments, one can mathematically construct the "efficient frontier" of portfolio choices (i.e., those promising the maximum expected return at varying levels of risk). Things get even more interesting if one also assumes that all investors construct portfolios this way, that because they all have access to the same information and use the same analytical techniques, they reach the same risk/return conclusions about the universe of investments, and, finally, that they all behave "rationally" with known, stable risk tolerances.

By the 1960s, a group of academics had built a full-blown capital asset pricing model (CAPM) theory out of these assumptions. The theory explains why securities prices are what they are at any point in time, and why these prices may change at the next point in time. An elegant by-product of the CAPM theory is that everyone holds some combination of the market portfolio of risky securities and the risk-free asset, with the risky/risk-free proportions determined by each investor's risk tolerance. Naturally, in a world of risk-averse investors, the risky market portfolio is priced to offer an expected positive "risk premium" over the risk-free portfolio.

It is one thing to build elegant theory; it is quite another to get investors to believe that it explains how the real world works. Yet, that is (more than less) what happened between the 1960s and the 1990s. How did academia (with strong support from the marketing-savvy investment community) pull this off over the course of the last 30 years? In three phases:

1. Show that "active management" on average, underperforms passive management after fees, and is therefore at best a sideshow.
2. Show that asset mix policy is the most important investment decision.
3. Show that stocks outperform bonds and T-bills over the long run not only in theory, but also in practice.

By the late 1990s, these three "proofs" of CAPM's validity had become household "truths" not only to most pension and endowment fund investment committees, but to millions of individual investors around the globe as well. In this context, the launch of Siegel's *Stocks for the Long Run* was true to its dust jacket billing. It was indeed a seminal event. It confirmed what the investing public and their advisors wanted to believe (again, from the dust jacket): ". . . . when long-term purchasing power is considered, stocks are actually safer than bank deposits!"

WHAT IS WRONG WITH THESE "PROOFS"

What is wrong with these three "proofs"? In short, everything:

- On average, "active management" must underperform passive management, net of fees, because securities trading is a zero-sum game before fees. It is a "truism" that has nothing to do with the validity (or not) of the CAPM and its underlying assumptions. The CAPM does imply that there is absolutely nothing any single investor can do to systematically "outperform the market" on a risk-adjusted basis. Over the last 30 years, we have seen a great deal of evidence to the contrary.
- Similarly, the famous asset mix policy studies by Brinson et al. do nothing but reflect back an obvious truism. If you try to explain the return variance over time in pension funds made up of stable mixes of well-diversified stock and bond portfolios, it must be asset mix that explains the bulk of the fund return variance. Again, this has nothing to do with the validity (or not) of the CAPM and its underlying assumptions. It simply means that when you consciously choose to make asset mix the most important determinant of fund return variance, it will be so.
- Finally, studies showing that for most historical time periods in most capital markets, stocks have generated higher returns than bonds or bills (e.g., Siegel's *Stocks for the Long Run*), do not "prove" that investors are risk averse, rational, and well informed, or that a 5 percent equity risk premium (ERP) versus bonds is assured in the "long run." Indeed, when history is segmented into a series of sequential, coherent investment regimes, a very different conclusion emerges. Now ERPs become predictably positive or negative over 10- to 20-year time periods.

We elaborate on this critical latter point below.

WHAT IF "REALITY" IS NOT A RANDOM WALK?

What if "reality" is not a CAPM-driven random walk world with a constant 5 percent ERP expectation, but a sequence of coherent investment regimes, alternately shaped by pessimistic and optimistic investor mind-sets? How would this change our views on the determinants of the ERP at any point in time? Our views on asset mix policy and "stocks for the long run"? Before we head down this path of inquiry, we'd better check and see how well the facts square with this "alternating coherent investment regimes" theory.

Table 21.1 presents powerful evidence that the facts and the theory square very well. Each of the six sequential coherent investment regimes displayed in the table stays in place for 10 to 20 years before being swept away by the next regime. Successive regimes are indeed dominated alternatively by waves of investor pessimism and optimism. The gloom of the World War I decade gave way to the roaring 1920s, which in turn gave way to the despair of the dirty 1930s followed by yet other major and minor world wars in the 1940s and early 50s (i.e., World War II and the Korean War).

It took most of the 1950s and 1960s (i.e., Pax Americana I) to dispel the notion that the developed world's only choices were depression, communism, or war. Then came the scary 1970s with its Vietnam, Nixon, "Limits to Growth," oil crises, budget deficits, and ever-accelerating price and wage inflation. This set the stage in the 1980s and 1990s for Thatcher's, Reagan's, and Volker's "Triumph of Capitalism," "the Fall of the Wall and the Peace Dividend" "the New Economy," and finally "the Market Bubble" (i.e., Pax Americana II).

Do these regimes and their investor mind-sets affect capital market pricing? Let us see.

TABLE 21.1 Six Coherent Investment Regimes

Investment Regime	Investor Mind-Set	Approximate Time Span	Dividend Yield Change	Realized ERP*
The World War I Decade	Pessimistic	10 years	5% → 7%	−(5)%
Roaring Twenties	Optimistic	10 years	7% → 4%	+12%
Dirty Thirties/Fateful Forties	Pessimistic	20 years	4% → 7%	0%
Pax Americana I	Optimistic	20 years	7% → 3%	+8%
Scary Seventies	Pessimistic	10 years	3% → 6%	−(3)%
Pax Americana II	Optimistic	20 years	6% → 2%	+9%

Source: Stock returns are based on data from Elroy Dimson, Paul Marsh, and Mike Staunton. *Triumph of the Optimists* (Princeton, NJ: Princeton University Press, 2002). Bond returns are based on a hypothetical CPI-linked bond with a real yield of 2.5%.

INVESTMENT REGIMES, DIVIDEND YIELDS, AND ERPS

Note in Table 21.1 that in each of the three pessimism regimes, the stock dividend yield rises materially as the mood of pessimism becomes embedded in the collective investor mind-set. It rises from 5 percent to 7 percent in the World War I Decade, from 4 percent to 7 percent over the Dirty Thirties/Fateful Forties period, and from 3 percent to 6 percent in the Scary Seventies. This is rational behavior by investors who are losing confidence "in the long run." They want money now, not later.

Similarly, note that in each of the three optimism regimes, the stock dividend yield falls materially as the mood of optimism becomes embedded in the collective investor mind-set. It falls from 7 percent to 4 percent in the Roaring Twenties, from 7 percent to 3 percent in Pax Americana I, and from 6 percent to 2 percent (actually well below 2 percent at the peak of the bubble!) in Pax Americana II. Note that in each successive "optimism" regime, stock pricing became more ebullient as the regime progressed, reaching its all-time nadir in March 2000.

This increasing ebullience through the twentieth century raises important questions about investor "rationality." Did future prospects genuinely become brighter with each successive optimism regime? Or did investors just convince themselves (became convinced by others) that this is so, without fundamental justification? There is indeed a possible argument that a "genuinely brighter future prospects" dynamic was at work in the twentieth century. However, there is no guarantee of its continuance in the twenty-first century.

With the strong relationship between investment regimes and equity pricing already established, the numbers in the "Realized ERP" column in Table 21.1 should come as no surprise. The results confirm that the historical 5 percent "long-term" ERP was probably not created by a static CAPM-driven random walk world. Much more likely, the 5 percent was the accidental outcome of a particular sequence of alternating coherent investment regimes, with big positive ERPs alternating with smaller, but materially negative ERPs for extended periods of time. If that is the case, the primary focus for rational investment policy making at any point in time is the nature, shape, and likely duration of the current investment regime, and not some nebulous "long run."

THE POST-BUBBLE BLUES DECADE

Unfortunately, with the death of the optimistic 20-year Pax Americana II investment regime as we exited the twentieth century, history suggests that investor pessimism will increasingly shape the first regime of the twenty-first

TABLE 21.2 Assessing the ERP for the Post-Bubble Blues Decade—What Can History Teach Us?

Investment Regime	Investor Mind-Set	Approximate Time Span	Dividend Yield Change	Realized ERP
Average pessimism experience	Pessimistic	13 years	4% → 7%	−(3)%
Average optimism experience	Optimistic	17 years	7% → 3%	+10%
Post-Bubble Blues Decade	Pessimistic	10 years+?	2% → ?	−(?)%

century. In Table 21.2, we dub it the "Post-Bubble Blues Decade," and we are barely into it. Things have not gone well thus far, as the "alternating coherent investment regimes" model would predict.

How much longer will the current Blues regime dictate stock pricing? What will its dominant characteristics be? How high will the dividend yield eventually go? How should all this shape today's investment policies for pension and endowment funds? Will Jeremy Siegel recant his "stocks for the long run" belief after our debate next week? All questions for future chapters.

"Persistent Investment Regimes" or "Random Walk"? Even Shakespeare Knew the Answer

"There is a tide in the affairs of men which, taken at the flood, leads on to fortune. Omitted, all the voyage of their life, is bound in shallows and in miseries."

William Shakespeare

THE AMBACHTSHEER-SIEGEL DEBATE REVISITED

The reviews on the March 25 Ambachtsheer-Siegel "stocks for the long run ... or not?" debate were good, at least from an entertainment perspective. As one attendee put it, "a lively boxing match, with both parties landing telling body blows."

Frankly, the 500 Commonfund conference attendees would have been better served with a decisive Ambachtsheer knockout punch. In other words, a decisive victory for the view that major secular shifts in stock market valuations result not from random draws out of some politico-economic black box, but from discernable long-term shifts in investor psyches. The "regime" theory holds that such shifts alternate between optimistic and pessimistic mind-sets, take many years to complete, and then stay in place for many more years once the shift has occurred.

Why do we believe that a decisive victory for this viewpoint would have been a good thing? No, this is not about ego. It is because such a victory would have decisively moved 500 influential institutional investors away from seeing the 2000 to 2003 period as just a piece of rare bad stock market luck, soon to be replaced by much happier draws out of the stock market returns box. The absence of such faith would require them to fundamentally reexamine their "investment business models" whether endowment or pension fund related. We have been arguing for the need of such a fundamental reexamination since the late 1990s.

All this gets us to the goal of this chapter: to make the "knockout" punch case that the "persistent investment regimes" theory is far more than just an interesting idea. Indeed, this perspective has been, and continues to be the soundest foundation on which to construct investment policies for pension and endowment funds. To make the case, we argue from observation to theory, and then back again. You will see that it all the pieces fit together very well.

HISTORY ON OUR SIDE

Let us start with Table 22.1, which summarizes the six coherent investment regimes of the twentieth century. Note that the facts indeed fit the theory nicely. Clearly identifiable regimes dominated by increasing pessimism about the future alternate with equally recognizable regimes dominated by increasing optimism. Each regime lasts 10 to 20 years. In the "increasing pessimism" regimes, stock valuations (as indicated by rising dividend yields)

TABLE 22.1 The Six Investment Regimes of the Twentieth Century

Investment Regime	Dividend Investor Mind-Set	Approximate Time Span	Yield Change	Realized ERP*
The World War I Decade	Pessimistic	10 years	5% → 7%	−(5)%
Roaring Twenties	Optimistic	10 years	7% → 4%	+12%
Dirty Thirties/ Fateful Forties	Pessimistic	20 years	4% → 7%	0%
Pax Americana I	Optimistic	20 years	7% → 3%	+8%
Scary Seventies	Pessimistic	10 years	3% → 6%	−(3)%
Pax Americana II	Optimistic	20 years	6% → 2%	+9%

Source: Stock returns are based on data from Elroy Dimson, Paul Marsh, and Mike Staunton. *Triumph of the Optimists* (Princeton, NJ: Princeton University Press, 2002). Bond returns are based on a hypothetical CPI-linked bond with a real yield of 2.5%.

are far more conservative at the end of the regime then they were at the beginning. This leads to the realization of subdued or even negative equity risk premiums over the course of the regime. In the "increasing optimism" regimes, the reverse is true. Here, stock valuations are far more aggressive (as indicated by much lower dividend yields) at the end than they were at the beginning. As a result, investors happily realize fat equity risk premiums while the regime is in place.

All well and good after the fact, Jeremy Siegel pointed out during the debate, but how helpful is the "regime" theory today, in a forward-looking sense? In other words, how do you know where you are in an investment regime at any point in time? How do you know it has ended until well after the fact? Similarly, how can you discern the shape of a new investment regime without being well into it? Our short answer at the time was "with considerable difficulty, but not impossible with the right frame of mind and tool kit." Here, we provide a considerably longer answer based on personal experience over the course of the last 15 years.

THE INVESTMENT RETURNS STORY: HOW TO TELL IT

We wrote a seminal essay in December 1988, titled "Prospective Investment Returns: What's The Best Way to Tell The Story?" (it was used in the Level III CFA study guide for many years). There, we suggested that historical returns needed to be adjusted at four levels before they became useful for investment decision making:

> **Level 1: Current Bond Yield Curve-Based Adjustments.** Today's yield curve offers a better reflection of today's expectations about future inflation and fixed income returns than the historical experience embedded in past bond and bill returns.
>
> **Level 2: Apparent Biases-in-History Adjustments.** Known anomalies in the historical returns (i.e., pegged interest rates at artificially low levels, or a secular rise in stock market valuation) should be removed.
>
> **Level 3: "We're Not Just Anywhere in History" Adjustments.** Capital markets history naturally segments into a series of differing investment "eras," each with its own distinct flavor. Investor mood and memory matter in setting return requirements and hence securities pricing. What is that mood and those memories today?
>
> **Level 4: "The World's a Different Place" Adjustments.** There may be material socioeconomic developments going on today and tomorrow for which there simply is no historical precedent. That does not mean such developments can be ignored. Judgments must be made.

This framework has served us (and hopefully many others) well in telling and retelling the prospective equity risk premium story over the course of the last almost 20 years.

THE "INVESTMENT REGIME" GAME: SPOT TODAY'S WELL BEFORE IT'S OVER, AND TOMORROW'S BEFORE IT'S GONE ON TOO LONG

Let's be more specific: Just exactly how has this framework served us (and others who used it) well? Consider the following chronology of events extracted from selected past writings by the author since December 1988:

- **Late 1980s.** Argued that we had been living in the increasingly optimistic "Return of the Invisible Hand Regime" since the early 1980s. Foresaw a continuation into the 1990s of the healthy stock and bond market returns experienced during most of the Reagan-Thatcher-Volcker 1980s.
- **Early 1990s.** Emerging new theme was the required resolution of serious financial imbalances that had developed in the corporate, financial, personal, and public sectors. Success in this emerging "Degearing Regime" would mean a period of modest economic gains, continued declines in long bond yields, and a modestly positive risk premium on stock returns.
- **Mid-1990s.** Recognition that there was an even more optimistic third leg to the unfolding "Invisible Hand"/"Degearing" subregimes. This third leg would combine the benefits of the regained economic and political freedom of the 1980s, and the benefits of regained financial freedom in the first half of the 1990s, with emerging evidence of large productivity-driven economic gains (e.g., an earlier essay dated January 1997 was titled "We Are All Schumpeterians Now"). Long bond yields should fall further during this emerging "New World" period, while the historically high-equity valuations (and hence modest prospective equity risk premium) seemed justified and sustainable.
- **Late 1990s.** Rapidly rising equity prices (and hence rapidly falling dividend yields) lead to the disappearance of a prospective equity risk premium altogether. An earlier essay dated February 2000 was titled "Thinking the Unthinkable: Risk in the 21st Century." It urged fund fiduciaries to place themselves in the optimism-driven late 1920s, and then again in the optimism-driven late 1960s. In both cases, the world would look starkly different (and poorer) only a few years hence.

Surely, with the frothy equity market conditions of early 2000, the time had come to hedge against the palpable risk of a major regime shift from optimism bordering on "irrational exuberance" toward increasing pessimism.

- **Early 2000s.** Increasing conviction that a major regime shift toward increasing pessimism was indeed under way. Essay titles in early 2001 and early 2002 included "Investing Without an Equity Risk Premium: A Brave New World?" and "The 10% Equity Return Illusion: Possible Consequences." In March 2003, renamed the completed 1980 to 2000 investment regime "Pax Americana II" by combining the increasingly optimistic "Invisible Hand"/"Degearing"/"New World" subregimes. Tentatively dubbed the new post-2000 regime the "Post-Bubble Blues Decade."

In what ways was this almost 20 years of playing the "spot the investment regime" useful?

"REGIME SPOTTING" VERSUS "RANDOM WALK": WHICH IS MORE USEFUL?

Most fundamentally, "regime spotting" is useful because it forces the spotter to continue to ask the right questions, even though the answers are not always obvious. Looking at our own experience, the approach kept us seeing the unfolding investment sub-regimes within "Pax Americana II" as basically investor friendly, hence fostering increasing optimism.

The approach correctly identified long bonds as being likely undervalued throughout most of the 20-year "Pax Americana" regime. (Why? Because investors developed a violent distaste for bonds in the prior "Scary Seventies" regime). At the same time, we accepted the relatively high stock valuations (and hence modest prospective equity risk premiums) apparent from the late 1980s to the mid-1990s as regime justified. However, when the prospective equity risk premium calculation began to hit zero in the late 1990s, the risk alarm bells went off. The prospects of a regime shift became palpable, calling for resolute risk control measures in pension and endowment funds.

Meanwhile, what did the "stocks for the long run" random walk folks learn over this same 15-year period? Unfortunately, they took the wrong message from their high equity return–driven fund returns in the 1990s. They thought it proved the "stocks for the long run" thesis to be right, and hence that risk control was for sissies. They were wrong because their theory was wrong.

THEORY ON OUR SIDE, TOO

Speaking of theory, we note that William Shakespeare, that great student of human nature, was already a "regime shift" believer 500 years ago ("There is a tide in the affairs of men ..."). Economists John Maynard Keynes and Joseph Schumpeter made much of the presence or absence of "animal spirits" in their theories of how wealth was created or not. Paul Samuelson has characterized the stock market as "micro efficient" but "macro inefficient," with Robert Shiller offering a plausible psycho-finance explanation for this "macro inefficient" reality.

The latest attempt to formalize "the theory of regime shifts" is that of Woody Brock, who devoted 17 pages to it in a September 2002 study (www.sedinc.com). He postulates two processes that jointly determine the long-term persistence in stock market valuation, followed by regime shifts that move the valuation up or down for extended periods of time. One of these processes is the generation of news about socioeconomic developments. The other process governs the evolution of investor beliefs about future stock returns. Both processes are serially correlated (i.e., persist) over time, as well as interrelated with each other (i.e., influence each other) in complex ways. Thus it follows that stock market valuations should be "sticky" for extended periods of time, then shift to a new valuation level, where they again become "sticky" for an extended period of time, and so on. Here is a theory that fits the facts!

FELLOW TRAVELERS

We must note that we did not undertake our "spot the investment regime" journey alone. Fellow travelers provided important insights along the way. We have already noted Woody Brock's important contribution. We would also like to acknowledge those of Bill MacDonald (for his "New World" insights), Rob Arnott (for torturing the historical capital markets returns until they finally confessed to the "true" story), and Peter Bernstein (for his never-ending stream of insights about how the past influences the future). The quest continues for all of us.

CHAPTER 23

The Fuss about Policy Portfolios: Adrift in Institutional Wonderland

"Curiouser and curiouser!' cried Alice."

Lewis Carroll

TEMPEST IN A TEAPOT . . . OR NOT?

Our good friend Peter Bernstein put the institutional investment community in a tizzy earlier this year by pronouncing that policy portfolios (i.e., the practice of managing investment funds with fixed policy asset mix benchmark weights) should be abandoned. The phone lines burned. The industry media wrote articles. It became the number one topic of lunchtime conversations. Hands were wrung. Peter, oh Peter, why would you say such a thing? Have you become, heaven forbid, one of those . . . evil market timers?

After a summer of keeping the institutional investors waiting with bated breath, Peter gave them his answer. Policy portfolios have become a substitute for thinking, he said. The time has come to go back to investment basics. Every investment fund has a liability counterpart. That is where our benchmark thinking should take us. Only in asset-liability space can we think constructively about risk, and how much of it the balance-sheet stakeholders can, want to, or should undertake.

In short, the reason why policy portfolios should be abandoned is that they have become a dysfunctional barrier among investment professionals, the fiduciaries accountable for setting risk policy in pension and foundation balance sheets, and the beneficiaries/stakeholders in those balance sheets.

151

How does someone (specifically, this writer) who has had this viewpoint, and has been strenuously arguing for it for years, react to these developments? Let us tell you. The first reaction was envy (". . . how come they listen to him more than to me?"). The second reaction was to heap scorn on an institutional investment community so far adrift that, when confronted with the patently obvious, it is seen as a radical new insight (". . . . an industry adrift on a sea of irrelevance"). The third reaction was to be thankful to Peter for getting everyone's attention, and to sit down at the keyboard and write this chapter.

Below we retrace some of the history behind why liabilities matter in setting investment policy. We also demonstrate that when this fundamental idea is put into practice, the investment paradigm does indeed shift away from the policy portfolio–based investment paradigm that continues in vogue today. A much more powerful paradigm that integrates asset risk and return with liability risk and return takes its place. These conclusions are supported by new results from CEM Benchmarking Inc. (CEM). We conclude this chapter with the view that the barriers to the much needed paradigm shift (i.e., from an assets-only to asset-liability framework) actually occurring are not so much technological as they are institutional. That makes them much more difficult to knock down.

DUALITY IN FINANCE: A BRIEF HISTORY

The idea that an investment fund is the asset yin to some liability yang is not new. Indeed, the fundamental idea of duality in finance can be traced all the way back to the invention of double-entry bookkeeping during the European Renaissance. Since then, every credit has had its counterbalancing debit. When accumulating credits and debits are transformed into a balance sheet, they become assets on one side and liabilities on the other. This necessary duality in turn has become the foundation of modern financial management and reporting.

Financial intermediaries forget this necessary asset-liability duality at their peril. One of the first stories we heard when joining Sun Life in 1969 was how management in the 1920s got caught up in the equity bull market of those times. The resulting mismatch between equities on the asset side of the balance sheet and the insurance policies on the liability side pushed the company into technical bankruptcy when the bottom fell out of the stock market in the 1930s. A government bailout saved the company (and many other insurance companies doing the same thing). The lessons of the 1930s affect insurance company balance-sheet management and regulation to this day.

It appears that every class of financial intermediary has to learn the financial duality lesson in its own way in its own time. The material mismatch risks embedded in the balance sheets of the savings-and-loan industry did not catch up with it until the 1980s and 1990s. In the hedge fund sector, Long-Term Capital Management (LTCM) thought it was managing its mismatch risk, but had so much leverage that when financial markets misbehaved for only one fatal month in 1998, the LTCM balance sheet blew up. The combination of falling stock prices and interest rates since 2000 has now turned the spotlight on the risk management practices of pension and endowment funds. The record for the three-year period ending 2002 shows that these practices, too, have been sadly inadequate to the task.

FINANCIAL DUALITY IN PENSION AND ENDOWMENT FUNDS: BUILDING THE CONCEPTUAL FRAMEWORK

Why so sadly inadequate to the task? It certainly wasn't the absence of a balance sheet–oriented conceptual framework within which to manage pension and endowment funds. If we take the passage of the Employee Retirement Income Security Act of 1974 (ERISA) on Labor Day 1974 as the catalyst for the need to create such a framework, it appeared almost instantaneously. By July1976, Jack Treynor and co-authors Pat Regan and Bill Priest came out with a startlingly clear and clairvoyant little book titled *The Reality of Pension Funding Under ERISA* (Homewood, IL: Dow Jones-Irwin, 1976). In it, the authors set out the key issues around funding and managing corporate defined benefit (DB) balance sheets, which they argued should be attached to the balance sheets detailing the other corporate assets and liabilities and managed in that context.

Marty Leibowitz took over in the 1980s with a series of lucid articles that focused on the technology of immunizing the balance sheets of financial intermediaries with long-duration liabilities such as DB pension plans. We also made our initial public argument in favor of balance-sheet management rather than assets-only management in the 1980s, with the publication of the book *Pension Funds and the Bottom Line* (Homewood, IL: Dow Jones-Irwin, 1986).

Our award-wining 1987 *Financial Analysts Journal* article "In Defence of a 60-40 Asset Mix" was intended to counterbalance Martin Leibowitz's articles that argued for 100 percent immunization. Our counterpoint was that some pension plan balance-sheet mismatch risk was acceptable as long as the fiduciaries understood what the extent of that balance-sheet risk exposure was, and as long as they held a reasonable expectation of an adequate payoff from undertaking the mismatch risk.

The 1990s saw the development of a balance sheet–oriented performance measurement framework for pension and endowment funds. Its focus was and is: How's the balance sheet doing? Specifically, net of risk and expenses, is the investment process adding any value in a balance-sheet context? In other chapters, we have been reporting results in this context gleaned from the CEM databases for over 10 years now. Indeed, some new results follow below. The point here is that the ongoing assets-only focus of the institutional investment community can't be blamed on the absence of an integrated asset-liability investment paradigm. It has been around for decades.

NEW INSIGHTS FROM THE CEM DATABASE

Our friends at CEM have just sent us some new information on the performance of pension and endowment funds for various time periods ending with 2002. Here are some of the more interesting findings:

- The median five-year total mismatch risk (i.e., the volatility of the balance sheet surplus return) for the U.S. funds in the CEM database was a dangerously high 20 percent (there are 89 funds with an aggregate value of $900 billion with five-year continuous histories). This 20 percent volatility reading is over twice the historical mismatch risk associated with the standard 60-40 asset mix relative to a liability portfolio of typical duration and inflation sensitivity.
- When mismatch risk due to asset mix policy and mismatch risk due to active management are measured separately, the medians came in at 20 percent and 2.5 percent, respectively. In other words, asset mix policy contributed eight times more risk to the median balance sheet than active management did during the last five years. Indeed, total balance-sheet risk and asset mix policy risk both came out to the same 20 percent. Thus, the marginal risk of active management was zero over this period, despite its separate clocking at 2.5 percent. How can this be? Because policy risk and active risk were negatively correlated over the five-year period.
- A major reason why policy risk blew up to an outsized 20 percent over the 1998 to 2002 period is that, usually, stock returns and interest rate movements are negatively correlated (i.e., generally, stocks do better when rates are falling than when they are rising). This relationship reversed itself over the measurement period, with stock prices and interest rates both rising and (mainly) falling in tandem. This meant that during this period, as fund assets were falling because of falling stock prices, fund liabilities were rising at the same time because of falling interest rates.

- Despite being the major balance-sheet risk contributor, passively implemented asset mix policy portfolios underperformed fund-specific 100 percent liability-matching strategies by a median −19 percent per annum over the 2000 to 2002 period. Put differently, while the median policy portfolio had a three-year return of −5.6 percent, the liability-related three-year hurdle rate exploded to +13.5 percent as interest rates fell precipitously. So, cumulatively, the asset mix policies chosen by these 89 funds reduced their end-of-1999 funded ratios (i.e., asset/liability ratios) by a shocking median 47 percentage points over this three-year period ending 2002. On an aggregate balance sheet of $900 billion, that works out to a three-year "loss" in the many hundreds of billions of dollars for the 89 funds.
- The median active management contribution was a +0.9 percent per annum over this same period before expenses, but only 0.5 percent per annum after expenses, or say, a cumulative 1.5 percent over the three-year period. That works out to $14 billion "profit" on assets of $900 billion.

The short of these findings is this: While the active investment managers were making a few billion dollars in profits for these 89 funds over the course of the last three years, the policy portfolio decisions of these 89 funds were at the same time costing their sponsors many hundreds of billions of dollars in balance-sheet losses. Clearly, there is something wrong with this picture.

ENTER ORGANIZATIONAL DYSFUNCTION

So what is wrong with this picture? Simply put, the answer is organizational dysfunction. With a few notable exceptions, no one is accountable for dynamically managing balance-sheet risk in pension and endowment funds. So the most important risk doesn't get managed at all (no, static asset-liability studies using historical data that always give the 60-40 answer don't count!). Had the asset mix policy risk been dynamically managed over the 1998 to 2002 measurement period, that risk would have never been allowed to balloon to the 20 percent volatility level indicated by the CEM database. Any fund managing to a 10 percent maximum risk budget would have been forced to reduce equity exposure as the risk needle went through 10 percent on its way to 20 percent.

Why is no one in the pension and endowment fund worlds accountable for watching the balance-sheet risk needles and acting when required? There is no conspiracy here. It arises from a whole lot of well-meaning people doing the best they can within the confines of their own silos. There are human resources silos where people worry about pension benefits (its equivalent in the endowment world is the granting silo). Then there are treasury/investment silos where people worry about asset management. Outside of the organization, there are the external actuarial, accounting, consulting, and investment management silos, each with their own principles, practices, and conventions.

Hovering uncomfortably on top of all these internal and external silos are the funds' governing fiduciaries (sometimes called trustees, sometimes board, pension, or investment committee members). While these bodies are in theory accountable for balance sheet risk policy, in practice they are typically not equipped to make decisions that can withstand the test of adequate knowledge and due diligence necessary to make such decisions. Why is this usually the case? Because they have not been given the tools and the information needed to discharge their responsibilities. And why is this? Again, there is no conspiracy here. It is simply because there is typically no single executive to whom the governing fiduciaries can (or are willing to) look to, to come up with a functional integrative asset-liability investment paradigm, and a feasible business plan to implement it effectively. So, instead, everyone looks to outside "experts" for advice and comfort.

DECISIONS BY DEFAULT

As a consequence, instead of being guided by effective, integrative, dynamic balance-sheet risk management processes, pension and endowment funds continue to operate largely by a series of simple heuristics and rules of thumb supplied by outside "experts." That is why the vast majority of funds continue manage around the no-brainer "policy portfolios" that Peter Bernstein decries. Is there a better way? As we have shown in other chapters, absolutely! Will the pension and endowment fund management "industry" move to this better way? Not until the funds develop stronger, more effective internal governance processes that insist on balance-sheet risks being managed in a "best practices" manner. In short, change for the better will not be coming anytime soon.

CHAPTER 24

Shifting the Investment Paradigm: A Progress Report

"The significant problems we face cannot be solved at the same level of thinking we were at when we created them."

Albert Einstein

THE "POLICY PORTFOLIO" DEBATE CONTINUES

It was at the NMS Investment Management Forum in Phoenix in January last year that Peter Bernstein questioned the value of policy portfolios in managing pension and endowment funds. Peter's questioning touched off a heated debate on the future value of the "old" institutional investment paradigm, and whether there is a superior "new" paradigm that should replace it. This debate has now spilled over into the new year. Indeed, it was the lead-off topic at the recently concluded NMS Forum, in which we were invited to participate. All 500 seats for this year's sequel were already taken last fall. Obviously, the "old versus new investment paradigm" debate continues to attract serious attention.

This chapter commences with a summary of the arguments we made at the recent Forum against continuing with the "old" investment paradigm, and why we believe the time has come to shift to a "new" one. From there, we take a stab at the question of whether, or to what degree, the institutional investment community is actually "getting it." Paraphrasing Albert Einstein, has institutional thinking advanced enough to be able to solve the significant problems embedded in "old" paradigm thinking? We conclude by observing that while it is still pretty dark out there, unmistakable glimmers of light have begun to appear at the end of the investment paradigm tunnel.

A LENS TO SEE THE WORLD

A paradigm is a lens through which to see the world. The "old" lens through which the institutional investment community has been seeing its world has three key components:

1. On average, stocks have outperformed bonds by about 5 percent per annum in the past. Looking ahead, this 5 percent equity risk premium is also available in the future, as long as you are patient enough.
2. A 60-40 equity-bond mix provides enough diversification over shorter-term periods to create long-term sustainability in most pension plans and foundations, while still providing a 3 percent risk premium over a 100 percent bonds policy. This is a good reward/risk "deal." (Indeed, the experience of the 1990s persuaded many that even a more aggressive 70-30 mix can pass the prudence test.)
3. Given components 1 and 2, the bulk of the resources allocated to managing pension and endowment funds can focus on generating "alpha" (i.e., additional net return) relative to a passively implemented 60-40 (or 70-30) policy portfolio.

The question now comes down to this: Is this a good lens through which to see the world?

WHY THE "OLD" LENS DISTORTS

We believe this "old" lens in fact distorts reality. Here are three reasons why:

1. The prospective equity risk premium is *not* always 5 percent, even over long-term periods. It can be predictably high, normal, or low, with "normal" about 2.5 percent rather than 5 percent.
2. A 60-40 (or 70-30) asset mix policy is *not* always a good reward/risk "deal" for the stakeholders in pension plans or foundations. There are two reasons: First, such a policy will not always offer sufficient reward per unit of properly defined risk. Second, in some situations, such a policy is just absolutely too risky, regardless of whether the prospective reward is sufficient or not.

3. As components 1 and 2 of the "old" lens do not stand up to closer inspection, component 3 no longer automatically follows. Now devoting the bulk of a fund's resources to attempt to generate a modest amount of policy portfolio–relative additional net return for a modest amount of policy portfolio–relative additional risk may no longer be prudent.

Each of these three reasons deserves elaboration.

A VARYING EQUITY RISK PREMIUM

To confirm that the equity risk premium is indeed predictably high, medium, or low, look at Figure 24.1. The chart plots almost 200 years of equity risk premium predictions (using a simple rule of thumb) on the horizontal axis, against what actually happened (i.e., the excess return of equities relative to bonds) over the 10-year period after the predictions were made, on the vertical axis. Note the predictions on the horizontal axis range from −3 percent to +15 percent. The actual 10-year outcomes on the vertical axis range from −8 percent to +20 percent.

Now here's the critical question: Is the relationship between the equity risk premium predictions and the subsequent 10-year outcomes purely

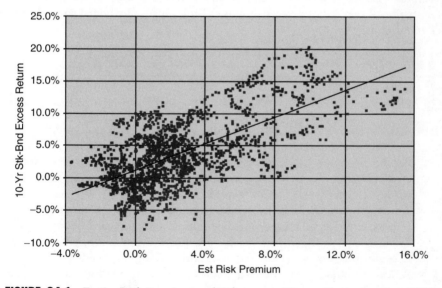

FIGURE 24.1 Equity Risk Premium and Subsequent 10-year Excess Returns, 1810 to 1991
Source: Robert D. Arnott and Peter L. Bernstein. "What Equity Risk Premium Is Normal," *Financial Analysts Journal,* March–April 2002).

random? Or is there a positive relationship? Clearly, the latter is the case. Generally, high predictions lead to high outcomes and low predictions to low outcomes. What is the rule-of-thumb equity risk premium prediction today? About +1.5 percent. What does the chart say about subsequent 10-year outcomes when the prediction is +1.5 percent? The historical 10-year outcome range with predictions in the +1.5 percent area has been about −7 percent to +10 percent.

We do not know any material reasons why this range should not also frame 10-year equity-bond return prospects today. If it does, the case for placing most of the risk chips in pension and endowment funds on a policy portfolio with 60 to 70 percent equity exposure is not strong. Seems like lots of risk and not enough reward. Figure 24.1 also makes clear that even if the rule of thumb produced an expected equity risk premium today higher than 1.5 percent, a policy portfolio with 60 to 70 percent equity exposure may still be too risky in some situations. The pension funds of defined benefit (DB) plans sponsored by corporations struggling with poor operating results and weak balance sheets come to mind.

Finally, the chart shows graphically that in a world of varying equity risk premium prospects, and varying abilities of fund stakeholders to withstand disappointing outcomes in 5- to 10-year time frames, focusing largely on "alpha" games where the realistic stakes are a net 0.5 percent of extra return for 2 percent of extra risk makes little sense. The board game Trivial Pursuit comes to mind.

A NEW LENS

So we need a new lens. Its components are:

- **A set of investment beliefs** grounded in good theory and confirmed by real-world experience. An important element of such a belief set should be the notion of a predictably varying equity risk premium. Other elements will reflect views on the return-generation processes in various capital market sectors and the predictability of those processes.
- **An integrative investment model** that directly links a varying return opportunity set to stakeholder income needs and risk tolerances. The essence of a successful model is to capture the linkages among fuzzy expectations, transactional friction, and stakeholder needs.
- **A decision-making protocol** that can dynamically integrate components 1 and 2 into "value" for fund stakeholders. The essence of a successful protocol is effective human interaction. Thus, its foundation must be alignment of economic interests, good governance, and good organization design.

What are the implications of seeing fund management through this new three-component lens?

A HIGHER LEVEL OF THINKING

Here are some further thoughts, being mindful of Einstein's observation that they must be at "a higher level" than used to construct the "old" investment paradigm:

- While John Maynard Keynes's 1936 opus *The General Theory of Employment, Interest and Money* was meant to address the economics of depression, it contains a very powerful chapter on investment beliefs. With some restatement, Keynes believed that capitalism embodies two distinct types of investment processes. "Long-horizon" investing is all about the projection and valuation of future cash flows. "Short-horizon" investing is all about zero-sum trading in financial instruments. The mistake we make today is to try and blend these two radically different investment processes together. Why is the long horizon/short-horizon distinction so important? Because the returns on long-horizon investments are intrinsically predictive, to some degree. In contrast, whether the returns on short-horizon investment processes (think market-neutral strategies) are predictive is purely in the eyes of the beholder.
- There is no place for "policy portfolios" in this new investment paradigm. The integrative investment model sketched out in Figure 24.2 makes clear why. The only relevant benchmark now is the risk-minimizing portfolio that looks most like the liabilities the investment fund is meant to cover. Moving to the right on the horizontal axis implies taking on increasing mismatch risk relative to the liabilities. The vertical axis measures increasing amounts of excess return relative to the risk-minimizing portfolio. The 10 percent on the horizontal axis might represent the "risk budget" (i.e., mismatch risk versus the risk-minimizing portfolio) that fund management must work within. The 3 percent on the vertical axis might represent the minimum required price of risk (MRPR) that should be earned with a 10 percent risk budget. The ellipse indicating the target performance area suggests that now all that matters are balance sheet–relative results, and not policy portfolio–relative results. Thus, that is what should be measured.
- Other chapters in this book provide statistical evidence that good governance and organization design matter. They lead to mission clarity, delegation clarity, effective strategic planning and execution, and a high level of trust within the organization. These factors in turn drive superior organization performance, and getting them right is just as important as getting the investment beliefs and the investment model right.

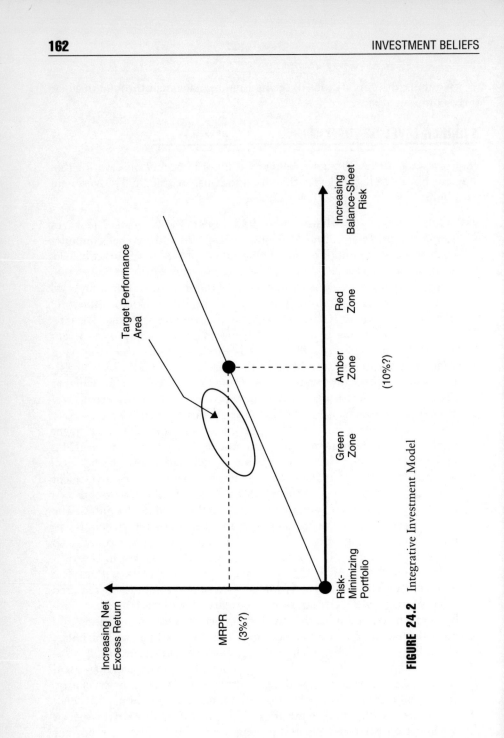

FIGURE 24.2 Integrative Investment Model

If this is the new standard against which to evaluate the practices of today's institutional investment community, how does it measure up?

GLIMMERS OF LIGHT

Most of the discussion at the NMS Forum fit the "old" investment paradigm far better than the new. It's still pretty dark out there. However, we noted two important glimmers of light. First, a number of investment fund executives observed that they were being pressed by their boards "to become more tactical." We take this to mean that some boards are beginning to understand there is no such thing as a single investment policy for all seasons. Instead, balance sheets should be managed dynamically, sensitive to changing seasons. These boards are on to something important!

The second glimmer was the fact that the Forum agenda listed a number of sessions that focused on the importance of good fund governance. In one such session, my prior book co-author Don Ezra reviewed the "excellence shortfall" work we collaborated on in the mid-1990s, and how that work supported the thesis that good governance and organization design really matter. Later in the day, Nancy Everett (now president and CEO at General Motors Asset Management) moderated yet another panel on fund governance and organization design. She also opened her session citing the important findings of the mid-1990s "excellence shortfall" work reviewed earlier by Ezra.

Do these glimmers mean that the end of the old investment paradigm tunnel may be in sight? It would be nice to think so.

CHAPTER 25

Whose "Investment Beliefs" Do You Believe?

"In classical investment theory, all agents are assumed to know the true probabilities of all future events, given the state of the world today ..."

Woody Brock
September 2004

WRITING AN "INVESTMENT BELIEFS" STATEMENT

Just as we had resolved to craft a personal statement of investment beliefs, Woody Brock's new quarterly report arrived in the mail, featuring his "Reconstruction of Modern Portfolio Theory." In the summary of his findings, he wrote: "These results fundamentally vindicate the views of commentators such as Peter Bernstein, Gary Brinson, Keith Ambachtsheer, Rob Arnott, Jeremy Grantham and others who have been critical of much status quo thinking about asset allocation for many years. ..."

Apropos of the above, this chapter starts by defining some ground rules to guide the articulation of a statement of investment beliefs that can withstand the dual tests of reason and empirical evidence. Next, we retrace the 35-year evolution of our own thinking about defensible investment beliefs. Then we compare our own conclusions with some of Woody Brock's, as inferred from reading his 47-page treatise, and confirmed with Woody in a brief e-mail message. The chapter concludes by observing that our investment beliefs also are at odds with those embedded in the classical capital asset pricing model (CAPM), and which Woody takes exception with in his own treatise.

INFERRING BELIEFS FROM ACTIONS

Investment people don't talk much about their investment beliefs. Certainly not in the careful, systematic manner that the topic deserves. So we are usually left with having to infer investment beliefs from investment behavior. If people manage pension funds with constant policy portfolios, it must be because. ... If people move to private markets and hedge fund investing it must be because. ... If people hedge currency risk it must be because. ... If a portfolio manager sells security A and buys B, it must be because. ...

The challenge we set for ourselves in this chapter is to get behind these "becauses" and see what we can reasonably say about the "investment beliefs" that justify them. When you do that, an immediate fork in the road presents itself. Investment decisions are based either on implicit, intuitive forecasting processes that cannot be modeled, or on explicit, objective processes that can. Intuitive approaches are intellectual dead-ends in the sense that they cannot be replicated and tested empirically. Objective forecasting approaches, however, can be tested empirically, and can be converted into optimal portfolio construction rules.

Table 25.1 shows how we made this important point in our first-ever *Financial Analysts Journal* article in 1972. The point of the decision matrix is obvious. The quality of security and market forecasts should play an important role in how portfolios are managed. The matrix also raises a critical question: What are realistic assumptions about the quality of such forecasts?

TABLE 25.1 Decision Matrix About Forecasting Ability

| | | Market Return Forecasting Ability | |
		Good	Poor
Specific	Good	1. Run concentrated portfolio.	1. Run concentrated portfolio.
Security		2. Manage beta around long-term average desired.	2. Keep beta at desired long-term average.
Return Forecasting	Poor	1. Run well-diversified portfolio.	1. Run well-diversified portfolio.
Ability		2. Manage beta around desired long-term average.	2. Keep beta at desired long-term average.

Source: Keith P. Ambachtsheer, "Portfolio Theory and the Security Analyst," *Financial Analysts Journal*, November–December 1972.

MEASURING PREDICTIVE ABILITY

A good part of our activities in the 1970s focused on measuring the predictive ability of securities return forecasts made by analysts directly, or indirectly through fundamental rating schemes. Our intellectual inspiration for this predictive ability measurement work came from Richard Brealey, whose similar measurement work preceded ours, and from Jack Treynor. In collaboration with Fisher Black, Jack formally extended portfolio theory to include return predictions conditional on the assumption of limited positive predictive ability (see "How to Use Security Analysis to Improve Portfolio Selection," *Journal of Business,* January 1973). In our own case, we would go on to contribute three more articles (in 1974, 1976, and 1979) to the predictive ability measurement question. The 1974 article, in the *Journal of Portfolio Management,* would coin the term *information coefficient* (IC), which celebrated its 32nd birthday this year.

What level of predictive ability were various human- and computer-based forecasting models able to achieve over the course of the 1970s? Here are some of the key findings (all statistically significant):

- Brealey set the original benchmark by finding a positive average IC of 0.15 among the security return predictions of 15 British institutional investors.
- In the 1972 *Financial Analysts Journal* article, we reported an IC that peaked five months after the forecast date at 0.22. The coefficient was based 250 U.S. stock ratings made by eight analysts in the Sun Life investment department, where we worked from 1969 to 1972.
- By 1974, we (and colleagues) had built a business out of measuring ICs and using the predictions to rebalance client stock portfolios. We reported average six-month stock and industry ICs of 0.16 and 0.14, respectively, and average annualized portfolio net excess returns of 3.6 percent, based on 16 clients and 40 sets of forecasts.
- In 1979, we (with James Farrell) combined Value Line and Wells Fargo's DDM stock rankings to produce an average six-month IC of 0.15 and annualized average net excess portfolio returns of 6.7 percent (information ratio [net alpha divided by tracking error] was a healthy 1.0) over the three-year period from Q4 1973 to Q4 1976.

What do these IC findings mean? They provide overwhelming evidence on the existence of stock excess return-forecasting models during the 1970s of sufficient predictive accuracy to generate healthy net portfolio "alphas." The implication is that during the 1970s at least, the efficient markets hypothesis (EMH) did not hold. Under the EMH, the measured ICs would average out to 0.0, and not 0.15. The consistently healthy information ratios produced by some "fund of hedge funds" managers over the course of the past 10 years suggests that the EMH at the individual securities level does not hold to this day.

WHAT ABOUT MARKET TIMING AND STRATEGIC ASSET ALLOCATION?

Measuring the ICs of return forecasts for securities markets as a whole is a different kettle of fish. Why? Staying with a six-month forecasting horizon for a moment, a single horizon forecast for, say, the equity risk premium (ERP) to be realized now produces a sample of one. To accumulate a reasonable sample of 30 such predictions implies waiting 15 years, long enough for the world to have changed considerably in many ways. That is not all. Even if you were prepared to back-test and assume that an ERP forecasting process had an IC of 0.15, so what? How much are you prepared to bet on a single forecast assumed to have such modest predictive accuracy? At the individual security selection level explored above, we had the law of large numbers on our side. For example, in the cited 1979 study, the security universe was 200. From an active management perspective, the ERP forecast would simply become the 201st return forecast for the six-month period. No big deal.

What happens if we shift the ERP forecasting horizon out to five years? Ten years? Twenty years? Can we count on sufficiently high ICs to make large bets on long-horizon ERP forecasts? Let's start with what logic can tell us. We developed a view in the 1970s that long-horizon stock and bond market pricing is best understood from an "era" perspective. For example, understanding that the Roaring Twenties were followed by the Dirty Thirties, the Fateful Forties, the Boomer Fifties–Sixties, the Scary Seventies, and then the Dynamic Eighties-Nineties is critical to understanding ERP behavior over the course of the last 80 years.

EXPECTED ERP POWERFUL PREDICTOR

Unsurprisingly, equities were priced to produce a post-World War I high ERP at the start of the Roaring Twenties, and a low ERP by the end (so stocks outperformed bonds during the 1920s). By the late 1930s, the expected ERP was high again (bonds had materially outperformed stocks). The expected ERP stayed high from the late 1930s all the way into the early 1950s (so stocks outperformed bonds strictly on a "divided yield plus growth" basis over this period). The falling ERP from the early 1950s to the late 1960s produced yet another extended period of stocks outperforming bonds. Then came the Scary Seventies, when stock and bond returns both went into the tank. By the early 1980s, stocks and bonds were both priced to produce future mega-returns again, which in fact they did, with stocks going into "bubble" mode in the last half of the 1990s. As the 1990s ended, the expected ERP had hit zero. Since then, it has opened up to a modest positive 2 percent spread again.

What is the essential lesson in this recount of history? It is as simple as it is powerful: The odds of stocks outperforming bonds on a long-horizon basis are high if the expected ERP is high (i.e., 5 percent or better). The odds are poor if the expected ERP is zero or worse. In IC terms, the expected ERP is a strong IC predictor of subsequent long-horizon (i.e., 5- to 15-year) relative stock-bond returns. Is there direct empirical evidence to support this conclusion? Yes, there is. We have already cited the 2002 *Financial Analysts Journal* article by Rob Arnott and Peter Bernstein ("What Risk Premium Is Normal?") in previous chapters. The authors use a simple model to calculate the expected ERP, starting in the early 1800s and ending in the late 1900s. Then they correlate the predictions with actual subsequent 10-year experience. The resulting IC is a breathtaking 0.70. To state the obvious, investors ignore forecasts with this level of predictive accuracy at their peril.

ENTER WOODY BROCK

When Woody sent us his "Reconstruction of Modern Portfolio Theory" piece, our response was that we would comment, once we had set out our own key "investment beliefs" first. They would provide a framework for assessing Woody's 10 propositions, and the supporting logic behind them:

- Woody's paper divides logically into an examination of beliefs about return-generation processes, and about their implementation implications. We agree that the distinction is important. Our own quest for better answers in the 1970s also started by separating return forecasts (including assumptions about their quality) and their portfolio rebalancing implications.
- Woody asserts that understanding the basis of the active/passive management dichotomy is important. We agree, stating so clearly as early as 1972 (see Table 25.1). Indeed, we went further, suggesting that there is a continuum between pure passive management (IC = 0), and increasingly active management as justified by increasingly bold assumptions about ICs.
- Woody asserts that in his new framework, the tactical/strategic dichotomy disappears. In our framework, excess return prospects (and hence

the value of active management) are driven by both levels of forecasting ability, and the time path of that forecasting ability. The empirical results cited above suggest there are two types of processes separated by forecasting horizon. "Short-horizon" predictive processes appear to peak in six-month time frames, with ICs in the 0.15 area. The key to turning these low-quality forecasts into reliable net excess return components is the use of the law of large numbers (i.e., large securities universes and multiple forecasting sources). By definition, "long-horizon" predictive processes have much longer workout periods (10 years in the Arnott-Bernstein study). The key to turning long-horizon predictive processes into reliable net excess return components is not the law of large numbers, but high predictive accuracy (IC was 0.70 in the Arnott-Bernstein study). In short, there is no tactical/strategic dichotomy in our framework either: just differing predictive processes with differing IC paths that need to be optimally integrated.

- Woody asserts that his "Rational Beliefs Equilibrium" (RBE) model, combined with Markov Chains, offer the best hope to improve the predictive accuracy of security markets return forecasting processes. This is a testable hypothesis. What ICs are processes based on these beliefs capable of generating over what time path? This seems to us to be the question that Woody needs to address next.

There are other key points in Woody's paper related to portfolio implementation implications. However, that takes us back to pension fund governance and management, a topic already covered in Part Three of this book.

IN CONCLUSION

Robust "investment beliefs" meet the dual tests of sound logic and empirical verification. It has been a good experience for us to recount the 35-year evolution of ours, which is:

- Our IC measurement work in the 1970s convinced us there are many forecasting methodologies with modest but economically useful predictive accuracy over short horizons. This likely continues to be the case today.
- The predictive power of low-IC forecasting processes is enhanced by optimally combining them. That has been the secret of success of the good "fund of hedge funds" managers in recent years.
- Broad capital market pricing assessments require a much longer time horizon. For example, the twentieth century experienced maybe seven

"eras" where stocks and bonds were priced quite differently in measurable ways, both in absolute terms and relative to each other. So realized stock, bond, and ERP return experience should also have been predictably different. The Arnott-Bernstein paper provides strong empirical support for this belief.

All this leaves us with two final questions. First, with the availability of positive low-IC, short-horizon relative-return forecasting processes at the individual security level for many decades, why has "active management" been, on average, unsuccessful? Second, with the availability of high-IC, long-horizon absolute-return forecasting processes at the asset class level for many decades, why do so many institutional funds operate with frozen "constant policy" portfolios? The integrative investment theory (IIT) set out in "Beyond Portfolio Theory: The Next Frontier" (Part One, Chapter Four) offers insight on how these two questions are best answered. IIT explains why having sound investment beliefs is not enough. There must also be an effective governance and risk management framework in which these beliefs can be put to good use. Without such a framework, sound investment beliefs might just as well not exist.

CHAPTER 26

Our 60-40 Asset Mix Policy Advice in 1987: Wise or Foolish?

"The old 60-40 equity-debt rule makes a lot of sense again..."
Keith Ambachtsheer

"In Defense of a 60–40 Asset Mix"
Financial Analysts Journal, September–October 1987

WHY ROLL THE CLOCK BACK 20 YEARS?

A client called the other day and said that our 1987 *Financial Analysts Journal* article "In Defense of a 60-40 Asset Mix" was the topic of conversation at a recent investment conference. A speaker at the conference had pointed out that there were inconsistencies between what we said in the article then and what we are saying and writing now. Sensing a learning opportunity, we went back and re-read what we had written about asset mix policy in the *Financial Analysts Journal* in 1987. Specifically, we wanted to find the answers to questions such as:

- What was the motivation for writing the article?
- How did we frame the risk issues at that time?
- How did we articulate our investment beliefs at that time?
- Why were we more comfortable with a 60-40 asset mix policy in 1987 than we have been in recent years?
- If we could be magically transported back to 1987 and were given the chance to rewrite the article, what would we say differently?

The reason for addressing these questions is more than just historical curiosity. There really is an important learning opportunity here. Not just for us, but for everyone interested in the evolution of the debate about pension fund investment policy and risk management. And what are the lessons to be learned? The goal of this chapter is to answer that question.

LEIBOWITZ'S IMMUNIZATION CAMPAIGN

Truth be known, the writing our "60-40" article in 1987 was a reaction to Marty Leibowitz's bond immunization campaign at that time. Over the course of 1986 and 1987, he had written no fewer than five brilliant articles on the rationale for, as well as implementation strategies for, immunizing pension plan balance sheets with dedicated bond portfolios. The arguments were persuasive. The math was compelling. There were, however, potential flaws in Leibowitz's arguments that needed to be aired.

The motivation for our "60-40" piece was to draw attention to these potential flaws. In 1987, inflation-linked bonds (e.g., Treasury inflation-protected securities [TIPS]) were still only a gleam in the eyes of Treasury officials. Thus, the immunization strategies proposed by Leibowitz would "work" only to immunize portfolios of nominal pension liabilities. We pointed out that if the intention of a given "pension deal" was to provide going-concern pensions linked to final average earnings, and to update those pensions for actual inflation experience, a 100 percent nominal bonds strategy would in fact create significant risks for the balance-sheet underwriters. Indeed, we showed that under reasonable assumptions, a 100 percent nominal bonds strategy was not obviously less risky than a 60-40 stock-bond strategy when invested against pension liabilities indexed to inflation, pre- and postretirement.

Indeed, we commented not just on the risk mismatch between nominal assets and inflation-linked liabilities implied by the proposed immunization strategy. The proposed strategy also implied tolerance for a situation where, despite a running inflation rate of 4 percent at the time, paying out only a nominal pension was implied to be smart policy. Put differently, long-bond yields were at a high 7.5 percent in 1987 because inflation was still running at a 4 percent rate. So it is a clever financial trick to invest pension assets at 7.5 percent and then let the real value of pensions decline at 4 percent per year. It may have been clever, but was it good human resources policy? Or even ethical if not fully disclosed and understood by plan members?

INVESTMENT BELIEFS IN 1987

If two investment strategies embody about the same risk exposure, logically, the one with the higher expected return should be preferred. So what did we think were reasonable long-term return prospects in 1987? Table 26.1 sets out our 1987 return expectations, as reported in the "60-40" article, along with a brief rationale for each asset class expectation. Note that at that time, we set the stock-bond risk premium at +2.5 percent. The implication is that the expected excess return of a 60-40 mix over a 100 percent bond strategy was 1.5 percent, making the 60-40 strategy clearly preferable to a 100 percent nominal bond strategy for pension plans with inflation-sensitive pension liabilities, given our equivalent risk assessment.

Fast-forwarding 10 years, it is instructive to see what the 10-year real returns actually turned out to be. Real estate in fact returned the expected 7 percent. Bonds and T-bills actually returned 5 percent and 2 percent real, respectively, somewhat above their 1987 expectations, mainly because the 10-year inflation rate came in at an actual 3 percent rather than the expected 4 percent. It was the 10-year real stock return that would come in wildly above expectations (at 13 percent rather than the expected 6 percent). What happened? It was purely a valuation phenomenon. Market participants were willing to pay twice as much for $1 of dividends in 1997 than they were in 1987.

INVESTMENT BELIEFS IN 1997

We celebrated the tenth anniversary of the *Financial Analysts Journal* "60-40" article with two essays in March and April 1997. Appropriately,

TABLE 26.1 Long-Term Real Return Expectations in 1987

Real estate	7%	With cash yields at 7%, assumes that cash flows increase in line with inflation. No change in the valuation basis
Stocks	6%	Dividend yield is 3% plus expected real growth of 3%. No change in valuation basis
Bonds	3.5%	Nominal yield of 7.5% mins a 4% inflation rate expectation. No change in valuation basis
T-bills	1.5%	Current relatively high yields should decline to more normal levels.

Source: Keith P. Ambachtsheer, "In Defense of a 60-40 Asset Mix," *Financial Analysts Journal*, September–October 1987.

they were titled "Is 60-40 Dead?" and "Beyond 60-40." The first essay noted that while the 10-year 1988 to 1997 real stock return of 13 percent was wonderful for the people that benefited from it, there was a consequence. The "cost" of a starting dividend yield of 1.5 percent in 1997 rather than a starting dividend yield of 3 percent 10 years earlier is a 1.5 percent decrement in prospective long-term return. The result is a material shrinking of the stock-bond equity risk premium (from 2.5 percent in 1987 to 1.25 percent in 1997, according to the "Is 60-40 Dead?" essay). Meanwhile, the essay also noted the advent of another important event: the issuance of the first tranche of TIPS by the U.S. Treasury, making the immunization of inflation-sensitive pension liabilities a "real" possibility at last.

So was 60-40 dead in 1997? The March 1997 essay argued that, if not dead, 60-40 was certainly no longer the "slam-dunk" that it was 10 years earlier, under the conditions we set out at that time. A materially lower-equity-risk premium in 1997, and the existence of inflation-linked bonds, had altered the balance of probabilities. For many pension balance sheets with inflation-sensitive liabilities, building up a TIPS portfolio now seemed to be a prudent thing to be doing. We also noted that the regular bond portfolios actually held by pension funds at that time were generally short on duration relative to the duration of the nominal component of pension liabilities. Extending the duration of those bond portfolios would increase return and reduce balance sheet risk at the same time. A rare free lunch!

For completeness, the April 1997 essay ("Beyond 60-40") argued that if pension fund fiduciaries believed that their plan could continue to undertake significant balance-sheet mismatch risk, the time had come to begin looking at potentially more rewarding long-term risk exposures than U.S. stocks. The essay went on to make cases for greater exposures to real estate, to commodities, to emerging markets, and, yes, to more of the right kind of active management.

THE RIGHT KIND OF ACTIVE MANAGEMENT

The previous chapter recalled why we have been a believer in the right kind of active management for over 30 years now. Our research in the 1970s convinced us of the existence of multiple securities return forecasting processes with low but statistically significant forecasting ability (i.e., "information coefficients" or ICs peaking at 0.15 in six-month forecasting horizons). Taken to its logical conclusion, the simultaneous use of multiple forecasting methodologies, coupled with the ability to be both "long" and "short," as well as the ability to control risk exposures, should produce investment outcomes with attractive reward/risk ratios. There is considerable evidence that this logic, in fact, plays out in practice, conditional on the amount of money under management not being "too much." We have been calling these kind of strategies "short-horizon risky" (SHR) strategies.

We have also been advocating a very different "right kind of active management." Its intellectual basis lies (for us at least) in the famous Chapter 12 of John Maynard Keynes's 1936 *General Theory of Employment, Interest and Money*. Simply put, this very different kind of active management seeks to purchase prospective long horizon cash flows at attractive prices. Writing in the middle of the Great Depression, Keynes had in mind new investments that would create new employment that was desperately needed at the time. Today, it matters less whether the prospective long-horizon cash flows relate to new or already existing investments. On the one hand, today's prospective long-horizon investment could relate to financing a new oil and gas pipeline from the Arctic. On the other hand, it could relate to selecting a portfolio of publicly traded corporations with the right mix of tangible and intangible long-horizon return potential characteristics. In either case, the intent is to "buy, hold, and nurture" rather than to engage in adversarial trading strategies. We have been calling these "long-horizon risky" (LHR) strategies.

WISE OR FOOLISH?

Given all the above, what is the verdict? Was our 60-40 asset mix policy advice in 1987 wise or foolish? Let's use the five elements of the integrative investment theory (IIT) introduced in Part One, Chapter Four "Beyond Portfolio Theory: The Next Frontier," to make the assessment:

1. **Agency issues.** Frankly, as we set out to provide a different perspective than that provided by Leibowitz in his five published articles, it was difficult to overlook the fact that the bond dedication arguments, elegant though they were (and are), were being made by a principal in a Wall Street firm specializing in bond trading. Further, we thought it important to recognize the diversity in pension plans, and in the organizations that sponsor them. So we described executives at the hypothetical but realistic Alpha Corporation, struggling with a number of agency issues (e.g., termination risk, tax arbitrage) as they sorted out the best investment policy for their corporate pension fund. Similarly, the board of trustees of the Public Sector Retirement System (PSRS) considered the potential impact of their investment policy decision not only on plan members, but also on state finances, and hence taxpayers.

2. **Governance.** We did not begin to dig into the intricacies of good governance and organization design until the 1990s.
3. **Risk issues.** We were pleased to rediscover that even back in 1987 we were already characterizing defined benefit (DB) pension plans as risk-sharing arrangements. So fiduciaries had a legal obligation to think through how risks were being borne by various parties subject to the "pension deal." We made a clear distinction between the default/termination risk embedded in corporate DB arrangements and the going-concern risks (e.g., related to contribution rates and benefit levels) embedded in all DB arrangements. We also noted the absence in 1987 of financial instruments that could immunize inflation risk.
4. **Investment beliefs.** Never having bought into the "efficient market hypothesis" in the first place, we have never had to recant it. This comes through clearly in Table 26.1, where we recount how we developed long-horizon return expectations in 1987. As importantly, when we repeated the process 10 years later in 1997, we observed that capital market pricing has changed in an important respect. Specifically, we noted that the stock-bond equity risk premium (in the United States at least) had halved from 1.25 percent from 2.5 percent 10 years earlier, and concluded that this change warranted a serious rethinking of investment policy.
5. **Financial engineering.** It was not until the late 1990s (and a further shrinking of the equity risk premium) that we declared that all mismatch risk relative to properly defined pension liabilities should be considered "active" risk. In other words, what mattered most was being aware of the degree of overall mismatch risk being undertaken, and that the net expected return on that overall risk exposure was adequate. This paradigm shift made the traditional distinction between "policy risk" and "active management risk" irrelevant. Hence, we expect that we will not be defending a 60-40 (or any other) policy asset mix again.

In closing, there is one final question to be addressed. Is there an overarching moral to this story? We think there is. The moral is that "truth," whether in 1987, 1997, or today, is never fully revealed. But there is value in attempting to discern it. That was true in 1987. It was true in 1997. And it is true today.

CHAPTER 27

"But What Does the Turtle Rest On?" A Further Exploration of Investment Beliefs

"When I was in grade school, I learned that somewhere in India there is a Hindu tribe whose members believe that the Earth and the sky above it rest on an elephant, and that the elephant rests on a turtle..."

Peter Fleck
Come As You Are (Boston: Beacon Press, 1992)

"BUT WHAT DOES THE TURTLE REST ON?"

Peter Fleck grew up in Amsterdam, had a successful career as a New York investment banker, and then became a theologian. In reflecting on the Hindu tribe belief, Fleck writes that he remembers asking his teacher "Yes, but what does the turtle rest on?" Much later in life, he understood: "In theology, there is a point beyond which no questions are asked. That point for most religious people is the turtle. ... "

Not so in other disciplines such as science and economics. Here, we never stop asking questions. Answers to initial questions now lead to further questions. So readers should not be surprised that when we began last fall to ask questions about investment beliefs, the initial answers would lead to further questions. For example, our initial questions led us to proclaim the belief that at a micro level, short-horizon individual security returns are marginally predictive, and that at a macro level, long-horizon asset class returns are strongly predictive. Of course, such beliefs about individual

177

securities and broad capital markets predictability lead to further questions. For example, what do we have to believe about capital market structures and participant behavior in order to justify our predictability beliefs? That is the profound "turtle" question we address here.

Before we do, it is worth a moment's contemplation why addressing questions about investment beliefs is so important. Logically, our investment beliefs should be the foundation on which we build and explain our investment policies and investment processes. So, for example, if a pension or endowment fund is run with a constant policy portfolio, and with its active managers required to closely track their benchmarks, what are the investment beliefs required to justify this behavior? If a corporate pension plan sponsor has a "return on assets" assumption for the pension fund of 8.5 percent, from what sources does management believe that net 8.5 percent will come? Maintaining an endowment fund payout policy of 5 percent should prompt a similar question: From what sources do the trustees believe the implied 5 percent net of inflation and costs will come? These are fundamental questions deserving well-founded answers.

THE EFFICIENT MARKETS HYPOTHESIS: FACT OR FICTION?

The efficient markets hypothesis (EMH) was, and continues to be, an elegant theoretical construct connecting now well-known assumptions about capital market structure, information creation and dissemination, and participant behavior into a now well-known asset pricing protocol. The implication is that asset prices always incorporate all available information rationally, instantaneously, and without costs. The only choice investors need to make is how much market (i.e., beta) risk they are prepared to undertake. Over time, they expect to be rewarded by earning a risk premium sufficient to compensate them for the beta risk undertaken. Active management has no positive payoff in the EMH world.

Over its 40-year life, the EMH has become considerably more that just an elegant theoretical construct. For many institutional market participants, the EMH has become the turtle on which their investment policies and processes rest. Specifically, they choose an asset mix policy (or adopt one suggested by advisers) with the intent to stick with that policy through thick and thin, as suggested by these same advisers. Of course, most institutional investors do engage in some active management on the side, but not to a degree that could materially impact the fundamental reward/risk choice embedded in their not-to-be-varied asset mix policy decision.

This convergence between behavior implied by the EMH and the actual behavior of many institutional investors raises a profound question: What if the EMH in fact does not represent the best available description of capital market structure, information creation and dissemination, and the complete behavior patterns of all market participants? What would be the asset pricing consequences of a better description of reality? And what if these asset pricing consequences suggest that the behavior of many institutional market participants described above is in fact value-reducing rather than value-enhancing? Surely, these questions loom large for all of us.

THE THREE STRIKES AGAINST THE EMH

Ironically, just as many institutional investors and their advisers appear to have adopted the EMH religion, a growing number of academics and industry thought leaders have become agnostics or outright, outspoken EMH atheists. The unfolding critiques of the EMH can be categorized into three broad themes:

1. **Observed asset price changes not random.** A growing body of empirical evidence suggests that asset prices are at least partially predictable through a variety of forecasting methods. We ourselves presented some of this evidence in prior chapters.
2. **Perfectly informationally efficient markets are a logical impossibility.** If asset markets are perfectly efficient, there would be no payback to gathering and analyzing information, which in turn would lead to zero trading, which in turn would lead to market collapse. Only in informationally inefficient markets is there a payback from gathering and analyzing information, and equilibrium is reached only when the marginal cost of gathering and analyzing information equals its expected payoff.
3. **Human behavioral biases.** Many investors simply don't behave in line with EMH assumptions. Clinical studies have provided well-documented evidence of human investment decision biases due to overconfidence, overreaction, loss aversion, herding, psychological accounting, and miscalculation of probabilities.

So is there a better way? Is there an asset pricing theory that can deal effectively with these three strikes against the EMH?

ECONOMISTS AND "OPERATIONALLY MEANINGFUL THEOREMS"

Enter MIT's Professor Andrew Lo. His lead article in the recent 30th anniversary issue of the *Journal of Portfolio Management* offers an asset pricing theory that deals with all three of the broad criticisms launched against the EMH. He calls it the adaptive markets hypothesis or AMH. Interestingly, Lo positions his AMH not as an alternative to the EMH, but as a reconciliation between the EMH and the views of its critics. His masterful development of the AMH is well worth summarizing.

First, Lo contrasts the differing perspectives of economists and psychologists. Psychologists tend to build theories from the bottom up—through observation and experimentation. Mutual consistency among resulting theories is not critical. Economists go the other way—from abstract theories to empirical analysis. Now theoretical consistency is highly prized. It is this perceived need for theoretical consistency, Lo suggests, that has created much of the controversy and arguments about the validity of the EMH over the course of the past 40 years. He gently suggests that economists would do well to pay closer attention to the real world. To make his point, he quotes the great MIT economist Paul Samuelson, who is far less gentle:

> *"Only the smallest fraction of economic writings, theoretical and applied, has been concerned with the derivation of operationally meaningful theorems. In part at least, this has been the result of the bad preconception that economic laws deduced from a priori assumptions possessed rigor and validity independently of any empirical human behavior. But only very few economists have gone so far as this. The majority would have been glad to enunciate meaningful theorems if any had occurred to them. ...."*

Ouch! Keeping Samuelson's criticism of economists clearly in mind, Lo goes on to lay out his operationally meaningful AMH.

THE ADAPTIVE MARKETS HYPOTHESIS

If we are going develop an asset-pricing theorem that has a sociological dimension, Lo argues, then we must bring an evolutionary perspective to the task. This means building on psychological research that applies the principles of competition, reproduction, and natural selection to social interactions, and then setting the findings in a financial context. Placing the implications of this research in a financial setting is not a totally new idea, but almost so. It means starting with an understanding of what individuals hope to achieve with their financial decisions. The evolutionary perspective on this does not lead to the EMH's rational maximization of utility, but simply to a quest for economic survival.

This economic survival imperative leads directly to "bounded rationality," a concept first espoused by the Nobel prize–wining economist Herbert Simon. Simon observed that people are generally not capable of optimizing. Instead, they "satisfice." How do they make "satisficing" rather than optimizing decisions? Through trial and error. If something worked in the past, keep doing it. If something stopped working, try to figure out why, and develop a new decision rule. If this is how people make decisions, then a changing environment is problematic. With a regime shift, the old rules don't work anymore. Developing new, more appropriate rules will take time. Meanwhile, applying the old decision rules in the new environment will look misplaced and irrational to an all-knowing observer. This explains the apparent contradictions between the "old" EMH and the presence and persistence of behavior biases in financial decision making.

Thus, Lo concludes:

> *"The AMH can be viewed as a new version of the EMH, derived from evolutionary principles. Prices reflect as much information as dictated by ... environmental conditions ... and distinct groups of market participants ... pension funds, retail investors, market-makers, hedge fund managers. ... Some asset markets will be highly efficient ... other markets less efficient. ... By viewing economic profits as the food source on which market participants depend for their survival, the dynamics of market interactions and financial innovation can be readily derived. Under the AMH, behavioral biases will abound ... emotions become central to rationality ... acting as the basis for a reward-and-punishment system that facilitates the selection of advantageous behavior ... the outsize rewards that accrue to the 'fittest' traders suggests Darwinian selection is at work ... unsuccessful traders are eventually eliminated from the population. ..."*

While Lo suggests that much more work must be done for the AMH to pass the "operationally meaningful theorem" test, it already offers some surprisingly concrete implications.

THE AMH'S FIVE PRACTICAL IMPLICATIONS

Specifically, Lo enumerates five profound implications that flow directly from an AMH view of the investment world:

1. **Risk/reward relationships will be unstable.** Thus, for example, the equity risk premium at any point in time will be determined by the relative sizes and preferences of various market participant groups. These factors will in turn be influenced by past experiences. History now matters.
2. **Arbitrage opportunities are now possible.** Without the possibility of these opportunities, there would be no incentive to gather and assess information, which in turn implies the breakdown of price discovery processes.
3. **The popularity of investment strategies will wax and wane.** Without merger and acquisition (M&A) activity, risk arbitrage becomes unprofitable, as will high-beta strategies without an adequate equity risk premium. However, at some point, M&A activity will likely return; as will the reappearance of an adequate equity risk premium.
4. **Innovation is the key to survival.** If there is considerably more to successful investing than just undertaking beta risk, then consciously structuring to be successful will have a high payoff.
5. **Survival is the goal.** Under the AMH, the ultimate organizing principle for individuals and investment organizations is survival, not utility or reward/risk maximization.

Profound implications indeed!

THE AMH AND INTEGRATIVE INVESTMENT THEORY

We have built our own investment theorem called *integrative investment theory* or IIT (see Part One, Chapter Four, "Beyond Portfolio Theory: The Next Frontier"). The goal of IIT is to identify and integrate client/beneficiary value-creation drivers in an operationally meaningful manner. The five IIT value drivers we identified are agency issues, governance, risk framing, investment beliefs, and integrative implementation. What happens when we integrate Ambachtsheer's IIT with Lo's AMH? Are the two theorems logically compatible? Does combining IIT and the AMH produce further operationally meaningful insights?

The answer to these questions is "yes." IIT focuses on providing the innovation strategies that the AMH says are critical to financial survival.

So, for example, IIT requires that attention be paid to aligning economic interests between principals and agents. Without such alignment, principals will pay too much for too little value creation by their agents. IIT identifies good governance and organization design as an independent, additional value creator (i.e., over and above creating structures that align economic interests). Indeed, it is hard to imagine the development and implementation of innovation strategies without good governance and organization design. IIT sees proper risk framing as a contextual challenge, especially in risk-sharing situations such as defined benefit (DB) pension plans and educational or medical endowments. Proper risk framing requires the tools of modern financial engineering. Relying solely on heuristics and trial and error can be fatal!

In short, IIT says that in an AMH world, the best chance for sustainable clients/beneficiaries value creation (i.e., achieving financial survival over the long term) comes through interest-aligned, well-governed institutions with clear missions to create such value. The development and application of realistic, well-grounded investment beliefs are critical to this task. The AMH offers a firm foundation on which to rest such beliefs. It may become the investment world's new turtle on which everything else rests.

CHAPTER 28

Professor Malkiel and the New Investment Paradigm: Raining on the Parade?

"I conclude that considerable skepticism is warranted with respect to active portfolio management strategies, as well as strategies designed to alter asset allocations over time on the basis of relative valuations..."

Burton G. Malkiel
Journal of Portfolio Management
30th anniversary issue, September 2004

RAINING ON THE "NEW PARADIGM" PARADE?

Two key elements of the new fund management paradigm that we have been advocating are active management and dynamic asset allocation. So when Princeton's eminent Professor Burton Malkiel publicly expresses "considerable skepticism" that these two strategies can be employed successfully, there are two choices. You either ignore Malkiel's skepticism in the hope that no one will notice, or you address it. Perhaps foolishly, we pursue the second course in this chapter.

First, a word on our approach. The previous chapter featured Professor Andrew Lo's adaptive markets hypothesis (AMH). Lo was careful to position the AMH not as an alternative to the efficient markets hypothesis (EMH), but as an adaptation of it with different investor behavior assumptions. We intend to be equally careful here in squaring our views with those Malkiel expressed in his *Journal of Portfolio Management* article in

September 2004. Is there a way for both of us to be right? We think there is, and explain why in the pages that follow.

THE BASES FOR MALKIEL'S SKEPTICISM

Malkiel starts his discourse by observing that during the past 30 years, the academic community has been changing its mind about the validity of the EMH. Where once most were true believers in the EMH and its implications, now most are not. Why? Because the preponderance of the empirical studies conducted since those early EMH days have generated results inconsistent with it. The "value" and "size" effects were discovered, as were the "January" and other seasonal events. Then came the whole behavioral finance movement documenting that investors often don't behave like rational EMH-believing "utility maximizers." A behavioral finance view of the world should logically lead to profit-making opportunities. For example, herd behavior leads to a tendency for individual securities and markets to "overshoot" in both directions, thus creating "buy low–sell high" profit-making opportunities.

Next, Malkiel shares the results of a series of experiments to see if all these EMH-inconsistent discoveries do indeed represent profit-making opportunities. Specifically, he tests five money-making strategies:

1. Attempts to make money from the "value" effect (i.e., the discovered tendency of "value" stocks to outperform "growth" stocks) failed.
2. Attempts to make money from the "size" effect (i.e., the discovered tendency of small-capitalization stocks to out perform large-capitalization stocks) failed.
3. Attempts to make money from the short-term "momentum" effect at the individual securities level failed.
4. Attempts to make money from the long-term "momentum" effect at the individual securities level failed.
5. Attempts to make money from the long-term "valuation" effect at the total equity market level (i.e., buy when dividend yields or earnings/price ratios are high, sell when they are low) failed.

After failing to find ways to make money directly from strategies that flow from the EMH-inconsistent research findings produced by academia, Malkiel turns to the investment performance of professionally managed money in the mutual fund sector. Is there evidence that investment professionals can systematically make money for their clients in this sector?

Again, he comes up empty-handed, making the following three observations:

- Studies show that large pools of equity mutual funds underperform their benchmarks by averages in excess of 2 percent per annum over extended periods of time. This underperformance is pervasive. After 20 years, 90 percent of the still-existing funds underperformed their benchmark.
- Trying to pick winners within the mutual fund universe based on past performance appears equally futile. Studies in fact suggest that the best-performing funds in one period tend to be below-average performers in the next.
- There is, however, a mutual fund performance model with significant predictive power. The model's two key performance drivers are the fund's MER (i.e., management expense ratio) and its turnover ratio. In a sample of 990 funds, every 1 percentage point increase in MER was associated with an average long-term performance decline of 1.8 percent per year. Similarly, every 100 percentage point increase in portfolio turnover was associated with an average long-term performance decline of 1 percent per year. Both of these negative "performance driver" coefficients were statistically significant.

Turning the mutual fund performance model message on its head, Malkiel logically concludes that most investors are best served by funds that combine low fees with low turnover.

AN ALTERNATIVE CONCLUSION

Restating Malkiel's conclusion, he is telling investors not to play the investment game by the "high fees, high turnover" rules established by the mutual fund industry, and, of course, he is right. Today's mutual fund game is set up for clients to lose, and for the mutual fund industry owners and managers to win. However, what about an investment game designed for clients to win, rather than the services suppliers? Is it possible to devise such a game? If so, what would be its rules?

Parts One, Two, Three, and Four of this book frame our answers to these questions. Specifically, the integrative investment theory (IIT) we unveiled in Chapter Four sets out the five conditions required for clients to win, rather than lose, the investment game:

1. **Minimize principal-agent conflicts.** The informational asymmetry between sellers and buyers of investment management services is severe (what

else could explain millions of mutual fund buyers willingly giving up an average 2 percent per year of their hard-earned money to the sellers for no "quid pro quo"?). The only certain way for buyers not to be "gamed" by sellers in this situation is for the investing to be done by buyer co-ops. "Client value for client dollars" must be the organization's vision.

2. **Maximize good organization governance.** Structuring the investment organization as a buyer co-op is not enough. The organization also has to know what it is doing. This means that the same "good governance" rules all other organizations should live by also apply here. Effective governance in turn leads to effective management, sound organization design, and sound decision-making processes.

3. **Make "risk" client-relevant.** Stakeholders with financial interests in endowment funds face different risks than those with financial interests in shared-risk pension arrangements. The latter in turn face different risks than individuals accumulating retirement nest eggs on their own. Each context requires careful study as to what constitutes risk, and how much of that risk should be undertaken.

4. **Articulate clear, defensible investment beliefs.** Prospective investment expenses are generally highly predictable; prospective return volatility less so; and prospective returns still less so. But how much less so? Also, are certain types of volatilities and horizon returns more predictable than others? Over what forecasting horizons? Hard questions, yes. But absolutely necessary for well-governed "buyer co-op" investment organizations to answer, and review regularly.

5. **Implement and integrate effectively.** Winning outcomes require the continuous application of integrative thinking and modern financial engineering practices.

So Ambachtsheer's alternative conclusion is that minimizing investment expenses and turnover is not the only way for investors not to lose. Indeed, through well-governed buyer co-ops they can do better than not losing. They now have a reasonable prospect of actually winning!

WINNING EVIDENCE

What evidence is there that the proper application of IIT turns client/beneficiaries into prospective winners? Such evidence must have at least two elements. First, the evidence must show that investment organizations that meet the "buyer co-op" test as a class are a better collective "value for dollars" proposition than mutual fund organizations as a class. Second, within the buyer co-op class, the evidence should also show that well-governed buyer co-ops produce higher risk-adjusted returns than poorly governed buyer co-ops.

The chapters in Part Three documented that such evidence in fact exists for a buyer co-op class of institutional investors called *pension funds*. (See especially Chapter 19, "How Much Is Good Governance Worth?") First, why can we reasonably categorize pension funds as a class of buyer co-ops? Because the rationale for establishing pension funds is not fee-based profitability for some third party, but the provision of employee retirement income. All other things equal, the lower a pension fund's expense ratio, the less it will cost to produce a target pension. So there is a natural incentive for pension funds to maximize net returns, rather than expenses.

Malkiel cited evidence that mutual funds, on average, have underperformed their benchmarks by over −2 percent per year, approximating the average MER plus excessive turnover expenses. What about pension funds? In Chapter 36 in Part Six, we report comparable results for pension funds from the CEM Benchmarking Inc. (CEM) database. A sample of 3,513 annual observations accumulated between 1992 and 2004 on some 300 pension funds produced an average annual net excess return of +0.2% (t = 3.5). On a gross basis, annual excess returns averaged 0.6 percent versus an average expense ratio of 0.4 percent. These results are consistent with our expectations. Where mutual fund unit holders have, on average, been hit with the full force of very high management expenses on the one hand, pension fund stakeholders, on the other, earned sufficient excess returns to cover their much lower management expenses.

THE "GOOD GOVERNANCE" BOOST

Thus, on a net basis, CEM's pension fund sample performed materially better than Malkiel's mutual fund sample. However, even the pension fund sector as a whole did only marginally better than merely recovering its investment management expenses. What about performance within the pension fund sample? In a study published in the November–December 1998 issue of the *Financial Analysts Journal,* we reported a positive statistical association between the net excess returns of 80 pension funds and their "CEO scores."

These CEO scores were based on the pension fund chief executives' rankings of 45 statements related to the fund's governance, management, and operations. Out of the 45 statements ranked, 11 displayed a positive association with fund performance. Six of these statements were related to board behavior, four to management practices, and only one to operational practices. The overall CEO scores based on all 45 statements ranged from 3 to 6. The statistically derived CEO score coefficient was 0.4 (t = 2.0). Multiplying the score range (i.e., 3) times the CEO score coefficient (i.e., 0.4) provides an estimate of the value of good fund governance and management rather than poor governance and management: a 1 percent per year performance margin (i.e., 3×0.4). This work was recently updated, as described in Part Three, Chapter 19. The conclusions from this earlier study remain intact.

We stated in Chapter 19 that, in our view, this quantitatively derived 1 percent per year performance edge in fact understates what high-performance pension and endowment funds can accomplish. For example, Malkiel showed in his article that he could not devise simple money-making decision rules from academic research findings based on valuation and momentum. Highly effective pension and endowment fund management teams know that there is considerably more to generating excess return over time than applying simple decision rules to buying and selling stocks and bonds. You have to be an intelligent participant in private markets. You have to be able to separate the good hedge fund managers from the bad ones. You have to be able to define and manage the risks relevant to the context of your clients/beneficiaries. You have to create incentives both inside and outside the organization that align principal-agent interests. From personal experience, we know there are organizations (though few) that actually do all this!

WE'RE BOTH RIGHT

Professor Malkiel is right to advise individuals to choose well-diversified, low-cost investment options. Both good theory and real-world experience support his view. However, such a view is not inconsistent with our own that the client/beneficiaries of investment pools in the hands of "well-governed buyer co-ops" can do better. Both good theory and real-world experience support our view too.

The real trouble is the scarcity of investment organizations that can pass the "well-governed buyer co-op" test. It requires both vision and effective collective action to create such organizations. No wonder there are so few.

CHAPTER 29

The "Post-Bubble Blues Decade": A Progress Report

"We show that ignoring structural breaks affects equity premium forecasts, and results in overconfidence in their accuracy".
John Maheu and Tom McCurdy, December 2005

ANOTHER NAIL IN THE IID COFFIN

University of Toronto researchers John Maheu and Tom McCurdy have hammered another nail in the once-popular notion that the equity risk premium (ERP) is independently, identically distributed (IID). By using a Bayesian learning procedure, their working paper ("How Useful Are Historical Data for Forecasting the Long-Run Equity Premium?") documents the finding that over the course of the last 100 years, the excess returns of U.S. stocks over T-bills come from a series of statistically differing return regimes. The strongest structural regime breaks in the excess return series occurred in 1929, 1940, and the late 1990s.

Why should we care whether the equity risk premium is IID or not? Simply put, because if it is, we can project the historical 5 percent ERP realization forward at any point in time, regardless of whether stock market prices are "high" or "low." Indeed, in an IID world, there are no "high" or "low" stock prices. In this world, the expected ERP was the same 5 percent in 1929, in 1940, and in 2000, as it is today. This is not the case in a non-IID world. Now the expected ERPs in 1929, 1940, 2000, and today are allowed to be predictably low in 1929, predictably high in 1940, and once again predictably low in 2000. The goal of this chapter is to see what we can say about the expected long-term ERP at the start of 2006.

WHY NON-IID LOGIC WINS

First, what is the evidence supporting a non-IID view of the world? Chapter 25 noted Woody Brock's theory supporting the view that history is made up of alternating investment regimes, 10 to 20 years in length. He based his theory on the reality that history gives rise to a succession of powerful socioeconomic developments. This succession has enough cyclicality in it (i.e., serial correlation and mean-reversion), so that good news is followed by more good news over extended (i.e., 10 to 20 year) periods of time. Eventually, the "good news" string runs out, to be replaced by a series of "bad news" events over an extended (i.e., 10 to 20 year) periods of time. Eventually, the "bad news" string runs out ... and so on.

With some lag, equity prices reflect the mood of the times. Moods of hope and optimism eventually lead to high equity prices, and hence a low prospective ERP. As moods of hope and optimism give way to darker, more pessimistic mind-sets, equity prices eventually fall to reflect this mood change, and the prospective ERP rises.

Chapter 27 reviewed Andrew Lo's adaptive markets hypothesis (ADH), a non-IID view of the investment world based on a socioevolutionary perspective. This hypothesis derives its logic from research in the field of psychology, applying the principles of competition, reproduction, and natural selection to social interactions, and then setting the findings in a financial context. What do people generally hope to achieve with their financial decisions? Economic survival, rather than the maximization of utility assumed by classical investment theory. This economic survival motive leads directly to "bounded rationality," a concept first espoused by the Nobel Prize–winning economist Herbert Simon. He observed that people are generally not capable of "optimizing." Instead, they "satisfice" through trial and error. This leads to rules of thumb that people will continue to use to make decisions until these decisions begin to fail.

This is likely to happen, for example, in an investment regime shift wherein the decision rules that worked in the prior regime now don't work anymore. However, figuring out a new set of decision rules appropriate to the new investment regime will take time. So there will be a period of time when people, with the benefit of hindsight, appear to be acting irrationally. In relation to our ERP discussion, from an alternating investment regimes perspective, it means that investors will misprice equities for years on end. In regime shifts from pessimistic to optimistic, there will be a considerable period of time when equities are underpriced (i.e., the prospective ERP is too high). In regime shifts from optimistic to pessimistic, there will be considerable periods of time when equities are overpriced (i.e., the prospective ERP is too low).

INVESTMENT REGIMES IN THE REAL WORLD

The Brock and Lo non-IID views of long-run equity pricing square nicely with reality. In preparation for our "Stocks for the Long Run" debate with Jeremy Siegel in early 2003, we prepared the "Six Coherent Investment Regimes in the Twentieth Century" table (Table 29.1). Note that the six twentieth-century regimes alternate between extended optimistic and pessimistic market mind-sets 10 to 20 years in duration. Also note that equity market pricing follows the predicted script. Dividend yields fall during the optimism regimes and rise during the pessimism regimes. Stated differently, as the optimism regimes run their course, investors are willing to pay increasing amounts of money for $1 of dividends. The reverse is true in the pessimism regimes. Finally, note the secular rise in equity pricing over the entire 90-year period. Investors were willing to pay more for $1 of dividends at the end of Pax Americana II than they were at the end of Pax Americana I and at the end of the Roaring Twenties.

This framework for understanding equity pricing logic suggested that by 2000, with the duration of Pax Americana II approaching 20 years, we were due for a from-optimism-to-pessimism regime shift. We christened the new pessimism regime that would increasingly come into focus the "Post-Bubble Blues Decade," and speculated that some of its markers would be:

- A major break in equity prices would lead to broad acceptance by investors that there were material risks in investing in equities after all. This view would be reinforced by the very visible failures in corporate

TABLE 29.1   Six Coherent Investment Regimes in the Twentieth Century

Investment Regime	Investor Mind-Set	Approximate Time Span	Dividend Yield Change	Realized ERP*
The World War I Decade	Pessimistic	10 years	5% → 7%	−(5)%
Roaring Twenties	Optimistic	10 years	7% → 4%	+12%
Dirty Thirties/ Fateful Forties	Pessimistic	20 years	4% → 7%	0%
Pax Americana I	Optimistic	20 years	7% → 3%	+8%
Scary Seventies	Pessimistic	10 years	3% → 6%	−(3)%
Pax Americana II	Optimistic	20 years	6% → 2%	+9%

Source: Stock returns are based on data from Elroy Dimson, Paul Marsh, and Mike Staunton. *Triumph of the Optimists* (Princeton, NJ: Princeton University Press, 2002). Bond returns are based on a hypothetical CPI-linked bond with a real yield of 2.5%.

governance that were coming to light. Over time, these realizations could lead to a material adverse shift in the demand curve for equities relative to bonds.

- In a broader context, post-9/11 major acts of terrorism were likely. The global potential for major energy, environmental, and pandemic disasters also seemed to be on the rise.
- The "animal spirits"-dampening effects of "aging" in the developed economies would begin to be felt. These effects would manifest themselves in reduced gross domestic product and productivity growth and a greater aversion to risk taking.

Most importantly, the historical logic laid out in the table suggested that with the passage of time, the Post-Bubble Blues Decade would see investors eventually requiring a higher ERP, and that hence, the price they would be willing to pay for $1 of dividends would decline. Stated differently, dividend yields would eventually begin to rise.

WHAT SEEMS TO ACTUALLY BE HAPPENING?

All the foregoing gets us to the question at hand: How are we doing? Now that we are through the first half of this decade supposedly dominated by increasing pessimism, what seems to *actually* be going on? Here are some observations:

- The major break in equity prices that we experienced early in this decade does not seem to have adversely shifted the demand curve for equities relative to bonds as yet. At the same time, corporate governance practices are arguably improving.
- We have in fact experienced wars, further acts of terrorism, and tsunami/hurricane-related disasters of major proportions. There has been a visible adverse shift in the energy supply curve. An avian flu pandemic may be looming. However, none of this seems to as yet have created a major collective funk negatively impacting equity prices.
- Europe and Japan have arguably been in "aging"-related states of economic torpor. However, the rest of the world, led by the United States, China, and India, has been busy acting out Thomas Friedman's dynamic "the world is flat" theme. Now even Europe and Japan seem to want to join the party.
- All the above is playing out against a backdrop of historically low inflation and nominal interest rates. Real yield curves are also low, suggesting that loanable funds around the globe continue to be in ample supply despite generally robust rates of economic growth, and serious fiscal imbalances in the United States.

Placing all this in the context of the twentieth-century investment regime experience documented in Table 29.1, we conclude that investors have not found the actual 2001 to 2006 experience painful enough to produce a major downward revision in equity prices or, conversely, a major upward revision of the required ERP.

SOME ACTUAL NUMBERS

What actually happened with corporate cash flows and their valuation over the 2001 to 2005 period? Table 29.2, pieced together from data provided in the December 2005 issue of the *Bernstein Disciplined Strategies Monitor,* tells an interesting Standard and Poor's (S&P) 500 story.

The operating earnings of the 500 companies in this portfolio are now well above where they were in 2000. The amount of cash returned to shareholders via dividends and net share buybacks (NBBs) has grown even faster over the course of the past five years. At the same time, the market value of the S&P 500 portfolio has yet to reattain its bubble heights of five years ago.

Importantly, the Div/NBB yield of the index portfolio almost doubled from 1.5 percent in 2000 to 2.8 percent in 2005. At the same time, the real yield on default risk-free bonds fell from 3.7 percent to 2.0 percent. If we attach a long-term real growth rate expectation of 2 percent to the dividends/NBBs per share series, the projected ERP on the S&P 500 increased from a marginally negative expectation in 2000 (i.e., 1.5 percent + 2 percent − 3.7 percent = −0.2%) to a healthier +2.8 percent in 2005 (i.e., 2.8 percent + 2 percent − 2 percent = 2.8 percent).

TABLE 29.2 S&P 500 Index Cashflows and Valuations: 2000 to 2005

	Operating Earnings	Dividends Plus NBB*	% Payout	Index Value	Div + NBB Yield	TIPS Yield
2000	$56	$22	39%	1450	1.5%	3.7%
2001	$46	$19	41%	1350	1.4%	3.5%
2002	$48	$25	52%	900	2.8%	2.7%
2003	$56	$28	50%	1150	2.5%	2.3%
2004	$67	$32	48%	1200	2.7%	1.9%
2005	$74	$34	46%	1250	2.8%	2.0%

*Net share buybacks are estimates based on S&P 400 data.
Source: Based on data from *Bernstein Disciplined Strategies Monitor*, New York: Sanford C. Bernstein & Co., December 2005. Net Share Buy-Backs are estimates based on S&P 400 data.

THE BOTTOM LINE

The combination of rising dividends/NBBs, static stock prices, and falling Treasury inflation-protected securities (TIPS) yields restored the prospective ERP on the S&P 500 equity portfolio from no ERP at all to an almost 3 percent ERP over the course of five years. This is an unambiguously positive development for all investors. Having said that, the investment regime framework laid out in this chapter suggests continued caution is warranted.

Why? Because while history seldom repeats itself, it does echo. Any combination of future negative events still has the potential to create the kind of collective funk that could see the dividend/NBB yield rise well above its current 3 percent level. Remember, it rose to 6 percent in the Scary Seventies regime. So continue to diversify your risk exposures. "Stocks for the Long Run" continues to be a one-trick pony.

PART Five

Risk in Pension Plans

"Suppose an actuary had been asked for an opinion on the number of life-boats to be deployed on the Titanic on its maiden voyage. Under current actuarial practice, the actuary first assumes that the Titanic doesn't sink, this being more probable outcome. Since no lifeboats are needed if the Titanic stays afloat, the actuary can make any lifeboat recommendation and claim that it falls within the ambit of accepted actuarial practice. ..."

Malcolm Hamilton, FCIA, FSA

CHAPTER 30

Rethinking Funding Policy and Regulation: How Should Pension Plans Be Financed?

"PGGM provides a high-quality pension plan, with stable contributions that are kept as low as possible. . . ."
                                                                  PGGM Annual Report, 2001

THE DEVIL IN THE DETAILS

In an ideal world, all pension plans have the attributes cited in the 2001 Annual Report of PGGM, the 50 billion euro industry pension fund for the Dutch health care sector: high-quality pensions financed by low, stable contribution rates. The devil, of course, is in the details. Thus, in the real world, the sustainable financing of pension plans is akin to a never-ending high-wire balancing act involving multiple stakeholder groups today and tomorrow.

The equity bull market began to blur this reality in the late 1990s, as it seemed that high-quality pensions could indeed be financed with low, stable contribution rates simply by having a 60 to 75 percent asset mix weighting in equities. Indeed, in many defined benefit (DB) plans, it appeared that the return on the pension assets already accumulated would be sufficient to finance future benefit accruals without making any further contributions at all!

Today, with most DB balance-sheet surpluses having vanished like snow in springtime, the reality of pension finance as a high-wire balancing act between multiple-stakeholder groups has returned with a vengeance in countries with funded pension schemes. For example, Dutch pension funds are now debating new funding rules among themselves and with their regulator. British funds are trying to understand the true meaning of the new "minimum funding requirement" promulgated by their government. North American DB funds and their regulators are dusting off the current regulations for solvency valuations and the potential consequences of failing the solvency test. Meanwhile, in the DC world, there is a growing gap between pension aspirations and the capital required to finance it.

Given these new realities, a chapter addressing the issue of how to frame pension funding policy and regulation questions seems timely. We begin by exploring the nature of the multiple-stakeholder balancing act around financing pensions, and the nature of the financial and other interests that various principal and agent stakeholder groups have in pension plans. We first apply the results of this exploration process to defined contribution (DC) pension plans, and then move on to the DB context. In the process, we uncover four guiding principles that should make the financing and regulation of DB pension schemes more transparent and effective. See if you agree.

HOW MANY COURSE-CORRECTION TOOLS?

In a world of certainty, funding future pensions is a matter of simple arithmetic, with the calculations for DB and DC plans amounting to the same thing. In an uncertain world, however, contributions must adjust sufficiently over time in DB plans to finance the promised pension, while in DC plans, pensions must adjust sufficiently over time to match accumulating capital. At least, that is the theory.

As usual, reality is considerably more complicated. Why? For one thing, the available kit of course-correction tools is far greater than just contribution rate adjustments in DB plans and pension adjustments in DC plans. For example, contribution rates could be adjusted on the DC side, too, while on the DB side, benefits paid could be made contingent on the scheme's funded status. Simultaneously, investment risk can be altered over time (up or down) in both types of arrangements.

In principle, we can say the greater the number of course-correction tools at hand, the more likely it is that a pension scheme will continue as a going concern. As a corollary, however, we must also say that the greater number of tools at hand, the greater the need for decision-making structures that can competently use those tools to achieve pension plan sustainability over time.

MAKING FINANCING DECISIONS: IN WHOSE INTEREST?

In DC plans, the "who and how" financing questions seem, at first blush, relatively easy to answer. Employee and employer contribution rates are struck, a legal structure with investment options and record-keeping facilities is created, and the fate of participant account balances is reported on a regular basis. However, recent events involving large own-company stock positions in 401(k) plans in the United States suggest that when things seem too simple to be true, they probably are. The lesson learned there is that when basic diversification principles are violated in DC plans, these plans become lotteries rather than pension arrangements. A clear position by pension legislators and regulators on this diversification issue has yet to be articulated (i.e., should DC plans be subject to minimum diversification rules, or should plan administrators be held accountable for devising such rules?).

Behind this "here and now" diversification issue in DC plans lies the broader, longer-term issue of whether today's capital accumulations and tomorrow's contribution rates and investment returns will lead to adequate pensions down the road. This is an open question that cannot be answered with any degree of certainty. What can and should be done is to regularly convert today's accumulated capital, plus tomorrow's intended contribution rates and reasonable expectations of investment returns, into future pension projections. Effective early warning systems alert us to danger in time to take preventive measures.

Calculations of this type are, of course, required by law in the countries with funded DB plans. That is the good news. The bad news is that the potential number of "funded status" calculations that must be performed to meet various fiduciary, regulatory, and financial disclosure requirements is so great as to potentially confuse rather than enlighten. This confusion is often compounded by potential stakeholder conflict, and by principal-agent issues embedded in the financing of DB pension plans. Thus, it may be in the interest of certain stakeholder groups to put more money into the plan now (e.g., current and future pensioners worried about benefit security). At the same time, it may be in the interest of other stakeholder groups to delay making such additional contributions (e.g., current shareholders or taxpayers).

In theory, these types of potential conflicts are sorted out by "objective" actuaries and regulators through the establishment of clear funding rules based on sound actuarial and financial principles. Unfortunately, the application of sound actuarial and financial principles is not guaranteed. Thus, in practice, funding rules are often less than clear (e.g., the United Kingdom's minimum funding requirement) or, even if they are, often produce unintended consequences (e.g., corporate employers choosing to terminate schemes rather than subject shareholders to large cash call surprises).

So how do we sort out these various pushes and pulls, stresses and strains on DB pension plan funding? Can we build a decision framework that will lead to greater clarity and less discord than is currently the case? That is the question we turn to next.

AN ANALYTICAL FRAMEWORK FOR ASSESSING DB PLAN FINANCING DECISIONS

Consider a DB plan with an accrued pension liability of $100. The $100 is calculated with no anticipation of future wage or price increases, using the current market-determined nominal yield on long-term government bonds (say 5 percent today) as the discount rate. What if we wanted to include an appropriate reserve for future wage and price increases? The simplest and most objective calculation would be to substitute the market-determined real yield (i.e., inflation indexed) on long-term government bonds for the nominal yield (say 2.5 percent today, rather than 5 percent) as the new discount rate. Let's say this raises the liability to $130. If we wanted to add an additional piece that recognizes the likelihood that wage growth will exceed price inflation, the $130 might become $140.

Let's now consider a third liability calculation possibility. The DB plan manager believes the pension fund can earn a 2.5 percent excess return over the government bond yield over the long run. If that estimate turned out to be right, by how much could the pension reserve be reduced? We already know the answer for the inflation indexed reserve calculation of $130. It knocks the $130 back to $100. Say that it knocks the higher $140 reserve calculation to $110. Let's also say that it would knock the original ex-inflation reserve of $100 down to $70.

Having established, in theory at least, a funding target range for the DB scheme from a low of $70 to a high of $140, we can move to the other side of the DB scheme balance sheet. Let's consider cases in which the current pension fund market value is $70, $100, or $140. Next, let's identify five specific stakeholder groups, and see how they might respond to the funding target possibilities of $70, $100, or $140. Let's also see if their choice would be affected by whether the fund asset value was $70, $100, or $140 at the point of valuation. The matrix of possibilities is laid out in Table 30.1, along with our assessment of the "rational" funding target choices various stakeholder groups would make.

TABLE 30.1 Possible DB Scheme Stakeholder Funding Target Perspectives

	Current Fund Value		
	$140	$100	$70
	Rational	Funding	Target
Plan members—no contribution responsibility	$140	$140	$140
Plan members—with contribution responsibility	$130	$120	$110
Employer—good credit/high profitability	$130	$120	$110
Employer—poor credit/low profitability	$120	$100	$ 80
Regulator—minimum requirement focus	$100	$100	$100

"RATIONAL" EXPLANATIONS

Table 30.1 suggests that, depending on who you are, and depending on the current value of the pension fund, the range of "rational" funding targets under the circumstances set out above might be anywhere between $140 and $80. Here is why the range is so wide:

- Plan members with no responsibility for making contributions are interested only in having enough money in the plan to ensure receipt of a "fully loaded" pension upon retirement. That is $140 in our example.
- Plan members who do have a responsibility to contribute toward a funding shortfall must make a trade-off between less/more money now, and more/less benefit security later. We reflect that trade-off by suggesting they might prefer funding targets between $130 and $110, depending on the current value of the pension fund.
- Employers with high credit ratings and/or high profitability probably see the world similar to plan members with whom they share funding risk. So they, too, might prefer funding targets between $130 and $110, depending on the current value of the pension fund.
- Employers with poor credit ratings and/or low profitability have cash conservation mind-sets, so they will prefer to fund to a lower funding target. We suggest a possible $120 to $80 range, depending on the current value of the pension fund.

■ The regulator's job is to police pension scheme solvency. This means ensuring there are sufficient assets on hand to meet accrued pension obligations without any projection for future wage or price increases, using the current default risk-free long-bond yield as the discount rate. That is $100 in our example.

What does all this suggest about possible DB plan funding principles?

FOUR PRINCIPLES TO FUND BY

Four basic principles to guide funding policy for DB plans suggest themselves:

Principle 1. The "DB pension deal" must be clearly articulated, including what the target pension benefit is, which stakeholder groups are to bear what risks, and who is to be accountable for the articulation and implementation of the scheme's funding and investment policies over time.

Principle 2. Only "mark-to-market" asset and liability values have economic meaning; hence, only such values should be used to set balance-sheet funding targets and to assess the funded status of DB schemes over time.

Principle 3. Sponsors of DB schemes should be required to file a "statement of funding policy and goals" alongside the "statement of investment policy and goals." The funding policy statement should articulate the process through which the funding target is to be determined. It should also establish a "no action" funded ratio band, within which only the normal service cost contribution is made (e.g., "the funding target is 130 percent of the accrued pension liability with no projections; however, within a funded ratio band of 120 percent and 140 percent, only the normal service cost contribution will be made").

Principle 4. In the same way that regulators have moved investment regulations away from an "our arbitrary rules" toward a "your fiduciary obligations" philosophy, they must now do the same with funding regulations. Having said that, they should reserve for themselves the power to enforce special steps to protect beneficiaries when a DB plan fails the solvency test as we have defined it (i.e., market value of assets below the market value of the accrued liability with no projections).

Do the basic principles and rules that guide the funding of DB pension schemes need to be any more complicated than this? We don't think so. Do you?

Funding Policy and Investment Policy: How Should They Be Integrated in DB Pension Plans?

"Suppose an actuary had been asked for an opinion on the number of lifeboats to be deployed on the Titanic on its maiden voyage. Under current actuarial practice, the actuary first assumes that the Titanic doesn't sink, this being the more probable outcome. Since no lifeboats are needed if the Titanic stays afloat, the actuary can make almost any lifeboat recommendation and claim that it falls within the ambit of accepted actuarial practice. ..."

Malcolm Hamilton, FCIA, FSA

PRINCIPLES TO FUND AND INVEST BY

Times like the present confirm the wisdom of having clearly articulated funding and investment principles and policies for defined benefit (DB) pension plans. Without such principles and policies, the radical deterioration in plan funded status that has occurred since 2000 can lead to poorly conceived, knee-jerk decisions, or possibly just as bad, no decisions at all. This was the motivation for writing the previous chapter on funding policy issues for DB pension plans.

In that chapter, we asserted that there is a shortage of clear thinking about funding policy issues, both inside the actuarial community and (not surprisingly) outside it as well. We suggested that more coherent funding policy decisions require broad adherence to three key principles by plan sponsors, actuaries, and regulators alike:

1. The "DB pension deal" must be clearly articulated, including what the target pension benefit is, which stakeholder groups are to bear what risks, and who is to be accountable for the articulation and implementation of the plan's funding and investment policies over time.
2. Only "mark-to-market" (i.e., "fair value") asset and liability values have economic meaning, and hence only such values should be used to set balance sheet funding targets, and to assess the funded status of DB plans over time.
3. Sponsors of DB plans should be required to file a "Statement of Funding Policy and Goals" alongside their "Statement of Investment Policy and Goals."

In the Part Three and Four chapters on pension fund governance and investment beliefs, we asserted that there is an equal shortage of clear thinking about pension investment policy issues, both inside the investment community and (not surprisingly) outside it as well. We have been suggesting that more coherent investment policy decisions require broad adherence to nine key principles, including these three:

1. Fully define the pension contract, including the target benefit and who bears what risks in going-concern and termination contexts.
2. Regularly value the accrued liabilities using the current yield curve of default-free bonds, with and without wage and price inflation "best estimates." Compare the resulting liability "fair values" to the market value of plan assets, and assess how changes in the plan's "fair value" funded status (i.e., ratio of "fair value" assets to liabilities) might impact the future plan contribution rate and (possibly) the level of future pension payments.
3. Control balance-sheet risk by establishing a balance-sheet risk budget, which is then monitored regularly over time.

Unfortunately (or fortunately?), all of these fine principles are not the end of the story. As always, the devil is in the details. Consider the following three questions, for example:

1. Can a DB pension "contract" ever be fully defined? What do we mean by "fully defined"? Does it mean "no risk"?
2. Is there such a thing as a "normal" funding target for a DB plan? "Normal" in what sense?

3. Should there be a link between a DB plan's funding policy and its investment policy? How should we think about this question?

Hard questions? Yes! But they must be answered if DB pension plans are to survive the current difficult environment. We give it our best effort below.

WHAT MAKES DB PENSION "CONTRACTS" RISKY?

Holders of DB pension "contracts" are potentially subject to three kinds of risks:

1. **Default risk.** The plan sponsor becomes insolvent, and pension assets are not sufficient to cover all accrued pension liabilities.
2. **Inflation risk.** The pension promise is set out in nominal terms, rather than inflation-adjusted terms, and inflation adjustments are at the discretion of the sponsor. Alternatively, the promise is nominal, partially indexed, or fully indexed by formula, depending on the financial condition of the plan.
3. **Intergenerational risk.** The contribution rate required to bail out an underfunded pension plan becomes so high that the next generation of plan contributors is unwilling to make the required contributions.

Note that all three kinds of risks can be largely eliminated through the existence of a large enough pension fund of "matching" default-free bonds that "immunize" the accrued liabilities. Thus, it is only (a) when assets are insufficient and/or (b) when there is an asset-liability mismatch, that pension contracts become risky.

The greater the asset shortfall, and/or the greater the asset-liability mismatch, the riskier the pension contract becomes. It follows directly from this conclusion that funding policy and investment policy in DB plans are indeed intimately linked. Both have a direct impact on the riskiness of pension contracts. Further, more risk exposure from one source can be offset by less risk exposure from the other, and vice versa.

SHOULD DB FUNDING TARGET CALCULATIONS ASSUME THAT MORE RISK MEANS MORE RETURN?

What defines a "normal" funding target for a DB pension plan? Presumably, the goal is to set aside enough money now so that there will be enough money later to pay accrued pensions when they fall due. But assuming what return on plan assets? Is it the known return on default-free bonds with similar financial characteristics (e.g., duration, inflation sensitivity) as the accrued liabilities? Or is it the expected (i.e., presumably higher but uncertain) return on a pension fund with material liability mismatch risk?

Every financial economist we know would answer "the default-free bond rate." However, the majority of actuaries (so our spies in the actuarial community tell us) would answer "the expected return on the pension fund." Why? Because they assume the mismatch risk policy will pay off, and that hence plan assets will earn a risk premium over the relevant default-free bond rate. What the majority of actuaries don't seem to understand is that this kind of calculation puts considerable, unrecognized risks on DB pension balance sheets.

IS CURRENT "ACCEPTED ACTUARIAL PRACTICE" UNACCEPTABLE?

In a scathing critique of current actuarial practices in the United States, actuaries Larry Bader and Jeremy Gold ("Reinventing Pension Actuarial Science," July 7, 2002, www.soa.org) point out that current practice implies that, for example, in funding a $1.63 million pension payment 10 years hence, $1 million of 5 percent zero-coupon Treasury bonds is equal to a $628,000 equity portfolio with an expected return of 10 percent.

Would mainstream actuaries really trade $1 million of bonds for $628,000 of stocks "even up" today? Presumably not. Yet, they are willing to certify that $1 million of risk-free pension debt has a "liability" value of only $628,000 if it were invested in equities. In short, they are rolling the dice that the $628,000 will earn 10 percent over the 10-year period. What if it doesn't? Apparently, that is not their problem.

The majority of Canadian actuaries seem to be of similar "roll the dice" mind. An October 1998 discussion paper prepared for the Canadian Institute of Actuaries titled "Pension Plan Funding: A Fresh Approach" authored by nine of its members (www.actuaries.ca) was widely criticized for recommending (among other things) that the following minimum funding standard become part of "accepted actuarial practice":

> *"The minimum contribution is the amount required to ensure that the market value of a pension fund equals or exceeds the plan's wind-up liabilities five years after the valuation date with an acceptable level of certainty. ..."*

Thus, using the Bader-Gold example, the Canadian discussion paper not only recommends the $1 million calculation as the current liability basis (rather than $628,000), but also recommends adding an additional margin to that $1 million basis to reflect such risks as asset-liability mismatching. So, for example, a 20 percent margin would lead to a minimum funding target of $1.2 million rather than $1 million. Such thinking is apparently unacceptable to most actuaries. To paraphrase Canadian actuary Malcolm Hamilton, one of the authors of the discussion paper, when you assume that the *Titanic* will not sink, almost any number of lifeboats will do.

WHAT IS AN "ACCEPTABLE LEVEL OF CERTAINTY"?

All this leads us logically to the next question. How much of a margin is needed, using the words of the Canadian discussion paper, for the market value of plan assets to exceed the plan's wind-up liabilities somewhere (five years was their recommendation) down the road? Very little margin would be needed if the liabilities are immunized with matching default-risk-free bonds. Potentially, a lot of margin would be needed if the chosen investment policy results in a material asset-liability mismatch, and if most of the resulting "pension contract" risk is to be eliminated.

Assume, for example, a situation in which a DB plan is 100 percent funded on a "fair value" basis in relation to its target benefit level. Assume further that its mismatch risk is measured as an annual 10 percent volatility (i.e., annualized standard deviation) between its fund return and the market return on a portfolio of bonds constructed to match its accrued liabilities. This volatility level is consistent with a 60-40 asset mix policy and some "active" management in normal times. Finally, assume that this mismatch risk can reasonably be expected to produce an additional 1.5 percent of return per annum over the risk-minimizing portfolio over the long term. What would an appropriate funded ratio margin in excess of 100 percent be in this case?

We calculate that a five-year "one sigma" buffer works out to a required margin of about 15 percent (i.e., a target funded ratio of 115 percent). This would be an insufficient amount of margin in one five-year period out of six. A much more stringent "two sigma" buffer requires a much larger 40 percent margin, which would be insufficient in only one five-year period out of 40 under the simplifying assumptions used in the margin calculations (i.e., normal distributions, no serial correlations).

These calculations make an obvious point. It is simply too expensive to make DB pension contracts absolutely risk free, unless current balance sheets have large margins of assets over liabilities. That is generally not the case today. Absent such large margins, affordable contracts require that plan participants either accept lower income replacement rates as target pensions than is currently the case, or alternatively, plan participants are going to have to explicitly accept more risk in pension contracts (i.e., sponsor solvency risk, inflation risk, or intergenerational risk) than they currently perceive they have accepted. This is an unpleasant, yet necessary, message that will have to be conveyed to plan members.

SURPLUS OWNERSHIP

If the combined effects of a plan's funding and investment policies can lead to a balance sheet funded ratio in excess of one, a fully defined 'pension deal' must articulate the rules of surplus ownership. A recent paper by three Dutch authors (Theo P. Kocken, Huub F. van Capelleveen, and Janwillem Engel, "Proprietary Issues in Pension Funds from an Option Theoretical Point of View," www.cardano-riskmanagement.nl) offers a fresh new perspective on the thorny surplus ownership question.

The authors proceed from the same observation we have already made above: Most pension contracts are risky, with the risks capable of being characterized as a series of puts and calls that plan stakeholders have "issued" to each other. Specifically, sponsor solvency risk is like a put option that can be exercised by the employer under certain circumstances. Though the authors don't mention it, intergenerational risk sharing involves a similar put option exercisable by the current generation at the expense of the next generation under certain (often not spelled out in advance) circumstances. If the pension contract is fair, there are off-setting calls on the other side of the balance sheet.

However, there is also a going-concern sponsor promise to make additional contributions in the case of asset shortfalls. This is like a put option issued by the sponsor to plan members, requiring the sponsor to increase plan assets under certain circumstances. Finally, conditional inflation indexation is like a put option issued by current plan members to the sponsor, or to the next generation (i.e., under certain conditions, the sponsor [or the next generation] can reduce the pension liability by not granting inflation updates). Again, if the pension contract is fair, there are off-setting calls on the other side of the balance sheet.

Each of these puts and calls has a financial consideration (i.e., an implicit "option premium") attached to it. It is the relative values of these option premiums that determine the relative claims on surplus assets. The authors review a series of "pension deals" wherein surplus ownership ranges from 100 percent employer (i.e., value of pension default put is zero, the employer commits to making good asset shortfalls, and inflation indexation is unconditional) to 100 percent plan members (i.e., no sponsor obligation to make up asset shortfalls). They also show that for most realistic cases involving both conditional indexation and a sponsor obligation to make up asset shortfalls, a 50-50 surplus split is not a bad approximation.

CLEANING UP OUR ACT

For decades, most of the pension "industry" has gotten away with sloppy thinking, on both the asset and liability sides of the balance sheet. Proof once again that bull markets finesse brains every time. The coming decades will not be so easy. Now we will need clear thinking to get the funding and investment principles and policies of DB pension plans right, and we will need strong leadership to implement the necessary changes.

More specifically, a combination of clear thinking and strong leadership would lead to material changes in how DB "pension deals" are defined, how they are managed, and how they are regulated. Where do you stand? Do you want to build better, more transparent pension plans or defend the status quo? The time has come to choose.

CHAPTER 32

Resurrecting Ranva: Adjusting Investment Returns for Risk

"RANVA is a metric for people who would rather measure the right things imperfectly than the wrong things perfectly."
From *Pension Fund Excellence,* by Keith Ambachtsheer and
Don Ezra, 1998

RESURRECTING RANVA

Most new ideas never catch on. Some catch on quickly, but flame out with the passage of time. Then there are those very few ideas that take time to gain acceptance, but do eventually have a sustained impact on behavior. Co-author Don Ezra and I introduced the risk-adjusted net value added (RANVA) idea in our book *Pension Fund Excellence* (New York: John Wiley & Sons, 1998). It was to be a performance metric that would standardize pension fund returns not only for differences in investment expenses, but also for differences in risk exposure. As we wrote at the time, it was to be a metric that would measure the right things imperfectly, rather than the wrong things perfectly.

Eight years later, the best we can say for RANVA is that it did not catch on quickly and then flame out with the passage of time. Optimistically, it is still in the running as an idea taking time to gain acceptance, on its way to eventually impacting how performance of the globe's pension funds is measured and managed. The goal of this chapter is to assess RANVA's prospects of becoming an important performance metric in the global pension fund "industry." It proceeds by reviewing how RANVA was defined in the 1998 book and reviews actual RANVA results achieved by a large sample of pension funds as captured in the CEM Benchmarking Inc.

(CEM) database. The chapter reexamines the RANVA idea in light of this experience, and offers some further reflection on its conceptual foundation. It concludes with some thoughts on what the "tipping point" conditions for broad acceptance of the RANVA idea might be, and what we can do to create those conditions.

RANVA IN 1998

Our 1998 book asserted that "pension fund excellence" cannot be just an abstract ideal. It should also be confirmable through measurement. While no single metric can ever confirm that some standard of pension fund excellence has been attained, it is hard to imagine achieved investment return not being the foundation of an important "excellence" metric. But investment return relative to what? Historically, and even today, a common answer has been: relative to the returns on other pension funds. However, the problems with such comparisons are well known. For example, expenses between different funds can vary widely, so net returns are more comparable than gross returns. However, even net returns are not directly comparable. In a risk-averse world, earning 5 percent by accepting considerable risk that the outcome could have been far worse, cannot be as "good" a result as earning 5 percent without such risk.

Intuition tells us that the 5 percent outcome involving risk should get a "haircut," representing payment for the risk undertaken in achieving it. But how large should that "haircut" be? Conceptually, that depends on the reward people require for risk bearing. But how do we translate this notion practically? The 1998 book provided a brave "bootstrap" answer. It observed that a common internal rate of return (IRR) hurdle rate for risky corporate projects seemed to be 15 percent. Let's take this to be "the cost of risk capital." Now we need to bring this 15 percent hurdle rate requirement into a pension fund context. We might ask: Over the measurement period, what proportion of the pension plan balance sheet was "at risk"? Let's say the estimated balance-sheet mismatch risk had a sigma (i.e., annualized surplus volatility) of 8 percent, and that the balance-sheet capital "at risk" was defined as two sigmas, or 16 percent. Pulling these pieces together, if to justify risk exposure the 16 percent of the balance sheet "at risk" has to meet a "hurdle rate" expected return test of 15 percent, a total fund risk capital charge of 2.4 percent results (i.e., 15 percent $\times 2 \times 0.08 = 2.4$ percent). The implication is that the risky strategy needs to have a net expected return of 7.4 percent (i.e., 5 percent + 2.4 percent) to be as attractive as the risk-free net 5 percent return result.

Figure 32.1 provides a visual representation of this logic. The mismatch risk estimate is set out on the horizontal axis. It was 8 percent relative to the

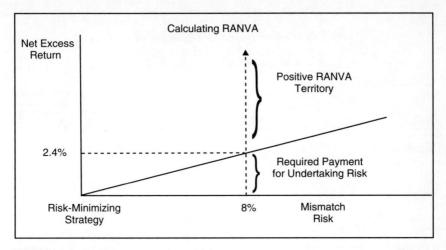

FIGURE 32.1　Calculating RANVA
Source: Keith. P. Ambachtsheer and D. Don Ezra. *Pension Fund Excellence.* New York: John Wiley & Sons, 1998.

risk-minimizing investment strategy in the numerical example above. The expected net excess return requirement is set out on the vertical axis. We calculated it to be 2.4 percent in the numerical example above. The diagram prompts important risk-related questions about the investment context. For example, is the risk-minimizing investment policy defined in relation to the payment obligations the assets are meant to cover? Is undertaking 8 percent balance-sheet mismatch risk the result of a conscious "new paradigm" risk-budgeting decision? Or does it just fall out of an asset mix policy based on a set of "old paradigm" historical rules of thumb?

Regardless of how these questions are answered, the diagram's main message should be clear: the first 2.4 percent of realized net excess return is just payment for undertaking risk. The RANVA clock only turns positive once that extra 2.4 percent has been earned.

MEASURING RANVA IN THE REAL WORLD

While the RANVA metric has maintained a distinctly low "real-world" profile since 1998, we noted above that CEM has been estimating realized RANVAs for a large sample of pension funds since 1998. In fact, it has been estimating two RANVAs per participating fund: a policy RANVA and an implementation RANVA. The former is based on the return behavior of the passively implemented asset mix policy relative to the "liability portfolio." The latter is based on the net return behavior of the active strategies relative

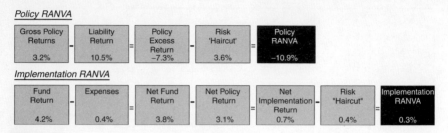

FIGURE 32.2   Average *RANVA* Estimates for 84 Large U.S. Pension Funds, 2000 to 2004
Source: CEM Benchmarking Inc., 2005.

to the "policy portfolio." The RANVA calculations for both are displayed in Figure 32.2. They are based on the average results of a sample of 84 large U.S. defined benefit (DB) pension funds (average value $13 billion) over the five-year period ending in 2004.

The numbers in Figure 32.2 tell quite a story. The overall theme is that over the course of the five-year period starting in 2000 and ending in 2004, the 84 large U.S. pension funds won a battle but lost the war. Specifically, on average, they generated 0.7 percent per annum of positive net excess return with their implementation strategies. The results remain positive even after a risk "haircut" of 0.4 percent (i.e., at +0.3 percent). At the same time, however, the asset mix policies of these funds produced a −7.3 percent per annum shortfall relative to their liability-related risk-minimizing strategies. The risk "haircut" calculation shows that the asset mix policy mismatch risk exposure in fact required a positive return increment of 3.6 percent over the risk-minimizing strategy to pay for the policy risks undertaken. So on a risk-adjusted basis, average asset mix policy–related underperformance over the 2000 to 2004 period was −10.9 percent per annum.

THE 2000 TO 2004 EXPERIENCE: LESSONS

What can we learn from these calculations? The following lessons come to mind:

- Conceptually, the RANVA idea makes as much sense in 2006 as it did in 1998.
- Practically, the 2000 to 2004 results confirm that "old" investment paradigm thinking still dominated over this period, with asset mix policy risk requiring a nine times greater risk "haircut" than implementation (or active) risk (i.e., 3.6 percent vs. 0.4 percent).

- Asset mix policy risk exposure over the 2000 to 2004 period produced a large negative result (-7.3 percent) even before applying the 3.6 percent risk "haircut." The hard-learned lesson is that material "ex-ante" risk does turn into excruciating "ex-post" pain every once in a while.
- Not surprisingly, many pension organizations are now reexamining the "ex-ante" risk exposure question in more integrated (i.e., liability-related) contexts. This more thoughtful and demanding approach requires addressing four fundamental questions. How should we value the liabilities? How big should the overall risk budget be? Which risk exposures have the best expected payoffs today? What risk-based "haircut" should we apply today in establishing our portfolio of risk exposures?

In short, the 2000 to 2004 experience is producing a widespread paradigm shift. The old, little examined investment "rule" of loading up on asset mix policy risk and then playing a trivial active management game at the margin is ending. The new, far more demanding investment "rule" of not prejudging where the risk bets should be placed, requires ongoing, explicit judgments and decisions regarding risk budgets, investment prospects, and where to set the risk-based hurdle rates. This is a world where the RANVA idea should eventually play an important role in measuring pension fund performance.

REMAINING BARRIERS

What are the remaining barriers to broad acceptance and use of RANVA that still need to be breached? We can think of three:

1. **Belief in the "new investment paradigm."** Continued growing acceptance is required of the reality that saving-investment intermediation processes are dynamically adaptive, with expert participants systematically capable of identifying investment opportunities with better RANVA prospects than participants with less expertise. In other words, broad acceptance that there really are skill-based differences in investment results to be measured.
2. **Belief in "pay for performance" arrangements.** Continued growing acceptance is required of the reality that skill-based differences should logically lead to compensation differences. However, if "pay for performance" arrangements are to pay for skill-based differences rather than risk differences, investment returns must be assessed risk-related return "haircuts" that reflect those risk differences.

3. **Consensus on how risk-based "haircuts" should be calculated.** We noted that the RANVA examples in the 1998 book were bravely "boot-strapped" by blending together (a) a 15 percent "cost of risk-capital" standard, (b) a "sigma" of 8 percent for balance-sheet mismatch risk, and (c) a 2-sigma "surplus-at-risk" convention. In its RANVA calculations, CEM currently employs a lower 12 percent "cost of risk capital" standard and a lower 1.65-sigma "surplus at risk" convention. The actual 2000 to 2004 average asset mix policy and implementation "sigmas" were an outsized 17.9 percent and a very modest 1.8 percent, respectively. While individual funds need to estimate their own investment component and total balance sheet "ex-ante sigmas," there is surely room for some industry standardization on the "cost of risk capital" assumption, and the "surplus at risk" calculation convention.

Let's see what we can do to knock these barriers down over the course of the next 12 months. The time has come to begin to measure the right things imperfectly, rather than the wrong things perfectly.

CHAPTER 33

Adjusting Investment Returns for Risk: What's the Best Way?

"Consider a put option that pays off only when a firm is insolvent. This put option provides insurance against the firm's insolvency. Its cost is an intuitive measure of insolvency risk and . . . measures the economic cost of avoiding bankruptcy."

Robert Jarrow

"Put Option Premiums and Coherent Risk Measures," *Mathematical Finance,* April 2002

RESURRECTING RANVA

The previous chapter asserted that creating comparability in investment results is critical to the pension fund industry's legitimacy, and that it requires two things. To be comparable, gross investment returns must be reduced to reflect all incurred investment expenses. Then the net returns should be further reduced to reflect the risks undertaken to earn them. Generally, small risk exposures require small risk-adjustment "haircuts," and large exposures large ones.

The previous chapter recalled that we introduced a specific risk-adjustment methodology some eight years ago that led to the metric RANVA (risk-adjusted net value added). After reviewing the methodology, and showing what kind of risk-adjustment "haircuts" it has produced in the CEM Benchmarking Inc. database since 2000, we listed the following three requirements for broad acceptance of a RANVA metric in the global pension fund community:

1. **Belief that skill-based differences in investment results exist.** For a RANVA metric to have any meaning, skill-based differences in investment results must really exist. If there are no expert investors capable of identifying and exploiting investment opportunities with superior RANVA prospects, there is nothing to measure. In other words, if all investors have equal skills, the implications of the capital asset pricing model (CAPM) will hold, and all outcomes different from CAPM-based expectations are just random noise.
2. **Belief in "pay for performance" arrangements.** Belief in skill-based differences in investment results should logically lead to a parallel belief in compensation schemes based on skill-based differences. However, if "pay for performance" arrangements are to pay for skill differences rather than luck differences, investment returns should be assessed "haircuts" reflecting the differing risk exposures undertaken.
3. **Consensus on how risk-based "haircuts" should be calculated.** The example risk-adjustment "haircut" of 2.4 percent in the previous chapter was based on a "bootstrap" methodology that combined (a) a 15 percent "cost of risk capital" return requirement, (b) a "sigma" of 8 percent for balance-sheet mismatch return volatility, and (c) a 2-sigma "surplus at risk" convention. There is nothing sacred about these three assumptions. Different combinations of assumptions would have produced different risk-adjustment "haircuts," and hence different RANVA results. Clearly, broad-based use of a specific RANVA metric is dependent on broad-based acceptance and adoption of a specific RANVA calculation protocol.

We do not believe that listed requirements 1 and 2 above are RANVA deal-breakers. Indeed, belief in the existence of skill-based differences in investment results, and in willingness to pay for those skill differences, is on the rise in the pension fund industry. That leaves requirement 3: broad-based acceptance and adoption of a specific RANVA calculation protocol. The purpose of this chapter is to lay the conceptual foundation for such an agreement by exploring the pros and cons of two possible RANVA calculation approaches.

THE "COST OF MARKET VOLATILITY" APPROACH

If the historical and future expected annual excess return of equities over bonds are taken to be 5 percent, and the excess return volatility 17 percent, a constant 5 percent/17 percent = 0.3 percent unit "cost of market volatility" results. So within this simple capital asset pricing framework, a 60-40 equity-bond mix would have an expected excess return of 3 percent (0.6 × 5 percent), with an excess return volatility of 10 percent (0.6 × 17 percent). However, we have already noted that if a pension fund with a 60-40 asset mix policy earns an excess return greater than 3 percent in any given year, it has not necessarily earned a positive RANVA. In a world where fund return outcomes above or below those based on the "cost of market volatility" are unpredictable random events, RANVA is always zero.

Only with the assumption that active management can add value is there a potential RANVA to measure. In the standard pension fund management framework, total fund excess returns are neatly divided into "policy excess return" and "active (or implementation) excess return" components. Usually, "policy excess returns" (e.g., resulting from the passive implementation of a 60-40 mix) are assumed to be driven by the known "cost of market volatility" plus an unpredictable random return component. "Implementation excess returns," on the other hand, are assumed to have a skill-based element to them. So making a RANVA calculation for active management is now appropriate. The calculation is straightforward. Taking the 2 percent implementation-related volatility embedded in the typical pension fund, for example, and taking the constant 0.3 percent "cost of market volatility," an implementation risk "haircut" of 0.6 percent results (2 percent × 0.3 percent). At a 2 percent active management risk level, positive RANVA is earned (and should be paid for) only after a 0.6 percent excess return risk hurdle rate is cleared.

The great benefit of this "cost of market volatility" approach is its simplicity. However, the approach also has its drawbacks. One such drawback is the determination of the relevant "price of market volatility." For example, the Robert Arnott–Peter Bernstein article "What Risk Premium Is Normal?" argues that, once history is adjusted for nonrepeatable events, the historical average "cost of market volatility" was a much lower 0.15 percent per unit rather than the "official" 0.3 percent that is often cited. Further, the prospective "cost of market volatility" seems to oscillate from high to low in successive 10- to 20-year periods in a partially predictable manner. For example, simple calculations suggested it had declined to zero in 2000, the final year of the last multidecade bull market. Did that imply that the hurdle rate for active risk should have been reduced to zero in 2000 as well?

Another drawback of the "cost of market volatility" approach is defining the relevant "market volatility" to price. Using cap-weighted stock portfolios as "the market" is convenient because they are well defined, and historical excess return/volatility relationships with bonds are readily available. But can we really ignore other investable, multinational, asset categories such as low-grade debt, private equity, real estate, commodities, and infrastructure? What happens to the historical and future cost of volatility when we add all these additional asset categories to the "market" portfolio? Also, what happens to the "no skill-based policy returns" assumption we started out with at the beginning of this section? Does it continue to be reasonable to assume that pricing across and within each of these additional markets is "efficient," with no players having skill-based advantages in any of them?

All of these questions suggest that the simplicity of the "cost of market volatility" approach to risk-adjusting pension fund returns may come at a high price. The high price is that we really don't know what the "cost of market volatility" is. Worse, it may not even exist.

THE "COST OF INSURANCE" APPROACH WITH RISK BUFFERS

Consider a pension plan balance sheet with $100 in assets and $100 in liabilities. For simplicity's sake, assume there is a single pension payment of $105 due in one year, and that there is a one-year riskless bond yielding 5 percent. Obviously, if the $100 of assets were invested in the one-year riskless bond, they would grow to $105 one year from now, just sufficient to make the $105 pension payment. This is an example of an immunization strategy producing a perfect asset-liability match, leading to a pension plan balance sheet with zero mismatch risk.

Now assume that the pension plan also has access to an expert investment team with a track record of generating an average excess return of 5 percent with a mismatch risk volatility of 10 percent. Should the pension plan take advantage of this attractive but risky investment opportunity? Logically, only if somebody is willing to underwrite the now possible balance sheet shortfall risk. So how much "capital at risk" should be provided, and what should the cost of this capital be? Or stated differently, given the risk exposure involved, what does the expected return on this risk capital have to be in order for someone to provide it?

These questions logically lead to the "cost of insurance" approach to calculating risk-adjustment "haircuts" set out in the Ambachtsheer-Ezra book *Pension Fund Excellence* (New York: John Wiley & Sons, 1998), used in the CEM Benchmarking Inc. pension fund performance studies since 1998, and reviewed in the previous chapter. We called our specific approach a *bootstrap* method, built very simply on a "capital at risk" (or more popularly, "value at risk") definition, and a specified required return on that "capital at risk."

Carrying on with the simple example above, let's examine the risky strategy more closely. It has an expected excess return of 5 percent and mismatch risk of 10 percent. Assuming normally distributed returns, this strategy has 0.3 probability of producing a one-year return less than the required 5 percent. In other words, without a risk capital buffer, there is a 0.3 probability that the risky strategy will lead to an inability to pay the full $105 one year from now. A 2-sigma $20 "capital at risk" buffer would reduce that probability to a minimal 0.003. However, now assume that the provider of this $20 of risk capital needs to see a 15 percent expected return (i.e., 10 percent in excess of the risk-free rate) to place it at risk. Therefore, at the total pension plan balance-sheet level, a 3 percent risk-based "hurdle rate" results (i.e., 15 percent of $20 is $3, and $3 in relation to the $100 asset base is 3 percent). As a result, plan assets will only earn positive RANVA if total fund return exceeds 8 percent (i.e., 5 percent for the risk-free rate plus an additional 3 percent to pay for covering the mismatch risk undertaken).

What can we say about this approach to establishing a risk-based "hurdle rate" for pension funds? On the one hand, it makes good intuitive sense; on the other, it is not based on any rigorous theory in financial economics. The resulting arbitrariness of the underlying assumptions in setting risk buffers and the required return on them will make it difficult to ever reach pension industry-wide agreement on a RANVA calculation protocol using this framework.

THE "COST OF INSURANCE" APPROACH WITH PUT OPTIONS

Can anything be done to address the arbitrariness problem? Rather than setting arbitrary balance-sheet risk buffers and cost of risk capital requirements, why not use the well-established theory of option valuation? The theory could be used to estimate the cost of a put option that would insure against the pension plan asset return falling below a specified return. Going back to the example above, what would it cost to insure a minimum one-year asset return of 5 percent with the adoption of the risky investment strategy with the 10 percent mismatch risk volatility? Assuming a simple Black-Scholes model with a constant interest rate of 5 percent, the answer is $4, or 4 percent of the $100 asset portfolio. Therefore, option theory has directly provided us with an objective, risk-based "hurdle rate" of 4 percent. Any total fund return in excess of 9 percent (i.e., 5 percent for the risk-free rate plus an additional 4 percent to pay for the put option) constitutes positive RANVA.

This flash of the blindingly obvious came to us courtesy of Birgir Arnarson, head of research and risk management, Kaupthing Bank, Iceland.

He sent us the draft of his paper titled "Pension Fund Risk Management" last year, which explores this put option approach to establishing a risk-based balance-sheet "hurdle rate." His draft paper in turn built on the ideas first expressed by Robert Merton and Robert Jarrow (see the quote from a 2002 Jarrow paper at the beginning of this chapter). Option theory is not based on subjective probabilities. Instead, it is based on the "no risk-free arbitrage" principle, the employment of risk-neutral probabilities implicitly observable in market prices, and the derivation of a hedging portfolio with a value equal to the put option premium. An added benefit of an option-based approach to risk management is that with the appropriate stochastic model for assets and liabilities, total balance-sheet risk can be decomposed more accurately into constituent factor risk components such as yield curve changes, credit risk, equity and real estate market risks, various active risks, and so on.

Paraphrasing Winston Churchill, this chapter is not the end of the search for the best way to adjust pension fund returns for risk. It may not even be the beginning of the end. But surely it is the end of the beginning. Ideally, the way forward should be based on a "cost of insurance" approach. This means the price of risk should be based on put option premiums that ensure predetermined minimum required balance-sheet outcomes. But can this approach be made practical enough to become operational? That is a question yet to be answered affirmatively.

PART Six

Measuring Results

"Information is data endowed with relevance and purpose."
Peter Drucker

CHAPTER 34

Pension Plan Organizations: Measuring "Competitiveness"

"Achieving 'best practice' in pension administration is no mystery. ... It results from good governance, accountable CEOs, clear assignment of responsibilities, supporting information systems, and an appropriate evaluation and reward system. ... "

Peter Skinner

"International Best Practice in Superannuation Administration,"

An Australian Fact-Finding Study, 1997

PENSION PLAN ORGANIZATIONS AND "LEGITIMACY"

Prior chapters have noted Peter Drucker's concern with pension fund "legitimacy" as long as 30 years ago. That is, their ability to serve stakeholder interests in both perception and reality. He foresaw that the collectivity of these plans, in their various manifestations, would provide the retirement income of a large part of the population, and at the same time "own" a large part of the developed economies' outstanding bonds and stocks. Thus, these plans would become potential socioeconomic powerhouses. However, that potential power would be properly directed only if pension plans could hold their own in a world of political, corporate, and labor union power centers with their own agendas.

In the past 30 years, public and private pension plans in North America, and in parts of Europe and the Far East, have indeed grown impressively in size and visibility. The pension "industry" is unseen no longer. But from a "legitimacy" perspective, are pension plan organizations holding their own? We would answer: "Better than Drucker anticipated, but with still considerable room for improvement." Why have things turned out better than Drucker anticipated? Because sufficient large-end pension plan organizations around the world have adopted "good enough" business models to define their missions, and built the necessary organizational structures to achieve them. Thus, many pension organizations have acquired measures of "legitimacy" in the eyes of their stakeholders. Why is there still considerable room for improvement? The chapters in Part Three asserted that many pension plan organizations have yet to achieve true mission clarity, and have yet to build true "high-performance" organizations to fulfill their missions in a transparent, cost-effective manner. Much of our own research and writing these past 25 years have focused on these improvement challenges.

This chapter is written in that spirit. Specifically, we argue here that for pension plan organizations to achieve "legitimacy," they must be able to prove that they are "competitive." That is, they must be able to show their plan members and the sponsor(s) that they would be the service(s) provider of choice, even though the alternatives may be (at least in the short term) only hypothetical. Such a demonstration in turn requires the development of highly focused benchmarking disciplines for the key services provided. Below, we update readers on the state of the art of "best practice" benchmarking in the pension administration field.

"PROVIDER OF CHOICE" FOR WHICH SERVICES?

The concept of "best practice" benchmarking for pension service(s) providers raises a larger question: What are the services? In the broadest sense, there are two. Historically, the "glamour" service has been the generation of investment returns on pension assets. Indeed, most of our own research and writing has focused in this area. However, more recently, pension service(s) organizations are beginning to understand that it may be in the "direct client contact" benefit administration services area (e.g., pension payments, communication and education, record keeping, etc.) where the "competitiveness" war will be ultimately won or lost.

This observation raises some rather fundamental questions about differing organization model choices for not-for-profit pension service(s) providers. Specifically, is it best to offer "direct client contact" services and investment services under a single organizational umbrella accountable for the delivery of both types of services? Or are separate organizational umbrellas better? Or does it matter?

Our view is that "dual services–single umbrella" organizations have a comparative advantage from a "competitiveness" perspective. Not only does this type of organization have ongoing, direct client contact, but it can directly relate its investment policy and implementation activities to a client base it knows. In contrast, single-service providers (i.e., either investment-only, or benefit administration–only) can only deliver a piece of a larger package. Thus, they face greater "legitimacy"-proving challenges. Consider these questions, for example. Who are our customers? Do we know what they want? How do we communicate with them? How do we relate to other service organizations delivering other pieces of the larger package? These are usually tough questions for the single-service provider to answer.

BENCHMARKING PENSION SERVICES

In 1991, CEM Benchmarking Inc. (CEM) began to benchmark the invest-ment operations of both single-service and dual-service defined benefit (DB) pension plan organizations. In 1997, CEM introduced a defined contribution (DC) pension plan benchmarking service that tracks both the investment and administrative sides of these DC (mainly U.S. corporate 401[k]) plans. Also introduced in 1997 was a benchmarking service for the benefit admin-istration operations of both single-service and dual-service DB pension plan organizations. Its intellectual foundation was Peter Skinner's seminal 1997 study, from which we gleaned the opening quote for this chapter.

The two chapters following this one will report the key research results emanating from the DB investments and DC plan databases (e.g., on performance drivers, on cost drivers, etc.). Here, we share some key findings about the structure and cost drivers of DB benefit administration services. It has been CEM's benefit administration benchmarking service that has grown the fastest since 1997. In 1998, eight major dual-service DB pension plan organizations (five American, one Australian, one Dutch, one Canadian) participated in the original study. In 1999 that number, now including some benefit administration–only organizations, grew to 20, and in 2000, it grew to 35. Since then, growth has continued, with 60 organizations participating in 2005. With an average member base of 348,000, these 60 organizations look after the benefit administration needs of close to 21 million customers in the United States, Australia, Canada, and the Netherlands.

COSTING THE BENEFIT ADMINISTRATION "BUSINESS"

How "competitive" are the 60 pension organizations that participated in CEM's annual benefit administration benchmarking study? Ultimately, the answer to that question is in the eye of each of the 21 million "customers" of these 60 organizations. Having said that, incurred costs are an important part of the answer. Knowing that the active member benefit administration cost range for the 60 participating organizations was $2 million to $115 million (average $23 million, all in U.S. dollars) is only marginally helpful.

Knowing that on a per-active-member basis (exclusive of supplemental benefits and major projects), the cost range was $14 to $427 (average $124) is somewhat more useful. Still, $14 to $427 is a huge range to contend with, requiring a major standardization effort. What are the major cost drivers that will have to be taken into account before per member costs become even close to comparable?

CEM research has identified four:

1. **Complexity.** There is a vast range of complexity levels embedded in the 60 retirement income systems. For example, some involve only one employer; others involve thousands. Some have only one benefit formula; others have many . . . and so on.
2. **Service level.** The 60 systems embody a vast range of service levels. For example, you can decide to have a sophisticated, immediate-response call-centre or none at all. You can offer one-on-one personal retirement counseling or none at all. . . and so on. (Service levels should not be confused with service quality. Usually, quality, which CEM has begun to measure separately, is free.)
3. **Volumes.** Generally, high volumes mean good potential economies of scale, and low volumes poor economies of scale. In other words, increasing size should drive down unit costs.
4. **Cost environment.** All other things equal, relatively high local cost environments should drive up relative unit costs and vice versa.

These four factors in fact "explain" 61 percent of the variance in unit costs in the CEM database (see Table 34.1).

TABLE 34.1   The Benefit Administration Cost Equation

"Normal" Cost =	Constant	+ Complexity	+ Service Level	− Log Volume	+ Cost Environment
Coefficient ($)	−132	+1.1	+1.3	−50.7	+5.4
(t-statistic)		(3.0)	(2.5)	(−2.8)	(1.7)
r-squared		61%			

Source: CEM Benchmarking Inc., 2001.

THE BENEFIT ADMINISTRATION COST EQUATION

The resulting benefit administration cost equation shown in Table 34.1 is a useful thing. It tells sponsors, fiduciaries, and plan members alike what the "normal" unit cost experience is for given levels of system complexity, service levels, volumes, and cost environment. So, for example, for the average database values of these explanatory variables, the average database active member unit cost of $124 per member indeed results.

More importantly, the equation also indicates how that "normal" cost of $124 per member should be adjusted up or down for differing levels of the four explanatory variables. For example, the equation indicates the following:

- The calculated complexity variable in the database (based on complexity ratings in 12 key activities) has an average value of 39 and a range of 10 to 86. The cost equation indicates that on average, all else equal, every 10-point decrease in system complexity implies a "normal" unit cost decrease of $11 per year. Clearly, reducing complexity in retirement income systems is a worthwhile endeavor!
- The calculated service level variable (based on service-level ratings in 10 key activities) has an average value of 65 and a range of 35 to 84. The equation indicates that on average, all else equal, every 10-point increase in the system service level will increase "normal" cost by $13 per year. Clearly, providing higher service levels does not come without higher costs. Of course, the higher service levels may well be worth the additional costs!
- The volume level variable (number of thousands of active and annuitant plan members) has an average value of 348 and a range of 31 to 1,442. The equation indicates that with every 10-fold increase in actives and annuitants, "normal" unit costs should fall $51 per year. Clearly, material economies of scale are evident over the 31,000-member to 1.4 million-member range in the CEM database.
- The cost environment variable (local administrative assistant salaries in $000s) averaged 33, with a range of 23 to 41. The equation indicates that with every one-point increase in the cost environment, "normal" unit costs need to be adjusted upward by $5. Clearly, location can impact costs.

In short, the CEM benefit administration cost equation permits each pension administration organization to calculate its own unique "normal" cost. That normal cost will reflect each organization's own ratings of complexity, service levels, volume, and cost environment. It is relative to its own unique "normal" cost that a system's actual unit cost can realistically be judged to be competitive or not. The equation is also a valuable strategic planning tool, indicating the cost implications of upgrading service levels and/or reducing system complexity.

BUILD OR BUY?

The question of whether to "build or buy" is closely tied to pension plan organization competitiveness. In other words, when should the not-for-profit pension plan organization build service delivery capability inside, and when should it outsource to the for-profit sector? In his 1997 study, Skinner guessed that for under-2,000-member plans, outsourcing benefit administration is always best, while for over-10,000-member plans, building internal capability will be most cost effective. In our 1998 book, *Pension Fund Excellence: Creating Value For Stakeholders* (Keith Ambachtsheer and Don Ezra, New York: John Wiley & Sons, 1998), we indirectly came up with a minimum 10,000-member range to cost-justify building an "inside" investment executive function.

With the continuing evolution of "best practices" benchmarking of both benefit administration and investment services, such guessing is now no longer necessary. Instead, pension plan fiduciaries can now make "build or buy" decisions guided by a solid knowledge base. Either way, they will be able to recognize a cost-competitive price when they see one.

Measuring DC Plans as "Value Propositions": The New Imperative for Plan Sponsors

"Around the world, it is the value provided to employees that marks the successful DC pension plan. Unfortunately, many DC programs lack a structured process for measuring that value...."
From the Mercer 2002 Global DC Plan Survey

SILK PURSES FROM SOWS' EARS

Winston Churchill once observed that democracy was a terrible system of government, but that the alternatives were worse. We might similarly say that defined contribution (DC) plans are terrible vehicles for providing predictable, adequate future pensions, but if the alternative is no plan at all, that would be worse. Thus, we face the collective challenge of turning sows' DC ears into silk pension purses. Where to start? We believe our Mercer friends have it right: by measuring DC plans as value propositions for employees. Unfortunately, their 2002 Global DC Plan Survey indicates that such measurement is not yet common practice. Thus, it is timely to explore what a DC "value" measurement system might look like, and what its results might teach us about how to pack more "value" into DC pension plans. We do so in this chapter.

CEM Benchmarking Inc. (CEM) launched its DC plan "value" measurement system in 1997 with initial participation by 62 U.S. corporations sponsoring 401(k) plans valued at $98 billion. By 2005, U.S. participation has increased to 84 sponsors ($297 billion), including 17 in the noncorporate category. The CEM "value" measurement studies focus on three fundamental questions for DC plan sponsors:

1. How "prudentially" is our plan being managed?
2. Are there areas requiring action?
3. How "competitive" is our plan compared to those of our peers?

Let us see what we can learn from eight years of CEM experience answering these questions.

MEASURES OF "PRUDENCE"

Measures of prudence should focus on the number and types of investment options offered, on the allocation of participant dollars to the options offered, on the investment performance of the total pool and the individual options, and on the costs incurred. Thus, for example, the CEM reports provide the following broad insights on the management of U.S. DC plans:

- The median number of investment options is now 17, including six domestic equities options, three balanced/lifestyle, two international equities, two bond, one stable value, one money market, one own-company stock, and one "other" (e.g., mutual fund window, self-directed brokerage, etc.).
- The average DC asset mix at the end of 2004 was 66 percent equities (including 13 percent in own-company stock, of which 9 percent was voluntary and 4 percent mandated), 30 percent fixed income, and 4 percent cash. Except for the own-company stock allocation, this average asset mix looks very similar to the typical DB fund asset mix.
- The average five-year (2000 to 2004) return at the total asset pool level was 1.2 percent including mandated own-company stock, and 1.5 percent without it.
- The median total plan cost was 42 basis points in 2004. This includes all investment management fees, as well as other costs such as record keeping and education.

While giving a broad indication of general experience, averages and medians cannot possibly tell the whole story. Variances from general experience, and why they exist, also need to be understood.

THE "OWN-COMPANY STOCK" PHENOMENON

For example, we noted above that of the average 66 percent equities exposure in the 84 U.S. DC plans, 13 percent was in own-company stock, of which 9 percent was voluntary and 4 percent mandated. Table 35.1 provides important additional details behind these averages:

- Out of the 84 plans that constitute the 2004 database, 54 had own-company stock positions, and 30 did not (of which 13 are corporate sponsors).
- While the overall average own-company stock weighting was 13 percent, the median weighting was only 6 percent. This implies heavy concentrations of own own-company stock in a relatively small part of the 84-plan sample.
- Table 35.1 confirms that the really heavy concentrations (i.e., over 23 percent of total assets) exist in only a quarter of the 84-plan sample.
- Much own-company stock investing is done on the plan participants' own volition (see the "Voluntary Weights" column).
- The annual return ranges for own-company stock performance provide graphic evidence of the "lottery ticket" effect of this asset class. For example, the high-low own-company stock return range in 2003 was high: +407 percent versus low: −14 percent. Even the Q1 to Q3 break spread was a wide +49 percent versus +20 percent range.

This "lottery ticket" effect settles down in a five-year time frame when measured in an annualized return context. There are, however, two important caveats. First, while the annualized return ranges are narrower, it should be remembered that five years' worth of compounding of $1 at 13 percent (Q1 experience) produces a very different amount of wealth than compounding $1 at −7 percent (Q3 experience). Second, notice that while the annual databases have 47 to 55 observations (i.e., funds with own-company stock exposure), the continuous database for the five-year 2000 to 2004 period has only 26 observations. Why? Some of the funds with very poor own-company stock performance in earlier years chose not to participate in the database in subsequent years.

UNDERSTANDING DC PLAN TOTAL RETURNS

A well-managed DC plan should produce competitive rates of return for its participants. One indication of such "competitiveness" is how well plan assets are performing at the total fund level versus the performance of a relevant benchmark portfolio. Further insight can be gained by assessing how well the DC total fund asset pool is performing versus the sponsor's DB asset pool on a risk-adjusted basis.

Table 35.2 displays the five-year preexpense return experience of the U.S. DC and DB asset pools in the CEM database. The "policy returns"

TABLE 35.1 "Own-Company Stock" Experience in the CEM Database

				Own-Company Stock Return Ranges					
	Mandatory	Voluntary	Combined	2000	2001	2002	2003	2004	5-Year
Max	59%	67%	67%	74%	124%	44%	407%	82%	21%
Q1	0%	13%	23%	26%	18%	0%	49%	27%	13%
Median	0%	4%	6%	1%	1%	−18%	33%	14%	5%
Q3	0%	0%	0%	−23%	−17%	−30%	20%	3%	−7%
Min	0%	0%	0%	−81%	−65%	−80%	−14%	−31%	−42%
Observations	84	84	84	54	59	47	55	53	26

Source: CEM Benchmarking Inc., 2004.

TABLE 35.2 DC Versus DB Total Return Experience (2000 to 2004, preexpense)

	Total Return		Policy Return		Implementation Return	
	DC	DB	DC	DB	DC	DB
Max	8%	12%	7%	10%	4.0%	5.6%
Q1	4%	5%	3%	4%	1.0%	1.6%
Med	2%	4%	1%	3%	0.3%	0.8%
Q3	−1%	3%	−1%	2%	0.1%	0.3%
Min	−12%	0%	−12%	1%	−1.0%	−2.1%

Source: CEM Benchmarking Inc., 2004.

are estimates of what returns the passive implementation of the chosen asset mixes would have produced. The "implementation returns" are the differences between actual and policy returns.

Note:

- The total DC and DB fund returns in the Q1 to Q3 range (i.e., middle 50 percent) are quite similar. However, the first and fourth quartile returns are materially different, with the DC funds experiencing a wider range of return outcomes than the DB funds.
- The policy return data explain that the wider range of DC plan return outcomes is due to "policy" effects. More specifically, it is due to the own-company stock effect, as this is captured as a policy effect in the Table 35.2 results.
- The "implementation returns" of the DB funds are somewhat higher than those of the DC funds, except at minimum values. Thus, in this sense DB funds were a better "value proposition" than DC funds over the 2000 to 2004 period, at least on a preexpense basis.

What about the cost performance of DC plans? The fact that plan participants pay an average 92 percent of total DC plan expenses makes this an especially sensitive question.

DC VERSUS DB PLAN COST PERFORMANCE

The cost data (expressed in basis points in relation to plan assets) displayed in Table 35.3 may surprise some people. There is a perception that DC plans cost far more to operate than DB plans. However, Table 35.3 indicates, at least for the plans in the CEM database, that this is not the case, with a median DC expense of 42 bps versus a median DB expense of 34 bps.

TABLE 35.3 DC Versus DB Cost
Experience in 2004

	DC	DB
Max	95 bps	111 bps
Q1	54 bps	46 bps
Med	42 bps	34 bps
Q3	28 bps	23 bps
Min	8 bps	1 bps

Source: CEM Benchmarking Inc., 2004.

Indeed, the cited DB expenses are all investment related, while the DC data include record-keeping expenses (median unbundled cost 7 bps) and communication/education expenses (median unbundled cost 1 bp). Taking these costs out of the median DC expense number would reduce it to 34 bps as well.

What are the explanations for the surprising equality in 2004 DC and DB fund operating costs? Two factors come to mind. One relates to asset mix differences; the other to sample bias:

1. The average combined DC fund weighting in own-company stock and GIC/stable value investments in the DC plan database was 33 percent. These asset classes do not draw explicit management fees. At the same time, the DB funds had an average combined weighting of 10 percent in high fee asset classes such as private equity and real estate, where the DC funds have a zero weighting.
2. CEM's sample of 84 DC plans is not a random one. First, the average plan dollar value is $3.5 billion, indicating the potential for significant scale economies not available to smaller plans. Second, even within the large plan sector, the CEM sample is not random. Only those sponsors able and willing to meet the stringent data requirements are in the sample, giving it a decided "best practice" flavor. Likely, these funds have a more intense focus on cost control.

It is only when individual DC investment options with fees are compared to their DB counterparts that the DC options often become materially more expensive, especially if those expenses reflect retail mutual fund fees (30 percent of total DC assets) rather than institutional-level fees (70 percent of total DC assets).

OTHER DC PLAN PERFORMANCE METRICS

There is more to offering "value" to DC plan participants than being able to demonstrate a strong fiduciary oversight discipline. Here is CEM's checklist of further "value" benchmarks:

- The employer's contribution matching strategy is an important DC plan feature. The database indicates that 79 percent of employers do some degree of matching. Of those who do, 34 percent match with company stock, 64 percent with cash, and 2 percent with some combination of the two.
- The most common match rate was 50 percent of employee contributions, up to a ceiling of 6 percent of salary.
- Hardship withdrawal and loan features were offered by 82 percent of the DC plans in the database. In these plans, an average 24 percent of plan members have taken advantage of this option, with an average loan balance outstanding of $7,353.
- A default investment option for undirected employee contributions was in place in 78 percent of the plan in the database.
- On the communication/education front, almost all sponsors offer both an automated telephone response system, and some type of written communication to participants. More interactive methods (e.g., call center, Internet/intranet, modeling software, workshops) have been gaining ground. Direct access to some form of investment advice is provided by 52 percent of sponsors.
- All these features led to an average 2004 employee participation rate of 74 percent, an average employee deferral rate of 8 percent, and an average account balance of $58,000.

Once again, there are further stories to be uncovered in the dispersions around the averages and medians. They are for another day.

"VALUE PROPOSITION": YES OR NO?

Can we pack more "value" into DC plans? The CEM benchmarking process suggests that for many plans, the answer is "yes." Fruitful places to look are (1) the sponsor's policies regarding contribution matching and own-company stock, (2) the optimal line-up of investment options, (3) rigorous control of plan expenses, and (4) creativity on the communication/education front.

Are those the places where you are looking?

CHAPTER 36

Measuring Pension Fund Behavior (1992 to 2004): What Can We Learn?

"Information is data endowed with relevance and purpose."

Peter Drucker

A WELL-ENDOWED DATABASE

CEM Benchmarking Inc. (CEM)'s database on defined benefit (DB) pension funds had its fifteenth birthday recently. Thus, it is timely to search for, find, and reflect on the lessons for pension fund management it contains. The search does indeed produce significant insights "endowed with relevance and purpose," as we will document in this chapter. This should not be surprising, as CEM has the only databases in the global pension fund "industry" that permit serious analysis in a "value versus cost and risk" framework. That makes its databases the most likely to elevate past information about pension fund performance and structure into knowledge that can be used to enhance future performance.

At the end of 2004, CEM's DB investment database contained data on 273 funds (163 American [\$2.1 trillion], 94 Canadian [C\$519 billion], 12 European [€448 billion], and 4 Australian [A\$26 billion]). Of the 273 funds, 132 were corporate, 103 public sector, and 38 industry/other funds. Average fund size was \$11 billion versus a median size of \$3 billion. Table 36.1 sets out the current average asset mix policies for funds in the four regions. The policy differences reflect a combination of differences in local investment cultures, local opportunity sets, and fund size. Regarding size, the Euro funds were by far the biggest, averaging €37 billion in market value. The U.S. funds averaged $13 billion, the Aussie funds A$7 billion, and the Canadian funds C$6 billion.

CURRENT INTERNATIONAL INVESTMENT POLICY AND IMPLEMENTATION STYLE DIFFERENCES

Table 36.1 indicates that U.S. funds, with the biggest equity and debt markets in the world, display the greatest home bias, with only 17 percent of assets invested in foreign markets. In contrast, the Euro funds have an average 40 percent invested in foreign markets, followed by the Aussie funds at 36 percent, and the Canadian funds at 33 percent. In terms of private markets investments (e.g., real estate, private equity, etc.), the Aussie funds have made the greatest inroads with 18 percent of assets, followed by the Euro funds at 12 percent, the U.S. funds at 10 percent, and the Canadian funds at 6 percent. The Aussies also have the lowest fixed income/cash policy weights with 22 percent, followed by the U.S. funds at 30 percent, the Canadian funds at 38 percent, and the Euro funds at 47 percent. When the total database was cut by sponsor-type (i.e., corporate, public sector, and industry/other), there were no material differences in asset mix policy between the sponsor types.

Looking at the passive/active management style splits, Euro funds were the most venturesome with only an average 16 percent in passive management, followed by all the other regions at 22 percent each. The Euro funds also favored internal management more than the others with an average 45 percent managed internally, followed by the Canadians with 16 percent, the Americans with 9 percent, and the Aussies with none. The external/internal split is also driven by fund size. The top half of the

TABLE 36.1 Current Pension Fund Asset Mix Policies Around the Globe

	Australia	Canada	Europe	United States
Domestic stocks	31%	25%	17%	45%
Foreign stocks	29%	31%	25%	16%
Domestic fixed income and cash	15%	36%	32%	29%
Foreign fixed income	7%	2%	15%	1%
Real assets	11%	4%	9%	5%
Private equity and hedge funds	7%	2%	3%	5%
Total	100%	100%	100%	100%

Source: CEM Benchmarking Inc., 2004.

total CEM database by size (funds over $3.0 billion) averaged 20 percent internal management versus only 7 percent for the bottom half (funds under $3.0 billion).

TEN-YEAR INVESTMENT POLICY AND IMPLEMENTATION STYLE TRENDS FOR U.S. FUNDS

What about 10-year trends? Specifically, we focus on the 26 U.S. funds that have been in the database for the entire 13-year period. This is a sample of generally large funds with an average 2004 value of $28 billion (median $9 billion). Figure 36.1 indicates that these funds had the traditional average 60-40 asset mix policy in 1992, with the "equity" allocated 47 percent in domestic stocks, 8 percent in foreign stocks, 7 percent in real estate, and 2 percent in private equity. Over the next 13 years, the equity content crept up steadily, reaching 73-27 by 2004, with the additional equity allocations going to foreign stocks and private equity. This observed behavior is consistent with the "equity risk is value" philosophy that gained increasing favor in the pension investment community as the 1990s progressed.

Figure 36.2 lays out the 13-year trend in implementation styles for the same 26 U.S. funds. Two developments are worthy of note. The first is that the average internal active management weighting dropped 6 percentage points from 1992 to 1999 (i.e., from 16 percent to 10 percent of assets).

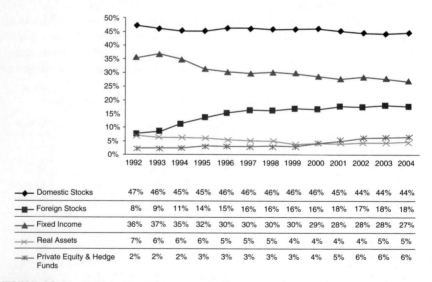

	1992	1993	1994	1995	1996	1997	1998	1999	2000	2001	2002	2003	2004
Domestic Stocks	47%	46%	45%	45%	46%	46%	46%	46%	46%	45%	44%	44%	44%
Foreign Stocks	8%	9%	11%	14%	15%	16%	16%	16%	16%	18%	17%	18%	18%
Fixed Income	36%	37%	35%	32%	30%	30%	30%	30%	29%	28%	28%	28%	27%
Real Assets	7%	6%	6%	6%	5%	5%	5%	4%	4%	4%	4%	5%	5%
Private Equity & Hedge Funds	2%	2%	2%	3%	3%	3%	3%	3%	4%	5%	6%	6%	6%

FIGURE 36.1 1992 to 2004 Asset Mix Policy Trends for U.S. Pension Funds
Source: CEM Benchmarking Inc., 2004.

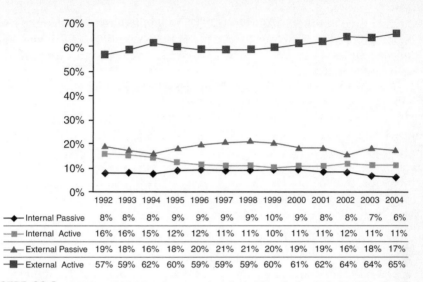

	1992	1993	1994	1995	1996	1997	1998	1999	2000	2001	2002	2003	2004
Internal Passive	8%	8%	8%	9%	9%	9%	9%	10%	9%	8%	8%	7%	6%
Internal Active	16%	16%	15%	12%	12%	11%	11%	10%	11%	11%	12%	11%	11%
External Passive	19%	18%	16%	18%	20%	21%	21%	20%	19%	19%	16%	18%	17%
External Active	57%	59%	62%	60%	59%	59%	59%	60%	61%	62%	64%	64%	65%

FIGURE 36.2 1992 to 2004 Implementation Style Trends for U.S. Pension Funds
Source: CEM Benchmarking Inc., 2004.

What happened there? Our guess is that as the bull market became the bubble market, it became increasingly difficult for pension funds to attract, and especially, retain internal investment talent. The second development is the apparent peaking of passive management over the 1997 to 1999 period. Note that the 1992 average passive weighting (combined internal plus external) was 27 percent. By 1997 it had crept up three percentage points to 30 percent. By 2000, the weighting had fallen below 30 percent again, returning back to 23 percent by 2004. What happened here? Our guess is that some pension fund managements began to realize that by the late 1990s, the "plain vanilla" passive management style had begun to contribute to the stock market bubble, with a few high-powered stocks increasingly driving both the return and risk characteristics of popular market benchmarks such as the Standard and Poor's (S&P) 500. Active management successfully counteracted this trend.

DID ACTIVE MANAGEMENT ADD VALUE?

So much for the investment policy and implementation style trends over the 1992 to 2004 period. What about the bottom line? Did the active management employed by the funds in the CEM database produce any value after accounting for expenses? To answer this question, all available U.S. and Canadian data over the 13-year period was employed, including data for those funds with less than a full 13-year history. Specifically, all possible "(annual total fund return)−(annual fund benchmark return)−(annual total operating costs)" calculations were made. The resulting 3,513 fund "net implementation value added" (NIVA) metrics were placed into a special database for analysis.

What story do these 3,513 total fund NIVA calculations tell? Figure 36.3 below begins to tell the tale. The average NIVA was +17 basis points (bps), with a respectable t-value of 3.5. This suggests active management did indeed add value over the 1992 to 2004 period! Even more interesting is the split of total NIVA into its three components. Average "gross in-category value-added" was an even more impressive +67 bps (t = 2.0), while "mix value-added" subtracted an average −14 bps (t = −4.2). Operating costs brought total fund performance down a further average −36 bps. These findings lead to two further important conclusions:

1. Even operating with a 100 percent passive implementation style costs money. So the proper benchmark against which to evaluate the +17 bps NIVA finding is not 0 bps, but the cost of pure passive implementation including all relevant overheads. This consideration reduces the benchmark NIVA from 0 basis points to, say, −10 bps. Thus a more realistic estimate of average NIVA experience of the pension funds in the CEM database relative to a pure passive alternative over the 1993 to 2004 period is +27 basis points.

2. This observed average NIVA of +27 bps would have been even larger had it not been for the calculated negative 13-year "mix" effect of −14 bps. This "mix" effect results from the funds doing something other than following the standard CEM protocol of rebalancing the asset mix weights back to those of the stated asset mix policy on January 1 each year. It is not totally clear to us why the funds' actual rebalancing strategies systematically underperformed versus CEM's standard rebalancing protocol over the 1992 to 2004 period. This is something worth further investigation (see Figure 36.3).

From here, we go on to dig further into two components of the total fund NIVA:

1. The "in-category selection alphas."
2. Total fund operating costs.

THE SELECTION "ALPHAS": GOOD NEWS AND BAD NEWS

Figure 36.4 below displays the "in-category selection alphas" for seven major asset classes for all U.S. funds in the CEM database. The "in-category

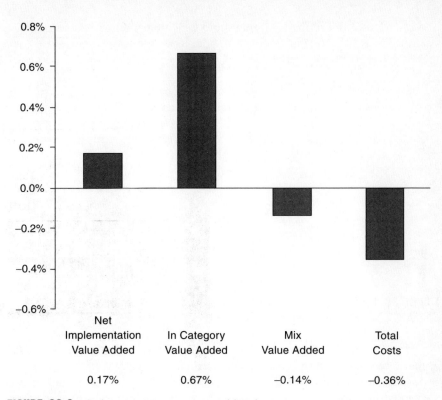

FIGURE 36.3 Did Active Management Add Value?
Source: CEM Benchmarking Inc., 2004.

alphas" are calculated by subtracting from the annual asset class return the return on a relevant benchmark portfolio selected by the participating fund. Note also that the direct costs associated with managing investments within each of the seven asset classes (i.e., either external fees or allocated internal costs) have been netted out.

As we study the results displayed in Figure 36.4, we should be mindful that the seven averages and standard deviations were calculated from very large actively managed samples that have accumulated over the 1992 to 2004 period. For example, the domestic large cap stocks category statistics are based on a sample of 1951 annual observations. Even the real estate and private equity sample sizes are 1,482 and 1,052, respectively. So from the perspective of standard tests of statistical significance, all the calculated average asset class net alphas easily pass the "null hypothesis" test, except for real estate. That leaves us with four positive asset class alpha results, and two negative ones. That is the good news.

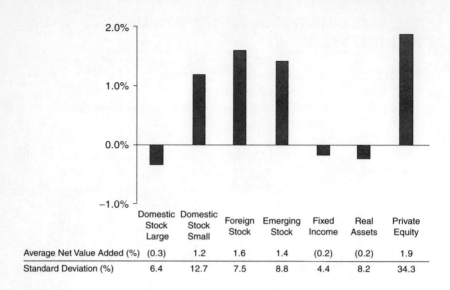

	Domestic Stock Large	Domestic Stock Small	Foreign Stock	Emerging Stock	Fixed Income	Real Assets	Private Equity
Average Net Value Added (%)	(0.3)	1.2	1.6	1.4	(0.2)	(0.2)	1.9
Standard Deviation (%)	6.4	12.7	7.5	8.8	4.4	8.2	34.3

FIGURE 36.4   Actively Managed Asset Class Alphas for U.S. Funds
Source: CEM Benchmarking Inc., 2004.

Having said that, the results also confirm that individual fund asset class alpha outcomes can vary greatly. That is the bad news. From a reward/risk ratio perspective, none of the average asset class alpha performances are very exciting. The attractiveness of average selectivity within foreign stock investing in developed markets scores best with an average reward/risk ratio of 0.2 (i.e., 1.6/7.5), and we suspect this success largely represents the systemic underweighting of Japan by most U.S. pension funds over the 1992 to 2004 period.

The very modest average 0.1 reward/risk ratio generated by the private equity asset class provides a very sober view of selectivity risk here. The 34.3 percent standard deviation suggests that being right on the asset class is not enough. It means that even though private equity as an asset class may perform well, you can still end up with terrible results in your fund. The implication is that, unless you have great confidence in your private equity manager selection skills, you'd better pay careful attention to manager diversification!

Of course, the observed great variance in private equity results could be given a much more positive spin. It suggests that good manager selection skills in this asset class have a very large payoff.

The Figure 36.4 statistics suggest that similar conclusions (both negative and positive) apply to the domestic small cap stocks and foreign emerging markets stocks asset classes.

IS THERE ALSO A PAYOFF FROM ACTIVELY MANAGING PENSION FUND COSTS?

Figure 36.3 indicated that total operating costs captured in the CEM pension fund database averaged 36 bps annually over the 13-year period. Table 36.2 provides important additional information. Note the database spans annual cost experience all the way from a miniscule 1 bp to a hefty 236 bps (based on 3,506 observations). Even the 10 to 90 percentile experience still encompasses a wide 14 bps to 59 bps range. This wide-ranging operating cost experience prompts an important question. Is there an "excess cost" performance drag in the same way that the analysis above suggested there was an "excess cash" performance drag over most of the 1992 to 2004 period?

The simplest way to answer this question is to regress fund performance (i.e., NIVA) against total operating costs. If there was an "excess cost" performance drag embedded in the database, it would show up as a statistically significant negative cost coefficient. This turned out to be the case. The statistically significant cost coefficient was in fact −0.50. Every basis point of additional operating cost reduced *NIVA* by an average −0.50 bps over the 1992 to 2004 period. While this is an important finding, it raises three important further questions:

1. Pension fund management should experience to significant economies of scale. What happens when we adjust for this scale factor?
2. Certain types of investment policies are much more expensive to implement than others. What happens when we adjust for this investment policy factor?

TABLE 36.2 Annual Total
Operating Costs

Low	1.1 bps
10th percentile	14.3 bps
1st quartile	22.7 bps
Median	33.8 bps
3rd quartile	46.8 bps
90th percentile	59.3 bps
High	236.2 bps

Source: CEM Benchmarking Inc.,
2004.

3. Operating cost structures may to some degree be country-specific. What happens when we adjust for this country factor?

All three questions have interesting answers:

1. The scale effect averaged −19 bps. For every 10-fold increase in fund asset value in the database (total range $16 million to $189 billion), total operating costs declined an average 19 bps. Thus large funds have a material cost advantage over small funds.
2. The incremental cost coefficients for U.S. stock, non-U.S. stock, real estate, and private equity mandates were +30, +47, +69, and +252 bps. These metrics indicate average total operating cost increases by shifting a fund out of bonds into U.S. stocks, non-U.S. stocks, real estate, and/or private equity, respectively. Thus, investment policy choices do materially impact cost experience.
3. Adjusted for scale and mix factors, Canadian funds experienced operating costs an average −15 bps lower than their U.S. counterparts. Why? Canadian funds generally chose simpler portfolio management structures and faced lower domestic external management fee structures.

Out of the total cost variance measured by a standard deviation of 19 bps for the full sample, these three cost drivers explained one half of the cost variance. So the question now is this: Are the three systematic cost drivers responsible for the measured "excess cost" performance drag coefficient of −0.50 bps? Or does the cost-related performance drag persist even after adjusting total operating costs for them?

We can answer this question by reestimating the fund performance versus fund operating costs relationship, but now using fund cost experience adjusted for differences in scale, asset mix, and country. If the "excess cost" coefficient remains statistically significantly negative, this would be an important finding. It would indicate that regardless of fund size, mix, or country, eliminating "excess costs," like eliminating "excess cash," has a positive performance payoff. The new "excess cost" coefficient was in fact −0.46. Thus, every basis point of additional scale-mix-country-adjusted "excess cost" reduced NIVA by an average 0.46 bps over the 1992 to 2004 period. This suggests that managing costs by ensuring that they have a positive payoff matters. It is the essence of "cost effectiveness."

The CEM database provided two examples of how a focus on cost effectiveness can increase fund performance. First, there was a modest statistical difference between the gross alphas of comparable externally and internally managed investment mandates. However, internal management was on average 30 bps less costly, and outperformed external management by an average 55 bps on a "net" basis. Second, every 10 percentage point increase in passive management was statistically associated with a 7 bps of additional NIVA. This suggests that significant exposure to very low-cost passive management together with concentrated active management was generally a cost-effective, value-producing combination over the 1992 to 2004 period.

TWO IMPORTANT LESSONS LEARNED THUS FAR

We close with a summary of two important lessons learned thus far:

1. In assessing the attractiveness of within-asset class active management, it is important to distinguish between average experience, and the variability of that experience. For example, over 1992 to 2004, active management was on average successful in 4 out of 7 major asset classes. However, with that average success came significant potential for individual funds to reduce return rather than enhance it.
2. A much surer way to increase fund NIVA was to carefully manage "excess costs." The value of having zero "excess costs" was easily worth as much as the total average value of active management, but without its downside exposure. There is a "free lunch" after all!

Can we identify other NIVA drivers? What happens when we introduce risk into the analysis? We addressed these questions in Parts Three, Four, and Five.

Pensions, Politics, and the Investment Industry

"...'Portable Alpha' has taken on several meanings because it is a supply-driven term shaped by each money management 'supplier.'..."

BernsteinResearch
Sanford C. Bernstein & Co.

Whither Security Analysis?

"The stories that follow explore the many ways investment banks now abuse the trust of their core customers—investors trying to build capital and companies trying to raise it. ..."

Fortune, May 14, 2001

"... we heard many comments about the conflicts of interest analysts face ... and about the pressures applied on some analysts by their employers and by the companies that they review or research. ..."

Securities Industry Committee on Analyst Standards,
April 2001

BUBBLE, BUBBLE, TOIL AND TROUBLE

Despite their stratospheric salaries, Street analysts did not distinguish themselves during the latter stages of the 1990s bull market. No statistic underscores this point more emphatically than one provided by First Call/Thomson Financial in October 1999 (i.e., within months of the top of the bull market). Their survey revealed that out of 27,700 analyst stock recommendations in their database, over 20,000 were in the "buy" category, while less than 300 (i.e., about 1 percent of all recommendations) were in the "sell" category. In a similar survey performed by Bloomberg in Canada, a measly 4 percent of all analyst recommendations were "sells" The obvious question these facts provoke is how any professional group can be paid so much for being so wrong.

A simplistic answer is that these security analysts really do provide a valuable service to investors, but that they got as carried away with the bull market's momentum as their clients did. There is probably some truth to that, but it can't be the whole story. In their own ways, the two quotes we cite above provide a more complete answer to the question. The fact is that during the last few years, there was so much more money to be made supporting the investment banking activities of the Wall Street firms the analysts worked for, that providing unbiased advice to investors simply was not a priority for many of them.

What, if anything, should be done about this reality? Whither security analysis? That is the question we address in this chapter.

FORTUNE TRASHES WALL STREET

The cover of the May 14, 2001, issue of *Fortune* magazine features the famous, but now forlorn face of Morgan Stanley's star Internet analyst Mary Meeker. Splashed across the cover is the question: "Can We Ever Trust Wall Street Again?" Three articles in the lead section of the magazine provide the context for the question. We summarize them as follows:

- "Where Mary Went Wrong" is the story of a security analyst who, by her own admission, became a stock promoter for Morgan Stanley and the Internet companies it took public. Thus, while she acknowledges that only 30 percent of Internet initial public offerings (IPOs) have a chance of becoming successful companies, virtually all of the companies she has been closely associated with have deserved "outperform" rankings (e.g., Priceline at $162, now $4, Yahoo at $237, now $19.50, Amazon at $106, now $15). She explains in the article: "It's a cool thing to take a company public" and "If you take a company public, and you are aggressive on the downside, it can be devastating. . . ." Yes, but not being aggressive on the downside can be devastating, too. It all depends whose interests you have in mind.
- "Betrayal On Wall Street" is the story of what *Fortune* calls "the IPO con game." In the past two years, issuing companies have collected $121 billion from IPOs, for which investment banks were paid $8 billion in underwriter fees. That $8 billion, however, was only the tip of the iceberg. *Fortune* suggests many of these IPOs were deliberately underpriced by investment banks, and then allocated to favored investment fund clients. These clients would then "flip" the IPO after a few weeks at hefty profits with the investment banks now acting as brokers, reselling the stocks to the general public at much higher prices. *Fortune* estimates that this process left $62 billion of issuing companies money "on the table" over the course of the last two years. Meanwhile, the investment banks earned additional profits through trading spreads

and commissions on the flip transactions, and on the additional business directed their way by the grateful investment funds that received the original IPO allocations. Thus they made money coming and going, and coming and going, and. ... "Hear No Risk, See No Risk, Speak No Risk" is the story of Winstar, "the former ski apparel shop that convinced the world that it could fly as a broadband company." Within a year of hitting $60/share and a market cap of $10 billion, Winstar would file for bankruptcy with $6.3 billion of debt on its balance sheet. This is not the place to repeat all the gory details set out in the *Fortune* article. Suffice it to say that security analysts working for Winstar's investment bankers managed to convince most of the world that Winstar's EBITDA (earnings before interest, taxes, depreciation, and amortization), while negative, was improving nicely. This company was going to be a big winner! For example, analyst Mark Kastan at investment banker Credit Suisse First Boston (CSFB) had a $79 price target on Winstar. The analysts did their job so well that even such major industry players as Lucent, Cisco, Siemens, and Microsoft became Winstar backers. Unfortunately, it seems that nobody was watching Winstar's balance sheet, where debt was piling up at an unsustainable rate. When Winstar announced that it could not meet interest payments, and with its share price at 14 cents, continuously bullish analyst Kastan finally downgraded the company to "underperform," admitting "at this point it makes no sense to continue our optimistic stance." Right.

It is one thing for the financial media to question the objectivity and value of sell-side security analysis; it is quite another if the securities industry itself or their regulators do so. Where are they on all this?

IS BETTER REGULATION THE ANSWER?

While the Securities and Exchange Commission (SEC) has expressed concerns about the cited conflicting roles of sell-side security analysts, it was the Canadian securities industry that was first off the mark in September 1999 in forming a task force to look into this issue. The Securities Industry Committee on Analyst Standards has just issued its draft report titled: "Setting Analyst Standards: Recommendations for the Supervision and Practice of Canadian Securities Industry Analysts." We believe any future securities industry effort in the United States would look very similar.

In framing their recommendations, the Committee observed:

1. Sell-side analyst conflicts of interest really are a problem.
2. Enforceable disclosure standards for research reports do not exist.

3. An enforceable analyst code of conduct does not exist.
4. Selective disclosure by companies to analysts is a problem.
5. Company pressure on analysts for positive coverage is a problem.
6. Failure by some investors to understand "that analysts have to balance varying degrees of conflicts of interest" is a problem.

The Committee's consideration of these issues has led to 28 specific recommendations. We highlight and summarize them as follows:

1. Research reports and media interviews should state any conflicts of interest in a clear, prominent manner.
2. Analysts should not issue research reports on companies where they are either on the payroll, or acting as an adviser to the company.
3. Research reports should clearly disclose sources of information, including site visits. The report-issuing firm should be clear about its recommendation terminology and categories, and report the proportion of recommendations that fall into each category.
4. Securities firms should have separate security analysis and investment banking functions, and clear codes of conduct should be established and adhered to. A "supervisory analyst" should be accountable for the quality and objectivity of research reports. Each firm should have a senior UDP ("ultimate designated person") with overall accountability for good firm conduct.
5. Public companies should have clear, even-handed communication policies, consistent with good corporate governance practices.
6. Investor education programs should "foster an understanding of . . . the role of analysts. . . ."

We have a somewhat schizophrenic view on these kinds of recommendations. On the one hand, it is self-evident that the Committee has done some good work, and has come up with some useful recommendations that deserve support. On the other hand, it is our view that recommendations of this kind fundamentally fail to address the current crisis gripping the securities analysis profession. We explain below.

REVERSING THE FINANCIAL FOOD CHAIN

We have observed previously that the financial services industry food chain tends to work in reverse, with the service suppliers on top and the ultimate customers on the bottom. The fundamental problem is one of informational asymmetry. In other words, most of the customers (whether individual investors, investment fund unit holders, or trustees of pension or other investment funds) don't know what they don't know, while the services suppliers do. The predictable general result is that the customers get too little value at too high fees, while the suppliers make too much money in relation to the value of the services they provide. The cited *Fortune* stories are simply graphic examples of this logic in action.

How do we get better outcomes from the customers' perspective? By reducing informational asymmetry. True, the cited Securities Industry Committee's recommendations try to do this. However, fundamental change cannot be brought about by making the "sell-side" behave a little better (although it can't hurt). Fundamental change can only come from strong, focused "buy-side" organizations with well-thought-out strategic plans on how to create value for their stakeholders. What might such strategic plans say about the role of security analysis? Our chapters on pension fund governance and investment beliefs in Parts Three and Four address this question.

WHAT IS SECURITY ANALYSIS, ANYWAY?

What kind of security analysis is useful from an ultimate "buy-side" customer perspective? We noted in our investment beliefs chapters that there are two potentially useful kinds: long-horizon analysis and short-horizon analysis. The focus of the former is the projection and valuation of uncertain future cash flows. The focus of the latter is the prediction of short-term changes in the market valuation of securities. No less an authority than John Maynard Keynes pointed out the radically different nature of the two approaches.

The first approach implies true, from first principles, long-term fundamental analysis of economies, sectors, and individual companies, new or old. It will be useful if it produces better-than-random long-term investment return projections with unbiased (and therefore offsetting) errors. Success with the second approach hinges on gaining short-term information advantages over other "active" market participants of sufficient magnitude and frequency to "outperform," net of fees and transaction costs, relative to some predefined benchmark. Now it no longer matters what you think the fundamentals are today. Rather, the game is to correctly predict the prices average opinion will produce tomorrow.

EVEN GOOD SECURITY ANALYSIS NEEDS CONTEXT

Our investment beliefs chapters provided the context for the profitable application of good long- and short-horizon security analysis disciplines.

Good long-horizon analysis disciplines can form the basis for profitable private markets investment programs in real estate, merchant banking, or venture capital. They can also provide the basis for an intelligent "core investing" alternative to purely passive index fund investing in exchange-listed securities. We noted that the most effective investment vehicle that uses short-horizon analytics with predictive content may be a diversified portfolio of long-short, market neutral strategies.

The point here is that successful "buy-side" investment programs must not only identify reliable predictive sources of long-horizon and/or short-horizon return forecasts. They must also create effective organizational structures to take advantage of them. Without carefully built structures, even potentially useful security analysis disciplines will not create value for the ultimate "buy-side" customers.

EFFECTIVE "BUY-SIDE" STRUCTURES

Now we have arrived at the heart of the matter. It is all about aligning economic interests. Specifically, what can be done to align the interests of the ultimate "buy-side" customers with those of investment analysts with genuine talent in either long- or short-horizon disciplines? The following recommendations suggest themselves:

- Foster the growth of knowledgeable "buy-side" organizations with mandates and incentive structures to produce "value at a reasonable cost" for the organizations' stakeholders.
- Foster decision processes inside these organizations to assess the degree to which it is advantageous to attract analytical talent inside the organization itself, or whether such talent needs to be accessed from outside the organization.
- If analytical talent needs to be accessed from the outside, what is the best way for the "buy-side" organization to access outside analytical talent? How are the optimal structures for accessing long-horizon and short-horizon analytical talent likely to be different?
- One desirable characteristic of relationships with outside suppliers of analytical talent is continuity. What can be done to ensure it?
- What kind of compensation arrangements will align economic interests? What are the implications for how performance should be measured?

These kinds of questions are not only relevant to large "buy-side" organizations such as Algemeen Burgerlijk Pensioenfonds (ABP), Teachers Insurance and Annuity Association–College Retirement Equities Fund (TIAA-CREF) or the California Public Employees' Retirement System

(CalPERS). We believe they are just as relevant to "buy-side" organizations of a much more modest scale. There is even hope at the retail level, as some shareowner investment cooperatives have shown.

IN CONCLUSION

The *Fortune* stories emphasize the disconnect between the "research" that most of Wall Street provides, and what genuine "buy-side" investment organizations need to be successful. Trying to make sell-side analysts behave better is commendable, but does not address the real problem. Only effective "buy-side" organizations can do that.

CHAPTER 38

Pension Funds and Investment Firms: Redefining the Relationship

Pumba: "What's eating Simba?"

Timon: "Nothing, he's on top of the food chain."

From Disney's *The Lion King*

WHO ARE THE SIMBAS OF THE PENSION INVESTMENT KINGDOM?

The Chartered Financial Analyst (CFA) Institute invited us recently to give one of the keynote addresses at their annual conference. We settled on the title that heads this chapter. Coincidentally, our friend and long time fellow-traveler Peter Bernstein invited us to guest write one of his Economics & Portfolio Strategy chapters (see www.peterlbernsteininc.com). Here, we offer the message shared with Peter's clients and CFA Institute Annual Conference attendees in Toronto. Readers will note an interesting shift in viewpoint here. Usually, we write to pension people about investment managers. Here, we write to investment managers about pension people.

First, what is the relevance of the cited Pumba-Timon dialogue about Simba, the up-and-coming young lion king? In previous writings, we have characterized the investment management community as the Simbas of the pension investment world. Over the past 30 years, it has been the investment management community that has been on top of the pension finance food chain, whether measured in terms of shaping investment mandates, structuring compensation arrangements, or simply in terms of public recognition, prestige, and personal wealth creation. The 1990s saw the beginning of a reversal of roles, as a small number of large pension funds began to claw their way up the food chain, determined to take their rightful place at the top.

We believe that this process will accelerate in the coming years. In short, the pension investment industry has begun to shift from a paradigm where the suppliers drive the behavior of customers, to one where the customers will increasingly drive the behavior of the suppliers. Why has the pension investment industry been supplier driven? Why is that now changing? What are some of the implications of the coming customer-driven new world? How should investment firms respond? We investigate these four questions below.

THE MONEY FLOOD

When *Pensions & Investments* editor Michael Clowes chronicled the post–World War II history of the U.S. pension investment industry, he appropriately titled his book *The Money Flood* (New York: John Wiley & Sons, 2000). A simple chart in the book showing U.S. pension asset growth over the past 50 years tells the tale. Over the first half of the period, pension assets barely got off the floor, reaching only $250 billion by 1975. Then they took off. The $1 trillion mark was hit around 1981, $2 trillion by 1986, $4 trillion by 1993, and $8 trillion by 1998.

Thus, without any detailed analysis, we have already identified one major reason why the pension investment industry has been largely supplier driven over the past 30 years. The "money flood" has had pension plan sponsors scrambling to get their pension assets managed. With the demand for investment management services growing so rapidly, it should come as no surprise that the supply side of the industry has been largely able to dictate the rules, both with respect to types of investment mandates, and with respect to compensation.

However, "excess demand" is not the only explanation for the observed supplier dominance during the past 30 years. Two other important forces were at play.

A QUESTION OF GOVERNANCE

In the mid-1970s, Peter Drucker foresaw the "money flood" while it was still a trickle (*The Unseen Revolution: How Pension Fund Socialism Came*

To America, New York: Harper & Row, 1976). However, he expressed a very different concern from the "excess demand" issue identified above. Who was going to be accountable for the stewardship of this immense asset pool, he wondered? Without strong governance mechanisms, he worried that pension assets would be used to further the aims of outside agents, rather than those of the inside principals.

The outside agents that Drucker had in mind were politicians, union leaders, and corporate executives. Clearly, in each case, one could identify possible motivations to use pension assets to further political, union, or corporate goals unrelated to, or even inimical to those of the direct pension plan stakeholders. Drucker might well have added pension industry services suppliers such as investment consultants and money managers to his outside agents list. The financial interests of these agents, too, do not always naturally align themselves with those of the pension plan stakeholders.

The bottom line is that, as is his wont, Drucker was onto something big well before the rest of the world figured out was he was talking about. In the pension economics and finance field in the mid-1970s, he identified good governance as a (possibly "the") critical element of successful pension fund "socialism" (or is it "capitalism"), while the rest of us were still totally absorbed arguing the true meaning of portfolio and capital market theory, and its alphas, betas, and information ratios.

ENTER THE ANTHROPOLOGISTS

Politicians, union leaders, and corporate executives occasionally did misbehave as Drucker predicted while the "money flood" ran its course through the 1980s and 1990s. But they did not abscond with the pension asset jewels in the wholesale way that Drucker feared they might. As we noted, it was in fact the investment management community that would derive the greatest financial benefit out of the "money flood." However, they would do so in a perfectly legal (and even admired) manner. As a result, Drucker's "good governance" issue never really showed up on the pension fund industry radar screen.

That is, until anthropologists William O'Barr and John Conley came out with their scandalous book *Fortune and Folly: The Wealth and Power of Institutional Investing* (New York: Irwin, 1992). After being allowed to study the day-to-day workings of nine major U.S. pension funds over a two-year period, they told the world (in the book preface): "After reading our book, you'll feel a little bit like the airline passenger who peeked into the cockpit at 30,000 feet and found there was no one in there."

Their specific observations included:

- The organization structures of the nine pension funds seemed to be more the result of historical accident than of any conscious decisions to excel.
- The most common cultural theme seemed to be efforts to shift responsibilities and to deflect blame.
- Much attention seemed to be paid to maintaining good personal relationships with outside suppliers such as consultants and investment managers.

The Drucker governance cat was back among the pension pigeons.

A CALL TO "EXCELLENCE"

The leadership of the pension fund management community did not much like the shot O'Barr and Conley had fired across their collective bow (what the executives of the nine unnamed funds thought is unprintable). But when 50 senior pension fund executives were asked in December 1995 what they estimated the "excellence shortfall" to be in their organizations, the median response was 66 basis points per annum in fund return foregone.

And what were the reasons for this "excellence shortfall"? The three top responses were (from *Excellence Shortfall in Pension Fund Management: Anatomy of a Problem* by Keith Ambachtsheer, Craig Boice, Don Ezra, and John McLaughlin, Cost Effectiveness Measurement Inc., 1995):

1. Poor decision processes (mentioned 98% of the time).
2. Inadequate resources (mentioned 48% of the time).
3. Lack of focus or clear mission (mentioned 42% of the time).

These are the classic symptoms of governance failure. Maybe there was something rotten in the state of pensions after all.

By 1997, these 50 qualitative judgments had been confirmed quantitatively by correlating rankings of pension fund governance quality with those of risk-adjusted fund performance. A study of 80 U.S. and Canadian pension funds found a "good-bad governance spread" of 1 percent per annum, and as a result, the significant cost of poor governance was confirmed (see Keith Ambachtsheer, Ronald Capelle, and Tom Scheibelhut, "Improving Pension Fund Performance," *Financial Analysts Journal,* November–December 1998). All these strands were brought together in the 1998 book *Pension Fund Excellence: Creating Value for Stakeholders* (by Keith Ambachtsheer and Don Ezra, published by John Wiley & Sons). Thus, through the 1990s, the call to excellence became increasingly difficult for pension funds to ignore.

WHAT DO "EXCELLENT" PENSION FUNDS LOOK LIKE?

So what do excellent pension funds look like? First and foremost, excellent pension funds have boards of trustees or pension committees who understand the difference between governance and management. As governors, they understand who the fund stakeholders are, what risks each bear, and where to draw the line between acceptable and unacceptable risk exposures. They understand that they can only do their job if the fund organization is capable of assessing these risk exposures on an ongoing basis. Finally, they understand that they must delegate the development and implementation of the strategic plan to the fund's executive.

In this governance context, the executive goal is clear: to manage a successful, ongoing process for the development and implementation of the fund organization's strategic plan. Critical elements of such a plan include:

- The identification of an asset portfolio that looks like the liabilities (i.e., the "liability portfolio").
- A prospective risk/return assessment protocol that references this "liability portfolio" as the risk-minimizing benchmark asset.
- An agreed-on cost-of-risk capital hurdle rate for the fund to establish the minimum required (or acceptable) net excess return per unit of balance-sheet risk.
- A risk budget that establishes the green-, amber-, and red-light risk zones at the total balance-sheet level.
- A breakdown of the total asset management operation into functional subgroups, each with their own risk budget allocation tied to the total budget.
- An organization design chart with optimal layering and delegation characteristics plus no preconceived biases toward either internal or external investment management.
- A compensation philosophy that aligns the economic interests of the stakeholders with those of the inside and outside agents performing the fund's work.
- An information system that meets the information needs of the governance, executive, and operations functions of the pension fund "business."

This is the blueprint that "best practice" pension funds around the globe are now adopting. Before we look ahead and explore the implications of this new blueprint for the investment management community, let's briefly look backward and see if it helps us explain the pension fund management world that was and why it was supplier driven.

A SUPPLIER-DRIVEN MARKET

We don't have to look back very far to find the pension fund management world that was. What was, still largely is, despite the recent clarion calls to excellence. William O'Barr and John Conley would have little trouble finding nine major pension funds today (let alone a host of smaller ones) that would fit their 1992 descriptions very closely. Such funds would still have weak boards of trustees or pension committees. These bodies are still at best uncertain about their roles, or worse, still have agendas not fully aligned with those of the fund stakeholders. They may or may not have a competent internal executive. Likely, they would have trouble distinguishing between competence and incompetence. In any case, they hire their own external consultants to second-guess the internal people.

What passes for a strategic plan in such organizations is largely imitative, driven by a need to shift responsibilities, deflect blame, and accommodate the supplier community. If others have 65-35 asset mixes, then they will also have a 65-35 asset mix. Never mind that it may suit the suppliers better than the stakeholders. If others use outside consultants to put together highly complex, expensive external investment management structures involving dozens of managers, then they will, too. Never mind that it may suit the suppliers better than the stakeholders. If others continue to pay asset-based management fees, then they will, too. Never mind that it may suit the suppliers better than the stakeholders. If others continue to define "risk" as tracking error versus commercially provided market benchmarks, then they will, too. Never mind that. . . . You get the idea.

Please note that this rant is not directed at the investment management community. As business people, you must take the market for your services as it is, not as it should be. My purpose here is to simply suggest that there are now forces in play that are moving the market that was (and largely still is) toward the one that should be.

THE TINY EQUITY RISK PREMIUM FACTOR

Luckily, the poor management practices spawned by weak pension fund governance mechanisms during the 30-year "money flood" haven't hurt fund stakeholders very much. The rising stock market tide over this period has floated nearly all pension fund boats, poorly governed or not. However, we have been among a small band of stock market observers arguing that all good things eventually come to an end. The positive equity risk premium string ran out some years ago. Even today, almost two years after equity markets peaked, the arithmetic of the market still doesn't work very well. (If you haven't already done so, just add today's stock market dividend yield to 80 percent of a realistic projection for long-term real gross domestic product growth, and compare the sum to today's real yield on the Treasury inflation-protected securities (TIPS) bonds. Can you get anything but a tiny positive equity risk premium out of that calculation?)

As far as we can tell, over 95 percent of the people involved in one way or another in the management of pension and endowment funds refuse to do this calculation. Or if they do it, they refuse to accept the "tiny equity risk premium" conclusion it leads to. Why won't they accept it? They will tell you that the conclusion must be wrong because, historically, equities have produced a solid 5 percent risk premium. Further, capital market theory asserts that investors are well informed, rational, and risk averse. So stocks must be priced to provide a positive equity risk premium. Finally, capitalism would come to a grinding halt without a reward for risk bearing. So there must be one.

This is not the place to systematically deflate each of these arguments. However, here are a few needles:

- The historical 5 percent risk premium calculation is time sensitive, usually including the 1990s period of extreme rising equity valuations. It is wishful thinking to project further valuation rises of this kind into future equity returns. Also, stocks have performed poorly over extended periods of time in history.
- Yes, many real-world investors are well informed, rational, and risk averse. However, many are not. Still others migrate between the former and the latter, or just simply march to their own, unique drummers (we would place most boards of trustees and pension committees we know in this latter category).
- Capitalism is not as fair and transparent as many idealists would like to believe (are you following the Enron story?). It is not at all clear that it will work as well for outsider shareholders over the next 10 to 20 years as it will for insider corporate managers and for Wall Street.

In short, we believe that today's 5 percent equity risk premium arguments may be straw houses, likely to be blown away by future winds of adversity.

If the 5 percent equity risk premium arguments are so easily countered today, why is it that most of the professional pension fund management community in its broadest sense (i.e., fund executives, consultants, money managers, Wall Street) continues to cling to the illusion of it? It is because the old pension fund management paradigm can't operate without a material risk premium. For example, without one, the rationale for the now standard "65-35" asset mix policy becomes questionable. Traditional passive strategies based on the standard commercial stock indexes no longer make sense. Traditional active alpha-generation strategies benchmarked against those same indexes also lose their rationale. In short, without a materially positive equity risk premium assumption, Humpty Dumpty would have a great fall. Let's keep the assumption so that he holds together.

"NEW PARADIGM" PENSION FUNDS: WHAT KIND OF INVESTMENT SERVICES DO THEY WANT?

We have already outlined what well-governed, "best practice" pension funds look like, and specifically, what the key elements of their strategic business plans are. Clearly, they have already put Humpty Dumpty's great fall behind them. They have moved on to a new pension fund management paradigm not dependent on a forever positive 5 percent equity risk premium. What kind of investment management needs do these "new paradigm" funds have? That is the question we tackle next.

To answer the question succinctly, we need to begin by understanding the organization design logic of the "new paradigm" funds somewhat better. Figure 38.1 helps explain what is fundamentally different here. The thinking now starts with the recognition that (a) there is a risk-minimizing "liability portfolio" they can invest in, and that (b) they can put on any combination of risky exposures within the constraint of the preestablished green, amber, and red risk zones, and the need to earn a net return in excess of the established cost of risk capital. In the schematic, the example cost of risk capital is set at 3 percent/10 percent = 30 basis points per unit of surplus volatility.

So the critical organization design question now becomes: What is the most useful way to break down the "risky investments" category into subsets? At a primary level, we firmly believe the answer is not "by asset classes," but "by forecasting horizon." Specifically, pension funds (and other investment funds) must make a fundamental distinction between risky strategies based on long-horizon views of future cash-flow prospects on the one hand, and those based on short-horizon views of absolute or relative changes in security prices on the other.

John Maynard Keynes made this critical distinction almost 70 years ago in *The General Theory of Employment, Interest and Money* (San Diego: Harcourt Brace, 1936), especially in the chapter titled "The State of Long Term Expectations." See Table 38.1 for two brief excerpts from this chapter. In more modern times, the distinction is a constant thread in David Swensons's story of his highly successful 14-year tenure as chief investment officer of Yale's endowment fund (see *Pioneering Portfolio Management*, New York: Free Press, 2000).

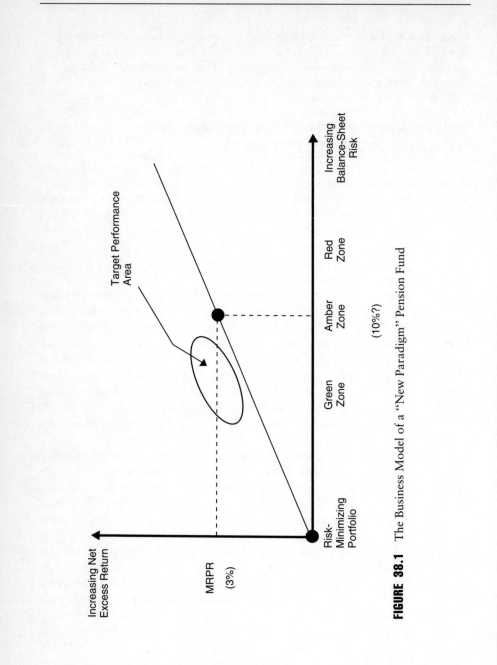

FIGURE 38.1 The Business Model of a "New Paradigm" Pension Fund

TABLE 38.1 John Maynard Keynes on Risky "Asset Classes"

Long-Horizon Risky Strategies	Short-Horizon Risky Strategies
"It is long-term investors who most promote the public interest. Yet it is they, wherever investment funds boards meet, who will in practice come in for the most criticism. For the behavior of long-term investors will seem eccentric, unconventional, and rash in the eyes of average opinion. Worldly wisdom teaches that it is better for reputation to fail conventionally than to succeed unconventionally."	"[Active management] is like a game of Snap, of Old Maid, of Musical Chairs. He is the victor who says 'snap' neither too soon nor too are managed by committees or late, who passes the Old Maid to his neighbor before the game is over, who secures a chair for himself when the music stops. These games can be played with zest and enjoyment, though all players know that it is the Old Maid which is circulating, or that when the music stops some of the players will find themselves unseated."

Source: John Maynard Keynes. *The General Theory of Employment, Interest and Money*. San Diego: Harcourt Brace, 1936.

With the forecasting horizon distinction made, it is clear that "new paradigm" pension funds will want to consider three types of strategies in the development and implementation of their strategic plans:

1. **Liability-relative risk minimizing strategies.** As an example, a fund with long-term, inflation-sensitive liabilities would probably settle on a long-duration TIPS portfolio as its risk-minimizing benchmark portfolio.
2. **Long horizon risky strategies.** They come in nonmarketable and marketable investments forms. Examples of the former are real estate, timber, merchant banking, and venture capital. An example of the latter is Warren Buffet's approach to managing the Berkshire-Hathaway portfolio. The common ingredient of all these strategies is the assessment and valuation of uncertain future cash flows.
3. **Short horizon risky strategies.** Any strategy driven by sufficient predictive accuracy to generate net positive excess return relative to the client's "liability portfolio" is a potential candidate. The challenge is to (a) identify sufficient individual candidate strategies that meet a set of predetermined selection criteria (e.g., sufficient transparency to monitor risk), and to (b) combine the selected individual strategies in a way that maximizes the overall "package" net information ratio (i.e., net excess return per unit of liability-relative excess return volatility). The common ingredient of all these strategies is that they are all zero sum and adversarial. There are always winners and losers.

The stage is now set to address the final question we set out to answer in this chapter. How should investment firms respond to this new, emerging set of market imperatives?

NEW PENSION FUND–INVESTMENT FIRM PARTNERSHIPS

We noted that "new paradigm" pension funds have no preconceived notion about which investment functions should be carried out in-house and which should be outsourced. It is a matter of comparative advantage and cost effectiveness. What is fundamentally different, however, is that these funds don't want a coterie of external managers that they (or their consultants) can hire and fire at will. They want long-term partners, and they want compensation arrangements that are transparent and make long-term economic sense to both partners. In that light, here are some issues external investment firms might consider:

- **Liability-relative risk minimizing strategies.** Do you have people on your staff capable of modeling client liabilities, and producing a matching risk-minimizing liability portfolio? Do you have the capabilities to actually manage such a portfolio over time? Have you developed, or do you have access to risk management tools that reference client liabilities as the benchmark?
- **Long-horizon risky strategies.** should you have a private markets investing capability? In the public markets, do you have the people with the skills and the mind-set to be long-horizon investors? How should "performance" be measured in a long-horizon portfolio of publicly traded securities? How active are you prepared to be in overseeing the governance processes of the entities issuing the securities you have positions in? What do "win-win" compensation arrangements between you and your partner/client(s) look like?
- **Short-horizon risky strategies.** Where are your comparative advantages in predicting the absolute or relative short-term price changes in publicly traded securities, derivatives, commodities, currencies, etc.? What research have you done to support your views? What investments are you making to maintain your comparative advantage? How many independent long-short absolute-return strategies can you create inside your own organization, and what are their dollar capacities? Are there enough to offer a diversified stand-alone "strategies package" to your clients and prospects? Or should you feed your individual strategy(s) into a diversified "package" your pension fund client is already managing? What do "win-win" compensation arrangements between you and your partner/client(s) look like?

Most of this thinking takes investment firms with large books of "old paradigm" business a long way from their familiar turf. How seriously should these firms take the emerging "new paradigm" fund market?

COULD YOU BE A "NEW PARADIGM" PLAYER?

Remember, the issue is not whether to abandon the still lucrative "old paradigm" market for your investment management services. Instead, it is whether you should run with the new Simbas of the pension investment kingdom. These "new paradigm" Simbas may still be few in numbers, but they are hugely rich in assets.

The scary question is: do you have anything of value to offer them?

CHAPTER 39

The New Pension Fund Management Paradigm: Feedback from Financial Analysts

"Leading pension funds around the globe are redefining their missions and their investment paradigms. This raises some important questions for investment firms. ..."

From the program of the 2002 CFA Institute Annual Conference held in Toronto, May 12 to 15, 2002

TEST DRIVING THE NEW PARADIGM

Our "new pension fund management paradigm" construction project is now complete. An invitation to address the Chartered Financial Analyst (CFA) Institute's 2002 annual conference offered a rare opportunity to "test drive" the new paradigm in front of a select audience of 1,000 financial analysts, employed in the main by investment firms from around the world. The speech title was "Pension Funds and Investment Firms: Redefining the Relationship," and the message (equally relevant to other long-term asset pools such as endowment funds) was set out in the preceding chapter.

Did the 45-minute message have an impact on the conference attendees? The post-speech "Q&A" session suggests it did. After a full 15 minutes of responding to written questions, time was up. With many question cards yet unread, session moderator Rossa O'Reilly jokingly suggested the remaining questions (and our answers to them) could form the basis for our next book. The suggestion stuck, with our answers to 15 selected questions filling the next few pages. Why is the post-speech "Q&A" session worth documenting as a separate chapter? For two reasons. First, the questions were for the most part intelligent and insightful, and hence worth repeating on their own merit. The second reason is that if we cannot provide credible answers to them, then "the new paradigm" we have been building effectively crashed during its first major "test drive" and should be hauled off to the scrap yard. Did the "new paradigm" survive? Read on and judge for yourself.

PENSION POLITICS AND ECONOMICS

The questions on pension politics and economics can be reduced to the four set out below. The first questioner zeroes right in on a very important strategic issue for corporate plan sponsors:

Q1:   *"For corporate DB or cash-balance plan sponsors, which is the proper balance sheet to focus on: the pension plan balance sheet by itself, or an extended corporate balance sheet which includes the pension plan?"*

A1:   *"Both the narrow and the broader perspectives offer important insights. From pension fiduciary and regulatory perspectives, the primary focus must be the pension plan balance sheet. If pension liabilities exceed pension assets, steps are required to redress the imbalance. However, from an overall corporate risk management perspective, the primary focus must shift to the extended balance sheet which includes all corporate assets and liabilities, including those accrued through the pension plan. For many 'old economy' manufacturing or services companies, deciding how much of their overall risk-carrying capability to allocate to their core and to their pension 'businesses' is one of the most important strategic issues they face. The U.K. pharmaceutical retailer BOOTS, for example, recently announced that they had immunized their pension plan balance sheet, thus freeing up all of their risk-carrying capability for use in their core business."*

A second questioner wonders if pension fund management is possible at all in the new "mark-to-market" world of disclosure:

Q2:   *"What is the relationship between how DB pension funds should be managed and how results are publicly disclosed? For example, pension scheme disclosure everywhere seems to be moving to a 'mark-to-market' philosophy. Can DB pension funds still be*

*managed effectively if balance sheet gains and losses are imme-
diately recognized? Or should the assets and liabilities just be
immunized?"*

A2:   *"You are quite right to observe that the 'new paradigm' management framework presupposes a 'mark-to-market' view of
the world. This is the proper view, as it embodies the only
truly objective basis for assessing DB balance sheet behavior
over time, and its status at any point-in-time. Some people do
indeed think that moving to a 'mark-to-market' philosophy elim-
inates any possibility for taking DB balance sheet risk. This
is not the case. What 'mark-to-market' does do is to promote
a more informed approach to risk management. For example,
it automatically raises questions such when, and under what
circumstances, should balance sheet imbalances in DB schemes
trigger changes in funding rates? What contingency reserves (if
any) should be kept as a hedge against potential asset shortfalls? In the old paradigm world, these kinds of questions
were the exclusive domain of the actuaries and their black
boxes. In the new paradigm world, this is no longer acceptable. Accountable, transparent risk management has become
everybody's business."*

A third questioner wondered if the new management framework for
defined benefit (DB) plans was relevant to the management of defined
contribution (DC) plans:

Q3:   *"Recent growth in pension schemes has been in DC rather than
DB plans. How relevant is the framework you propose for
capital accumulation plans where 'liabilities' are implicit rather
than explicit? Also, what kind of advice should plan participants
receive, and who should provide it?"*

A3:   *"The way our proposed framework deals with risk is directly
transferable to a DC context. The most certain (i.e., least risky)
approach to accumulating capital to support a future stream of
pension payments in real terms is to purchase a series of long term,
inflation-linked, default risk-free bonds. (As an aside, it is ironic
that these instruments are seldom offered as a DC plan investment
option! Why is that?). The most relevant way to frame risk and
reward for DC plan participants is to put them in a position
where they can assess the likelihood, and the degree to which any
risky investment policy they might consider could lead to a lower
accumulated capital amount (and hence pension) than the certain*

amount the least risky investment alternative would deliver. On the flip-side of the risk coin, what possible gains relative to the risk-free alternative could the risky investment policy deliver? Is the potential reward worth the risk? On the question of participant guidance and who should provide it, we see material principal-agent conflicts of interest as well as significant scope for future employer-plan member conflict. For example, where do the risk modeling inputs come from? From 'objective' history? (Which 'objective' history?) From the participants themselves? (What can they be reasonably expected to know?) Or from some outside 'expert' source? (Who qualifies as an 'expert?') How should the risky investment choices be categorized? Why? These simple DC questions, and the more profound questions they prompt, make us rather gloomy about the future of DC pension plans, at least in the way they are popularly constructed today. Informational asymmetry and misalignments of economic interests have led to typical DC structures that neither pool risks efficiently, nor create scale economies efficiently. With the 5 percent equity risk premium no longer around to bail everyone out, the legal community is rubbing their hands gleefully, as the cloth from which class action suits are tailored continues to pile up. Employers beware."

Finally, a fourth questioner demonstrated a keen awareness of a different type of principal-agent problem:

Q4: *"How long will it take for your 'new paradigm' to filter down to the many smaller pension and endowment funds? Will the pension consultants (i.e., the gatekeepers) ever buy in?*

A4: *"These are two separate, but related questions. Pension fund organization effectiveness is highly dependent on the clearly aligned separation of the governance, executive, and operations functions. Smaller funds have a tough time because they cannot afford a dedicated, internal executive function. As a result, the executive responsibilities end up diffused, partially shifted back to the governance group (i.e., a board or investment committee) and partially shifted to outside 'experts' (i.e., a pension consulting organization). In such situations, everyone is responsible, which really means no-one is. Too often, the result is disappointing performance. A hopeful sign here is that some consulting organizations have begun to accept 'managing fiduciary-for-hire' assignments, where they become explicitly accountable for the construction and implementation of the fund's strategic plan, and where their compensation is tied to (properly measured) performance."*

PENSION PLAN GOVERNANCE

Two questions addressed important pension plan governance issues. The first focused on the competence of boards of trustees (or pension committees):

Q5: *"Your proposed framework pre-supposes a board capable of understanding their role in it. Do you think that is the case? If not, what are the implications?"*

A5: *"Ensuring there is an effective risk management protocol in place should be one of a pension plan board's top priorities. Our framework provides it with such a protocol, with the board's role in that protocol clearly defined. Unfortunately, there can be a significant gap between what should be, and what is. Some boards are simply not capable of grasping what its job is. Other boards have the potential to understand, but never get the necessary coaching. Then they often fall prey to their own wiles, or those of external service providers with their own agendas."*

The second question also related to board effectiveness:

Q6: *"With the volatility of market returns, how confident are you that boards will stick with their policy decisions if they run into a few years of adversity?"*

A6: *"The proposed framework visualizes enterprise risk management as something dynamic rather than static. A good protocol places the board in a position to intelligently respond to a material change in the external or internal environments. Of course the key word here is 'material.' This is where a board must be wise enough to seek expert counsel, which in turn raises another critical question. There are far more people posing as 'experts' then there are experts. Boards that cannot first turn to their own internal executives for expert advice they trust, are at a huge disadvantage."*

THE NEW PENSION FUND MANAGEMENT PARADIGM

Again, the four questions on the new paradigm itself were "on the money." First, a question about the role of actuaries in the new paradigm:

Q7:   *"How do actuaries feel about your suggestion that pension liabilities should be 'marked-to-market' and represented by a risk-minimizing liability portfolio? Don't they think that valuing the liabilities is their job?"*

A7:   *"Marking pension liabilities to market is not a new idea. It has been around for decades. Many people (including some members of the actuarial profession) have never liked the idea of liabilities bouncing around the way the assets do. However, we shouldn't let their dislike stand in the way of effectively managing balance sheet risk. If we want to do that, then we must accept the obvious reality that just as changes in interest rates lead to changes in bond prices (and possibly equity prices), so do they lead to changes in liability 'prices.'"*

Next, a predictable, but nevertheless important, question about the measurement and quantification of balance sheet risk:

Q8:   *"Do you believe that volatility is a good measure of risk?"*

A8:   *"Risk is the potential for bad things to happen. In a pension plan context, the ultimate 'bad things' are default on pension payments or far more likely, an unanticipated increase in the contribution rate. Such 'bad things' can only happen when balance sheet liabilities exceed assets by a material amount. In this context, the potential volatility between the market value of the assets and the market value of the liabilities is indeed a good tool to help assess risk. This reality leads directly to one of the key elements in the proposed framework: the risk budget. The risk budget controls the maximum amount of asset-liability volatility permitted on the balance sheet. In Figure 38.1, the risk budget was delineated by the green, amber, and red zones on the horizontal axis, with the quantitative limit set at 10 percent."*

Also predictable was the next question, although our answer here is more fuzzy than we would like:

Q9:   *"How is the 'cost of risk capital' hurdle rate determined? Is it objective or subjective?"*

A9: *"We haven't seen or heard a lot of good discussion on this question. One approach is to attempt to establish what the 'normal' equity risk premium relative to bonds has been historically. Arnott and Bernstein attempt to do this in "What Risk Premium Is 'Normal?,' " published in the March–April 2002 issue of the Financial Analysts Journal. They come up with a 'normal' (i.e., expected) excess return of 2.4 percent. If we also assume a 'normal' excess return volatility of 20 percent, it implies a 'normal' reward/risk ratio of 0.12. Of course that still leaves the question as to whether the risk-bearing balance sheet stakeholders in any specific context are 'normal' in terms of their specific risk tolerance. A more direct approach to setting a 'cost of risk capital' hurdle rate is to ask directly what minimum return needs to be earned on 'surplus at risk' in a specific context. For example, a 15 percent minimum return requirement on the 20 percent of plan assets that represent 'surplus at risk' is equivalent to a 3 percent minimum excess return requirement at the total fund level. This assumes 'surplus at risk' is defined as a 'two sigma' event, and that the fund has a risk budget constraint of 10 percent. Are these kinds of deliberations 'objective' or 'subjective'? Highly subjective, of course, despite our pretence to the contrary."*

And finally, a question reflecting the insight that a good deal of time is being spent in the pension industry today attempting to square round circles:

Q10: *"What happens when the 'cost of risk capital' framework and the actuarial framework don't mesh? If done properly, the former framework tells you what your opportunity set really is, and where to position the balance sheet. The latter framework only tells you that if you want a contribution rate of 'x,' you need to earn a fund return of 'y.' "*

A10: *"You are right to observe that some plan sponsors and their actuaries and accountants feel compelled to choose fiction over fact when the going gets tough. So they will choose a required return of 'y' even if it is not realistic."*

PUTTING THE PARADIGM IN PRACTICE

We presented Table 39.1 to the financial analysts to demonstrate the point that "there are only three basic asset classes in the new paradigm." The "risk minimizing" asset class has zero excess return and excess return

TABLE 39.1 "Asset Allocation" in the New Paradigm

	Risk-Minimizing Strategy	Long-Horizon Risky Strategies		Short-Horizon Risky Strategies		
		A	B	A	B	C
Expected Excess Return	0%	2%	4.5%	0%	4.5%	10%
Excess Return Volatility	0%	20%	20%	2%	20%	5%

volatility relative to the liabilities. Long-horizon risky strategy "A" reflects a passive index fund strategy where the market equity risk premium is 2 percent. Overlaying short-horizon risky strategy "A" on top of its long-horizon counterpart (i.e., "A") reflects the average contribution of active management in the old paradigm world. We assert that the 60 percent equity component of the typical pension fund today is a combination of the two "A" strategies.

Long-horizon risky strategy "B" produces enough expected excess return per unit of balance-sheet risk to be included in the total fund asset mix. What are the components of this strategy? There are a number of possibilities. On the private markets side, there are a variety of private debt and equity opportunities (e.g., infrastructure investments, real estate, buy-out funds, etc.). On the public markets side, there are high-yield bonds and the shares of companies with an adequate projected return on investment relative to their acquisition price. The common orientation of all long-horizon strategies is the projection and valuation of uncertain future cash flows. If these processes are on average successful, the overall portfolio will produce the rate of return embodied in the projections.

What is short-horizon risky strategy "C?" It encompasses the successful market-neutral, adversarial trading strategies of the 1990s. Note that if they could be reliably replicated in this new decade, the search for the holy grail of investing would be over. Life is not that simple, of course. However, what if the search produced a bundle of market-neutral strategies with the reward-risk characteristics of short-horizon risky strategy "B" instead? Assuming zero correlation with its long-horizon counterpart (i.e., "B"), we asked the analysts, how much should we allocate to each, and what would the excess return volatility of the combination be? Further, we asked, if the overall balance sheet risk budget had been set at 10 percent, how much of the risk-minimizing liability portfolio would we have to acquire?

Some simple logic and arithmetic suggests that the two "B" risky strategies should be combined 50-50, and that about one third of the total fund should be invested in the risk-minimizing strategy. The resulting one third–one third–one third asset allocation has an expected excess return of 3 percent and an expected excess return volatility of 10 percent, thus meeting the risk budget constraint. If there was also a minimum "cost of risk capital" constraint of, say, 0.3, the mix would pass that test, too, with its expected reward/risk ratio of 0.3 (i.e., 3 percent/10 percent).

It was no surprise that this demonstration prompted some further questions from the assembled financial analysts:

Q11:   *"How can we have confidence that the expected return calcula-tions that underpin the long-horizon risky strategies that are part of the 'B' package are at all predictive?"*

A11:   *"The entire CFA Institute and its CFA program is predicated on the assumption that professionally conducted financial analysis is of value. This does not imply that risky future cashflows can be predicted accurately. They cannot. However, as long as the inevitable prediction errors are unbiased, and as long as the prediction process in aggregate is not completely random, good financial analysis should lead to a positive correlation between return expectations and realizations over time."*

Q12:   *"As more money is pushed into active market-neutral trad-ing strategies, won't the expected excess returns diminish? Are there not capacity constraints to successful short-horizon risky strategies?"*

A12:   *"Yes, there always are capacity constraints, and yes, expected excess returns will diminish as more money is allocated to histor-ically successful strategies. We conveyed that reality in Table 39.1 by contrasting the very high reported reward/risk ratios of the 1990s (Case 'C'), with the much more modest expectations of Case 'B.' Any fund that believes that even Case 'B' is not real-istic anymore should pass completely on the short-horizon risky strategies option."*

Q13:   *"Could you spell out for me how you got to the one third–one third–one third asset allocation?"*

A13:   *"Under the assumptions set out in Table 39.1, diversification between the two 'B' strategies is maximized with a 50-50 weight-ing. How much does excess return volatility decrease from the 20 percent assumed for each of the two strategies separately? The diversification formula suggests to about 14 percent if the two strategies are uncorrelated. However, the risk budget only allows a maximum 10 percent volatility. How do we get total fund excess return volatility from 14 percent to 10 percent? By introducing the 0 percent excess return volatility asset class (i.e., the risk-minimizing liability portfolio). How much of it do we need? With about 30 percent of the total fund in this asset class, total fund volatility reduces from 14 percent to 10 percent. Ergo, an overall one third–one third–one third allocation between the two 'B' strategies and the risk-minimizing strategy results. With two thirds of the portfolio having an expected excess return of 4.5 percent, the overall portfolio excess return is 3 percent."*

PERFORMANCE MEASUREMENT

What gets measured gets managed. So we had better measure the right things. CEM Benchmarking Inc. (CEM) has been measuring total fund excess return (net of all expenses) relative to the fund's own liability return since the mid-1990s. Many major U.S., Canadian, Dutch, and Australian funds now participate in this benchmarking discipline. On a more micro level, it becomes important to understand how the various portfolios contribute to the overall result. This becomes even more important if a component of compensation is tied to this contribution.

Once again, the financial analysts were on the right page with their questions:

Q14: *"How relevant are the market benchmark-based performance attribution systems that are so popular today, in your proposed strategic management framework?"*

A14: *"Any pension fund performance measurement system not grounded in a liability-relative, balance sheet–oriented perspective is a potential distraction from what is really important. Ideally, even the performance of fund components are evaluated from the perspective of (a) what contribution is this portfolio making to total fund net excess return? and (b) what contribution is this portfolio making to total fund excess return volatility?"*

Q15: *"What kinds of things should we measure that we are not currently measuring?"*

A15: *"The proposed framework offers some interesting new perspectives on what should be measured. For example, long-horizon risky strategies are only successful when they deliver returns over time that are, to some degree at least, in line with expectations. The development of expectations with predictive content in turn depends on developing informed views about the shapes of the uncertain future cash flows being acquired. Thus the focus for performance measurement in this investment sphere should be the accuracy with which investment professionals are predicting uncertain future cashflows in the fund's current and prospective long-horizon investments. Do you know of a performance measurement system with this focus? I don't."*

DID THE YARDSTICKS MOVE FORWARD OR BACKWARD?

We hope you agree that this "Q & A" exchange at the CFA Institute annual conference was instructive. The questions were impressive, and we hope that the answers did the questions justice. Collectively, we have indeed moved the pension fund management yardsticks forward.

CHAPTER 40

Reconnecting GAAP and Common Sense: The Cases of Stock Options and Pensions

"Information is data endowed with relevance and purpose."

Peter Drucker

CLOSING THE INFORMATION GAAP

The failure of simple investment arithmetic to produce a positive prospective equity risk premium as we entered the twenty-first century led us to a three-path characterization of future stock returns in previous writings. The least likely path was a continuation of the outsized excess returns of the 1990s. The more likely outcomes were (1) bond-like equity returns for many years or (2) the much more rapid reappearance of a significant equity risk premium through an up to 50 percent price reduction in the broad equity market indexes. In mid-summer 2002, events appeared to be conspiring to produce outcome (2) rather than (1).

Media coverage notwithstanding, outcome (2) is not a universally bad thing. Prospective equity returns are now higher. Enterprise-level risk management disciplines will now get the respect and attention they deserve. The effectiveness of both corporate and fund governance structures is now no longer taken for granted, as is the ability of generally accepted accounting principles (GAAP) to provide investors with data "endowed with relevance and purpose" as Peter Drucker once defined information. In short, Joseph Schumpeter's characterization of democratic capitalism as a process of "creative destruction" is still with us.

Two particularly vexing accounting issues receiving a lot of attention today are the GAAP rules regarding employee stock options and defined benefit (DB) pension plans. Both can be (1) highly material elements of employee compensation and (2) highly material items in financial statements. We show below that current GAAP rules fail Drucker's "endowed with relevance and purpose" test in both cases, and thus should be destroyed. Fortunately, the creative application of common sense can fix both failures. Schumpeter would be pleased.

WHEN ARE EMPLOYEE STOCK OPTIONS "EXPENSES"?

Never has an office clippings file grown faster than the one labeled "employee stock options." It seems like everyone has an opinion on this now hot topic. Some say such options are bad, allowing managers to rip off shareholders. Others say options align the interests of managers and shareholders, as long as they are properly used and disclosed. Some say options should be expensed as a component of compensation. Others say not, as option issuance involves no outlay of cash. GAAP flies in the face of common sense on the subject, permitting options to be expensed—or not. The media are fond of giving Warren Buffett the last word on the subject, quoting his now famous retort: "If options should not go into the calculation of expenses, where in the world should they go?"

The answer, of course, is: "On the balance sheet." Why? Because employee stock options represent capital transactions between a corporation and its employees. Specifically, the corporation issues legally enforceable claims to employees, giving them the right to purchase shares at predetermined prices over predetermined periods of time. This creates a corporate liability that should be recorded on its balance sheet. What does the corporation get in return? It gets access to the "human capital" represented by the employee option recipients. This claim sets up an intangible asset that should also be recorded on the corporate balance sheet.

How would this common-sense principle work in practice? Here are some guidelines:

- At first issuance, options are recorded as financial liabilities on the balance sheet at values established by the standard option valuation formula. An equivalent value is entered on the asset side as a "claim on human capital." As the two values are equal, there is no immediate expense to be recorded.
- With the passage of time, the "claim on human capital" asset is amortized to zero over the length of the option contract. The option liability is written up or down on a "mark-to-market" basis. Liability

increases (when the stock price rises) are recorded as financial expenses on the earnings statement, liability decreases (when the stock price falls) as financial gains.

- If the option is exercised, the "claim on human capital" asset is immediately written down to zero. The option liability is adjusted to the difference between the stock's market value and its exercise price, and the net result is moved off the balance sheet unto the earnings statement. (If the option expires unexercised or if the employee departs before the expiry date, both the asset and liability are extinguished, and the cumulative earnings statement impact is zero).

Is all this not eminently sensible?

THE COMMON-SENSE SOLUTION IN ACTION

While we would love to take credit for this common-sense solution, we can't. It was first suggested (as far as we know) by Reuven Brenner and Donald Luskin in the May/June 2002 issue of *The American Spectator*. Table 40.1 shows their estimates of how their proposal would have affected IBM's financial statements from 1995 to 2001. Note that by 2001, Brenner and Luskin suggest IBM's financial statements were underreporting assets and liabilities by $4.4 billion and $10.8 billion, respectively, and overstating pretax earnings by $5.4 billion. However, note that in 2000, pretax earnings were understated by $3.4 billion, as GAAP failed to account for the decline in the value of outstanding employee stock options in that year.

In short, we believe that the Brenner-Luskin approach meets the "endowed with relevance and purpose" test for information. It forces boards of directors to square an explicit value for the stock options being granted with the implied value of the "claims on human capital" the options are supposedly securing in the interest of shareholders. The approach correctly signals that the issuance of options effectively levers the corporate balance sheet, making it more risky and earnings more volatile. Maybe most importantly, the approach provides direct insight into whether the cumulative impact of employee stock option issuance is a win-win proposition for employees and shareholders alike with the passage of time. That, after all, is the information shareholders really want.

CURRENT PENSION ACCOUNTING RULES DEFY COMMON SENSE, TOO

The office clippings file on pension accounting has also been growing impressively. The media are having a field day with another obvious

TABLE 40.1 The Impact of Employee Stock Options On IBM's Financial Statements

	Options Issued (Mill)	Stock Price	As Reported			Restated for Options			Impact On		
			Assets ($B)	Liability ($B)	Pre-Tax Net ($B)	Assets ($B)	Liability ($B)	Pre-Tax Net ($B)	Assets ($B)	Liability ($B)	Pre-Tax Net ($B)
1995	26	$ 23	80.3	57.9	7.8	80.6	58.9	6.8	0.3	1.0	−1.0
1996	31	$ 38	81.1	59.5	8.6	81.6	61.8	6.9	0.5	2.3	−1.7
1997	43	$ 52	81.5	61.9	9.0	82.2	65.5	7.3	0.7	3.6	−1.7
1998	41	$ 92	86.1	66.7	9.0	87.3	74.6	4.3	1.2	7.9	−4.7
1999	43	$108	87.5	67.0	11.8	90.0	76.5	9.5	2.5	9.5	−2.3
2000	43	$ 85	88.3	67.7	11.5	91.8	73.6	14.9	3.5	5.9	3.4
2001	43	$121	88.3	64.7	10.9	92.8	75.5	5.5	4.5	10.8	−5.4

Source: Reuvin Brenner, and Donald Luskin. "Where Options Belong," *The American Spectator*, May–June 2002.

GAAP-driven inconsistency. How can it be, the media want to know, that while DB pension balance sheets have been devastated for over two years now by falling asset values and rising liabilities, corporations continue to report positive pension plan contributions to corporate earnings ($54 billion in 2001 for the 50 largest U.S. corporations, despite a $35 billion drop in pension fund values)? What's the "game"?

The essence of the "game" is very simple. Unlike any other financial business, GAAP permits the DB pension "business" to anticipate earning a spread between the return on the pension fund and the liability discount rate before it is actually earned. So even today, for example, the typical corporate sponsor continues to assume it will earn 9 percent on pension assets while valuing its liabilities using a 6 percent discount rate. So for every $1 trillion of pension assets and liabilities, GAAP permits publicly traded companies to print $30 billion in annual earnings forever, while the impact of investment losses can be spread over many years. Surely this defies common sense!

How does common sense inform us on what pension accounting rules "endowed with relevance and purpose" should look like? Here, unlike the case of employee stock options, we can refer back to our own previous work on this question. Indeed, we can go all the way back to the mid-1980s, when we testified to the Financial Accounting Standards Board (FASB) on their proposed Financial Accounting Standard (FAS) 87 pension accounting rules. A summary of what we said then, and say again now, follows.

SENSIBLE PENSION ACCOUNTING RULES

FAS 87's problems start with its convoluted definition of the annual "pension expense." It is an unpalatable mélange of three incompatible ingredients:

1. The annual service cost is the increase in the pension liability due to new benefits earned in that year. Service costs will always be a positive expense.
2. The net interest expense is the liability discount rate applied to the accrued liabilities, less the projected return on plan assets applied to the pension fund. This item could be a positive expense (in very underfunded situations), but is usually negative (because of the positive spread assumption permitted under GAAP we have already discussed).
3. Amortization costs arise for two reasons. First, plan amendments can lead to additional (and hence positive) prior service costs, which can be amortized over the future life of active participants. Second, experience gains relative to assumptions (negative pension expense elements) or

losses (positive elements) can be amortized using one of a number of permissible techniques.

What do you get when you mix all of these positive and negative pension expense ingredients together? Whatever it is, it surely fails the Drucker "endowed with relevance and purpose" test.

What approach would pass the test? Common sense suggests that as a first step, a clear distinction must be made between the estimated cost of the pension benefits earned in any given year and the gains or losses associated with running a dedicated pension annuity subsidiary. The former is clearly a component of total annual compensation, and hence a component of annual operating costs. The latter should be treated as the operating results of a corporate financial subsidiary, and should be reported on as such.

COMMON SENSE IN ACTION

How would these principles work in practice? Let's take manufacturing corporation X with a $5 billion annual wage bill. To get to total compensation for the year, we need two further items. One, the expenses related to employee stock options, have already been discussed. We noted that these expenses could be positive or negative in any given year. The other expense is the value of deferred compensation earned during the year related to pensions (and possibly other benefits such as retiree health care). Properly defined, the value of deferred compensation will always be a positive expense item. Assume that in the year X's wage bill is $5 billion, its option expense is $1 billion, and its deferred compensation expense another $1 billion. Thus, its total compensation expense for the year is $7 billion. Just to complete the picture, let's assume other operating expenses add up to $3 billion, and that revenues are $15 billion. Thus, X's pretax operating earnings are $5 billion.

Now assume that corporation X also has a deferred compensation–related debt servicing subsidiary, with mark-to-market assets and liabilities both equaling $10 billion at the beginning of the year. How should X report the results of this subsidiary in the coming year on its financial statements? Common sense suggests that X should report the market value of the subsidiary's assets and liabilities at the end of the year, and report the change in balance sheet surplus as a component of its pretax earnings. So if year-end asset and liability values were both $11 billion, for example, asset gains were offset by liability increases, and the earnings contribution of the subsidiary to X pretax earnings for the year is zero.

Table 40.2 displays the financial fate of Corporation X's deferred compensation–related debt servicing subsidiary under the assumptions that

TABLE 40.2 Typical 1997 to 2001 U.S. DB Pension Plan Financial Experience

End of	Assets	Liabilities	Funded Ratio	Surplus	Contributions to Pretax Net
1996	$10.0B	$10.0B	1	0	—
1997	$11.9B	$10.9B	1.09	$1.0B	$1.0B
1998	$13.7B	$12.1B	1.13	$16B	$0.6B
1999	$15.9B	$11.1B	1.43	$4.8B	$3.2B
2000	$16.1B	$13.2B	1.22	$2.9B	−$2.9B
2001	$15.4B	$14.2B	1.08	$1.2B	−$1.7B

Source: Based on average U.S. fund experience in the CEM database. CEM Benchmarking Inc. 2001.

(1) its end-of-1996 balance sheet had assets and liabilities of $10 billion, (2) the size and composition of its workforce held steady over the 1997 to 2001 period, and (3) that its asset and liability returns matched the average experience of U.S. pension plans in the CEM Benchmarking Inc. (CEM) database over the five-year period. Note that by the end of 1999, the subsidiary had contributed a cumulative $4.8 billion to X's pretax bottom line, only to see most of it dissipate in 2000 and 2001. Annual contributions to consolidated pretax earnings range from +$3.2 billion to—$1.9 billion. Relative to X's operating earnings of $5 billion, these are very big numbers. Is X managing its risks sensibly? What business is it in, anyway? Manufacturing or pensions? Do its shareholders know?

CARPE DIEM

A number of events since 2000 have conspired to create a renewed demand for accounting data endowed with relevance and purpose in the cases of employee stock options and DB pensions. Such GAAP windows do not open very often. May we seize the opportunity to get the rules right. Carpe diem![1]

---

[1] Since this chapter was written, the expensing of employee stock options has become mandatory. Accounting reform for pensions has occurred in Europe, and is imminent in North America.

CHAPTER 41

Is Sri Bunk?

*"... SRI presents a Zen-like paradox. It will only become
completely successful when it ceases to exist altogether. ... "*

Matthew Kiernan

Innovest Strategic Value Advisors

SRI AND ZEN

SRI, or socially responsible investing, has to rank as one of the most ambiguous concepts in the investment world today. To many of its supporters, the future of humankind hinges on the broad adoption of SRI principles by investors around the globe. To many of its detractors, SRI is a vacuous "do-gooder" concept that has been turned into a marketing gimmick by an investment industry forever looking for new ways to collect fees from a naïve investing public.

So what is SRI? Savior of the globe or marketing gimmick? After careful study, we conclude that SRI indeed presents a Zen-like paradox. It can only become a useful investment concept by disappearing from the investment lexicon altogether. This chapter shows how to make SRI disappear, but only after salvaging something very useful and valuable from the idea.

WHAT IS "SOCIALLY RESPONSIBLE INVESTING"?

To understand what people who talk about "socially responsible investing" mean by it, we turn to a July 2002 study titled "Do UK Pension Funds Invest Responsibly?" by David Coles and Duncan Green (www.justpensions.org). Coles and Green surveyed the SRI practices of 14 U.K. pension funds managing about 20 percent of all U.K. pension assets. Here are the four criteria they used to judge the SRI practices of these funds:

1. **Policies.** How clearly does a fund's Statement of Investment Policies and Goals articulate why social, environmental, and ethical issues should be considered in the fund's investment program?
2. **People.** Who is accountable for monitoring the social, environmental, and ethical performance of the companies the fund invests in?
3. **Implementation.** How is the assessment of social, environmental, and ethical issues integrated into the fund's investment and risk management processes?
4. **Transparency.** Is there an effective dissemination of the fund's SRI activities?

How well did the 14 U.K. funds score by these four criteria? According to the authors: "... *actual practice is substantially worse than we had expected. We can only conclude that poor practice by major pension funds on socially responsible investment is the norm.*"

Some examples will help explain why Coles and Green were so disappointed. In the majority of cases they found:

- **Policies.** Weak wording implying that the assessment of social, environmental, and ethical performance plays little real part in investment decision making.
- **People.** Nothing is done. No specialists are employed internally. No assessment is made of the SRI capability of external managers, nor is the activity outsourced to anyone else.
- **Implementation.** Funds rely on their external investment managers to consider SRI issues, but have no internal procedures to check how well they are doing so.
- **Transparency.** The fund Web sites provide no relevant information, probably because there is none to provide.

We have little hesitation extending these Coles-Green "poor practices" findings outside the United Kingdom, especially to North American funds. What are the consequences of the findings? According to Coles and Green, they are dire. The reputations of pension funds and their trustees are at risk, and governments are bound to step in and legally force good SRI practices on the institutional investment world.

A SLIPPERY SLOPE?

What are we to make of the Coles-Green findings and their suggested consequences? Would the integration of social, environmental, and ethical considerations into the investment processes of pension and endowment assets really create a better, greener, fairer world while at the same time enhancing investment returns? Or is SRI bunk?

It seems to us that the SRI movement, however well intended, places the trustees of pension and endowment funds on a very slippery slope. Whose social and ethical considerations are to be contemplated? Which environmental standards are to be adopted? Are the answers to these questions really so obvious that we can assign funds passing or failing SRI grades, and predict dire consequences for the failing funds? Is all this not a little too simplistic? Or worse, is all this not simply a marketing ploy too clever by half?

However, might there be a message somewhere inside all this SRI noise that could in fact be useful, if only we can figure out what it is? We think there is. The enduring message inside the noise is that sustainability matters. More specifically, there can be no long-term investment value creation without investment sustainability. Therefore, investment sustainability is worthy of careful study and analysis. Let's see what happens when we take the "R" out of SRI, and concentrate simply on long-horizon investing with a focus on sustainability?

SUSTAINABLE INVESTING

We have been promoting a major "rethink" of asset class definitions for years now, and steadfastly arguing that there are only three asset classes at the macro strategic level:

1. **Risk-minimizing.** Claims on default risk-free future cash flows that match future payment obligations with as little mismatch risk as possible in terms of both cash-flow duration and inflation sensitivity.
2. **Long-horizon risky (LHR).** Claims on uncertain long-horizon cash flows acquired at prices that reflect the investor requirement to earn a preestablished minimum risk premium. The greater the cash-flow uncertainty, the greater the risk premium required.
3. **Short-horizon risky (SHR).** Claims on uncertain profits earned through the execution of short-horizon adversarial trading strategies (involving both long and short positions) in listed securities and other financial instruments.

For most investment funds with long horizons and risk-bearing capabilities, the preponderance of their investments will typically fall into the LHR category. While commercial real estate and private equity may come to mind first as LHR assets, publicly listed corporations are in fact the largest LHR investment category, as long as they are approached with an investment rather than a trading mind-set. In practice, this reality is often confounded by the issuance and acceptance of "active management" mandates that attempt to blend elements of LHR and SHR investing together.

From a pure LHR investment perspective, today's stock price represents the present value of an uncertain long-horizon stream of future dividends (some people might say "earnings" rather than dividends, but recent events have demonstrated once again that "earnings" are too fuzzy a concept to take very seriously). The Gordon formula converts a stock's current dividend yield plus future dividend growth into its long-term return: $R = y + g$. In other words, long-horizon equity returns are all about a company's ability to sustain and grow its dividend payments to owners. It follows that the central focus of LHR investment analysis must be to assess that ability.

ASSESSING THE SUSTAINABILITY OF DIVIDEND GROWTH

The focus of traditional investment analysis was largely on "tangibles": How much plant and equipment did a company own? What return on assets was it generating? What were the company's future investment plans? What shape was its balance sheet in? What was the market paying for these tangibles in relation to their replacement cost? How did all these assessments translate into a realistic dividend growth projection? These were the questions at the heart of investment analysis not that long ago.

In his 2001 book *Intangibles: Management, Measurement, and Reporting* (Washington, DC: Brookings Institution Press,), Professor Baruch Lev argues persuasively that the size of the universe of companies where tangibles-based investment analysis continues to be of primary importance has fallen dramatically. For many corporations, it is now the shape of their intangible assets and liabilities that will determine their future economic prospects.

For these companies, a series of new questions is far more important: How strong are the company's brands and its customer loyalty? How effective is its research and development (R&D) program in protecting and enhancing its franchises? Does the company manage its risks effectively? Does it have enlightened governance, management, and human resources policies? Does it provide clear and timely information about its activities and finances?

These latter questions must be at the heart of investment analysis for most companies today. Asking them has nothing to do with getting good marks from the SRI police. It has everything to do with providing pension and endowment fund stakeholders with adequate, sustainable risk premiums on their LHR investments.

As an aside, we note that the flip side of the SRI movement is the CSR (i.e., corporate social responsibility) movement. Exactly the same arguments hold. CSR as a pure investor relations ploy is an empty gimmick. CSR as a commitment to maximize the value of a company's intangible assets and minimize the value of its intangible liabilities is just another way of saying it intends to create a sustainable stream of growing dividends for its shareholders in the new world. But if that is what it means, why does it need to be labelled CSR?

FROM SAYING TO DOING: A CASE STUDY

In the context set out above, a recent joint venture between the Dutch public employees pension fund Algemeen Burgerlijk Pensioenfonds (ABP) and the Canadian research boutique Innovest Strategic Value Advisors is noteworthy. They will jointly manage an LHR investment fund made up of companies in the MSCI (WORLD) universe. ABP will provide the investment analytics from a tangible assets/liabilities perspective. So its analysts will look at variables like balance sheet strength, return on equity, free cash flow, and various traditional valuation criteria.

Innovest for its part will provide the investment analytics from an intangible assets/liabilities perspective. So its analysts will focus on and assess a company's strategic governance capabilities, the quality of its human capital management, its franchise strength and R&D programs, and its ability to manage and possibly profit from environmental issues. Finally, each company's tangible and intangible asset/liability "alpha scores" are combined, based on their judged relative importance in each company's case.

Once again, the objective of this joint venture is not to score a perfect 10 on the SRI scale (though it well might!). Instead, the goal is to earn a healthy risk premium for ABP stakeholders in an investment environment different from that of previous decades in many ways. There is nothing new in this goal. What is new is the design of the analytical disciplines and tools being employed to achieve it.

REDEFINING THE SRI REVOLUTION

Some people claim that SRI will revolutionize institutional investing. We don't think it will, because the idea is too fuzzy to change investment behavior in any fundamental way. Having said that, we do believe that behind SRI lies an important reality that should impact how LHR investment analysis is conducted today and how its conclusions are implemented. A profound shift has occurred in the relative importance of the tangible and intangible elements in corporate wealth creation processes. For many companies, managing intangibles is increasingly what wealth creation is all about. Investors ignore this shift at their peril.[1]

---

[1]There has been a significant shift in both thinking and behavior in the SRI field since this chapter was originally written. The sustainable/responsible investing movement is indeed going mainstream. An important example is the United Nations Principles of Responsible Investing which have been endorsed by many of the world's leading investment organizations (www.unpri.org). See also the proceedings of a recent workshop on long-horizon investing organized by the Rotman International Centre for Pension Management (www.rotman.utoronto.ca/icpm).

Alpha, Beta, Bafflegab: Investment Theory as Marketing Strategy

"... 'Portable Alpha' has taken on several meanings because it is a supply-driven term shaped by each money management 'supplier.'..."

BernsteinResearch

Sanford C. Bernstein & Co.

GIVING ALPHA AND BETA A REST

Recent perusal of a spate of investment publications ranging from the news-oriented *Pensions & Investments* and *Investments and Pensions Europe* at one end, to the more analytical *Financial Analysts Journal* at the other, has led us to conclude that it is time to give the terms *alpha* and *beta* a rest. Two specific "tipping points" that sparked this conclusion were a study by Bernstein Research's Vadim Zlotnikov and Guillermo MacLean titled "Portable Alpha and the Beautiful Art of Language" (March 2006), and an article by Barton Waring and Laurence Siegel in the March/April 2006 issue of the *Financial Analysts Journal* titled "The Myth of the Absolute Return Investor." What struck us most about these two pieces is the extraordinary degree to which the investment industry is able to define the investment game to suit its own purposes, and to engage in semantics-focused debates that have little to do with the financial welfare of the industry's ultimate customers.

In the context of retirement savings, the financial welfare of the ultimate customers is surely best served by providing them with postretirement income streams that are adequate, affordable, and not subject to serious downside surprises. One would think that this worthy goal would frame both how the investment industry serving the pensions sector defines financial risk and how it articulates the risk/reward characteristics of available investment strategies. This chapter offers evidence that this is generally not the case. Instead, many investment firms focus on devising strategies they believe will enhance market share. Today, this is done by adapting investment theory to serve marketing needs, turning theoretical constructs such as alpha and beta into tools of persuasion. Not surprisingly, such strategies easily spark an industrial war of words about what is myth and what is reality. In the process, the larger questions of how to best serve ultimate customer needs are lost. The chapter goes on to restate and apply investment theory so that it focuses on customer needs, rather than those of investment firms.

THE BEAUTIFUL ART OF LANGUAGE

The Bernstein Research piece states up front that its goal is to help investment and advice firms think through their best business strategies in the current low-return environment. Authors Zlotnikov and MacLean conclude that the current hot "Portable Alpha" phenomenon is not some phrase *du jour* that will turn into a passing fad. Instead, investment firms will have to be able to articulate what they do, and how they add value, in the context of the new "Portable Alpha" framework. As a generic definition, this framework refers to financial engineering processes "that combine two distinct components—an index-tracking component plus an absolute-return engine ... this engine should not correlate with the index ... the index-tracking component is referred to as beta, and the engine as alpha. ...."

The bottom line of the piece is telling. The quest is not about achieving some precise definition of "Portable Alpha" or even about whether the concept is real or not. It is also not about the marketing prospects of specific "Portable Alpha" products. Instead, the authors argue, it is all about using the construct to frame what any specific investment firm brings to the table in the context of hedge funds, index funds, special-purpose funds, and derivatives-based strategies. In the authors' own words, these concepts now must be "put in the context of today's explosion of possible and constructible alpha constructs, as well as the creative uses of language in marketing as the means of shaping demand and supply of a variety of investment management services." Wow!

THE MYTH OF "ABSOLUTE-RETURN INVESTING"

In their *Financial Analysts Journal* piece, authors Waring and Siegel also write about the creative uses of language in the marketing of investment services. Their quarrel is with the term *absolute-return investing*. Specifically, they observe that in the current period of low prospective stock and bond market returns, the prospect of adding an "absolute-return asset class" into a pension fund's asset mix policy can be made to sound very appealing. So not surprisingly, absolute return–based marketing strategies have flourished. However, the authors quickly point out that there is really no such thing as pure absolute-return investing. Instead, *all* investing is ultimately benchmark relative. They support their assertion with examples. The return on a zero-beta hedge fund should be evaluated in a return on cash plus (or minus) alpha framework. The return on Warren Buffett's Berkshire Hathaway stock should be evaluated in a cost of capital (or blend of beta payoffs) framework.

Behind these specific examples lies their ultimate "everything is relative" argument. They state that the 40-year-old capital asset pricing model is "the foundation for how investment professionals understand and decompose total returns on portfolios today." This model shows how the total return on any portfolio can be decomposed into a market component (beta) and a manager-specific component (alpha). The authors call this "perhaps the most profound insight in modern finance." Why is this separation principle so important? One reason is that beta returns can be earned cheaply, while skill-based alpha returns are far more difficult and expensive to achieve. Also, alpha-earning capacity can be further enhanced by simultaneously being "long" attractive securities and "short" unattractive ones up to the point where a net-zero beta position is achieved. However, this does not make it an "absolute-return" strategy, but a "market-neutral, long-short" strategy. Got it?

INVESTMENT THEORY WITH THE END IN MIND

In a pensions context, what does all the foregoing have to do with providing people with retirement income streams that are adequate, affordable, and not subject to serious downside surprises? Stated differently, if we proceeded to derive a normative investment theory with this end in mind, would it look anything like alpha-beta theories (portable, stationary, or otherwise) discussed by Zlotnikov-MacLean, Waring-Siegel, and by a myriad of other current authors and investment conference speakers?

Let's find out.

We have already stated the goal of our theory: to provide people with retirement income streams that are adequate, affordable, and not subject to serious downside surprises. So a logical place to start is to define a strategy that would deliver a future payment stream with maximum certainty. This could be called the *risk-minimizing* (RM) portfolio. With long-term real interest rates at 2 percent or even lower, it costs a lot of money today to buy a stream of future pension payments that meet a reasonable "adequacy" test with an RM strategy. So people might want to trade off some future payment certainty for greater affordability potential. Simply put, they may be willing to take on some mismatch risk versus the RM portfolio in return for a chance at a better future pension at an affordable cost.

This raises the question of how to best characterize attractive risky investment strategies. Clearly, they should offer generous enough excess return prospects over the RM strategy to make undertaking the mismatch risk worthwhile. The nature of modern financial markets suggests two classes of risky strategies could be considered: One class focuses on earning short-horizon trading profits; the other on buying, holding, and nurturing long-horizon uncertain cash flows. Let's call the former "short-horizon risky" (SHR) strategies, and the latter "long-horizon risky" (LHR). SHR strategies are adversarial, producing winners and losers. The winners outpredict and outimplement the losers in short-horizon trading games involving various types of securities, financial contracts, or their derivatives. LHR strategies result in long-horizon cash flows that are smaller, equal to, or larger than expectations at the time of purchase. The nature of the cash flow–generating instrument could be a debt instrument, an equity ownership instrument, or a private contract between the selling and buying parties. LHR strategies may also produce winners and losers, but not necessarily. For example, if new owner(s) institute a superior governance process to oversee the operational aspects of their investment, which in turn leads to greater growth and stability in the investment's cash flow (e.g., dividend payments) than originally expected, there are only winners.

THE CRITICAL ROLE OF FUND GOVERNANCE

Simply getting the three categories of possible pension fund investment strategies straight cannot be the end of the investment theory story. Investment strategies can be implemented well or poorly. The critical "well-or-poorly" determinant is the motivation and the capability of a pension fund's governance mechanism. If the mechanism is weak, the best strategy categorization in the world won't help. Inevitably, funds with weak internal governance mechanisms are de facto managed "from the outside in" by collections of for-profit advisers and money managers who position themselves between the fund governors and the pension fund beneficiaries whose financial interests the governors are supposed to represent. Coming back to the basic thesis of this chapter, the for-profit suppliers of advisory and investment management services will continue to define the rules of the institutional investment game (including its language) as long as they are permitted to do so. Why? For the simple reason that it serves their financial interests.

How would the rules of the institutional investment game change if pension funds were managed "from the inside out" rather than "from the outside in"? Stated differently, what kind of difference would pension fund governance mechanisms that are strong in incentives and capabilities make? Here is a five-point snapshot. Such mechanisms would:

1. **Ensure that the "pension deal" is governable** in the sense that risk, and tolerances for bearing it, can be (and are) clearly articulated and managed.
2. **Delegate management of the fund to a competent CEO,** thus recognizing that it is foolhardy for an oversight body to try and manage a complex financial institution. The CEO becomes accountable for developing a strategic plan for the organization and implementing it.
3. **Insist that the fund has a clearly articulated set of investment beliefs** that can serve as the foundation on which investment strategy is articulated, implemented, and its performance measured.
4. **Insist on an organization design built for high-performance**—developing a proper balance between financial and nonfinancial incentives is critical.
5. **Institute a self-evaluation discipline** to ensure that the governance mechanism itself is, and continues to be, effective.

In short, pension fund governance mechanisms that are strong in the right incentives and capabilities would revolutionize institutional investing.

PENSION REVOLUTION

Seventy years ago, the great economist John Maynard Keynes lamented in his famous opus *The General Theory of Employment, Interest and Money* that there was too much "beauty contest" investing in the world, and not enough investment-driven real wealth creation. Peter Drucker made a similar observation in his 1976 book *The Unseen Revolution: How Pension Fund Socialism Came to America.* These "short term-ism" laments by Keynes and Drucker have not receded over the course of the past 30 years. If anything, "short term-ism" is getting a rougher ride from a more diverse group of voices today than ever before. What is going on here? An unpublished draft paper titled "The Problem with Corporate Governance" by Roger Martin, Dean of the Rotman School of Management, University of Toronto, sees "short term-ism" caused by a fundamental structural problem in the corporate governance chain (see www.rotman.utoronto.ca/icpm).

The paper argues that independent directors in widely held, publicly traded corporations have neither the incentives nor the capabilities to protect outside shareholders when they most need that protection. The result is a "short term-ism" mind-set by both inside corporate managers and outside investment managers.

A possible way out of this trap is the presence of a controlling shareholder interested in "moving upstream from creating [short-term] shareholder value to creating sustainable competitive advantage and defining moral purpose." Martin offers Ken Thomson (Thomson Corporation) as an example of a controlling shareholder who fits this "upstream" profile. We would go further and offer pension funds (and other natural long-horizon investors) as a much larger, potentially far more potent, class of major shareholders that should have an "upstream" mind-set. This would close the virtuous "pension fund socialism" circle Drucker foresaw 30 years ago.

However, we should all be clear about the caveat needed to close the circle: Pension funds must themselves have governance mechanisms that can pass the proper "incentives and capabilities" test. Without such mechanisms, institutional investment practices and language will forever be driven by the needs of the for-profit financial services industry. And we will have to live with alpha, beta, bafflegab forever.

CHAPTER 43

The Turner Pensions Commission Report: A Blueprint for Global Pension Reform

"A year ago, the Pensions Commission concluded that the pension system was heading for trouble. ... On November 30, the government-appointed body, chaired by Lord Turner, a former head of the Confederation of British Industry, set out a new destination for the pension system, and charted a course to get there."

The Economist, December 1, 2005

PENSION WISDOM FROM THE UNITED KINGDOM

To its credit, the U.K. Treasury has shown a persistent willingness to study pension reform. In 2000, it launched the Myners Review to study pension investment trends and practices, and to make recommendation for improvement. Then just two years ago, the Treasury launched the Turner Commission with the more ambitious aim of studying workplace pension system trends and practices as a whole and to once again make recommendations for improvement. In response, as *The Economist* noted, the Commission has produced a report that proposes a new destination for the United Kingdom's pension system and charts a course to get there. This chapter shows the Turner proposals have application well beyond the United Kingdom's borders.

We studied the Myners report carefully when it came out in 2001, praised what we liked about it, and critiqued aspects of the report we were less enthusiastic about. Here, we subject the Turner report to the same treatment. There is much to like about this report. It is thorough in its analyses and wise in its recommendations. We noted above that the broad sweep of its assessment and recommendations are not United Kingdom specific. They are relevant to all countries genuinely interested in reforming their pension systems. Thus, there is much in this report for all of us.

TURNER'S RECOMMENDATIONS

What is the essence of the Turner Commission recommendations? It boils down to these three actions:

1. Stabilize the pay-go Pillar 1 (i.e., universal) part of the national pension system so that it provides a transparent, minimum income floor for all (e.g., 30 percent of the medium wage), but at the same time adapt Pillar 1 to the reality of workforce aging and increasing longevity so as to stabilize costs (e.g., raise the age of eligibility gradually over a number of decades).
2. Increase funded Pillar 2 (i.e., workplace-based) pension coverage dramatically through auto-enrollment in a National Pension Savings Scheme (NPSS) for all workers who are not members of a workplace-based pension plan, but with an "opt-out" clause. The NPSS should target to raise income replacement from the 30 percent of pay target of Pillar 1, to 50 percent of pay for the median income worker. This implies an 8 percent NPSS contribution rate, to be split 5 percent for the worker and 3 percent for the employer. Total contributions should be capped at 3,000 pounds per annum. There should be autopilot, low-cost investment and annuitization options attached to NPSS. Again, "opt-out" options should be provided.
3. Establish NPSS as an arm's-length pension agency with its own governance, executive, and operations elements. Target an NPSS all-inclusive unit cost ceiling of 30 bps (0.3 percent) per annum.

Three simple (in concept, at least), but powerful recommendations! Recommendations that should be studied carefully for their relevance outside the United Kingdom as well.

THE POWER OF INTEGRATIVE THINKING

Myners was asked to study why U.K. pension funds were not investing in private equity, but he broadened his mandate to study pension investment practices in general. Similarly, Turner was asked to study dysfunction in workplace pensions, but he broadened his mandate to study the U.K. pension system as a whole. There is an important lesson in these two "broadening the mandate" decisions. In Chapter 12 we quoted Jane Jacobs as writing (in *Dark Age Ahead* [New York: Random House, 2004]): "Science has made little progress dealing with whole systems. It tends to become arrested in the stage of singling out isolated bits, with little grasp of how these interact with other bits of integrated systems." The point is clear. Trying to fix a smaller bit in a larger whole cannot be done well (if at all) without first understanding that larger whole. Solving complex pension problems requires system-wide integrative thinking.

The Turner report offers an excellent example of this logic at work. One of its key conclusions was that private-sector workplace pension plan coverage in the United Kingdom (just like in North America) is far too low, and more likely to shrink than grow in the future. So how to reverse this disturbing trend? We saw that Turner's answer was automatic enrollment of the entire noncovered segment of the U.K. workforce in NPSS, with an opt-out provision. This makes good sense, given the findings of a rapidly growing body of behavioral finance research that suggests people have a pretty good general idea what is "good" for them financially, but have a terrible time turning this general idea into a tangible action plan. However, you can't *force* workers to do the right thing, hence the automatic enrollment in a scheme that is "good" for them, but with an opt-out provision. Human inertia will take care of the rest. Likely, few will exercise their "opt-out" option, unless they really have a good reason to.

But Turner noticed there was a catch to the NPSS auto-enrollment proposal. Eligibility to a part of Pillar 1 of the U.K. pension system is means tested, thus targeting the lowest-income retirees. That in turn means this group has no incentive to participate in the NPSS, as participation would mean losing part of their Pillar 1 payments. Stated differently, under the current system, the effective marginal tax rate on NPSS retirement income is excessively high. Thus, the Turner Commission notes, a consequence of its recommendations is that future accruals of Pillar 1 pension rights must be universal, and not subject to means testing.

BLUEPRINT FOR GLOBAL PENSION REFORM

Readers know that we have been on our own quest to design the optimal workplace pension arrangement for some years now. In Chapter 11, for example, we wrote that Pillar 2 pension plans should ideally cover most of the workforce, and address two challenges in their design:

1. Pension plans should be designed so that workers are not left to make complex savings and investment decisions on their own.
2. Pension plans should be structured so that decisions are made solely in the interests of plan participants by arm's-length "expert" organizations.

These requirements led to the unveiling of TOPS (i.e., The Optimal Pension System), which is set out in Figure 43.1. TOPS has six critical characteristics, with the first three addressing the "human foibles"–related issues uncovered by behavioral finance research. The second three address the "agency" issues first articulated by Peter Drucker 30 years ago and underpinned by a series of research-based findings since that time.

The similarities between Ambachtsheer's TOPS and Turner's NPSS are noteworthy, but really not very surprising. If two unbiased, deductive reasoning processes start from the same research base and try to "solve" the same problem (i.e., design the optimal workplace pension arrangement), they should produce similar answers. Whether dubbed TOPS or NPSS, the widespread adoption of pension plans with the characteristics set out in the box can positively revolutionize Pillar 2 pension coverage and delivery in the developed and developing economies around the globe.

For example:

■ **In the United States.** What would have happened if the Bush administration had followed the Turner Commission approach and (1) stabilized Social Security and (2) introduced a U.S. version of the NPSS as two related but separate initiatives? Our judgment is that, had this been

TOPS: THE OPTIMAL PENSION SYSTEM

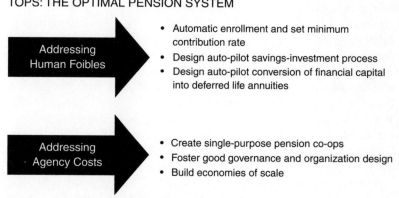

FIGURE 43.1   The Optimal Pension System

done, the United States would be a lot closer to genuine pension reform today than is currently the case. Meanwhile, sponsors of U.S.-based workplace pension plans in both the public and private sectors should be actively thinking about how to move their current defined benefit (DB) and defined contribution (DC) plans into TOPS/NPSS type of arrangements.

- **In Canada.** With a reasonably stable Pillar 1 structure already in place, systemic Pillar 2 problems should now be urgently addressed. The TOPS/NPSS design shows the way ahead. The basic formula could be applied nationally or on a province-by-province level. As in the United Kingdom, the means-testing element in the Pillar 1 part of the pension system will have to be eliminated. As in the United States, sponsors of already existing workplace pension plans in both the public and private sectors should be actively thinking about how to move their current DB and DC plans into TOPS/NPSS-type arrangements.

- **In the Netherlands.** There is already a reasonably stable Pillar 1 and broad Pillar 2 coverage through mandatory participation in workplace pension plans, and a regulatory process that will soon require "mark-to-market" valuation and risk buffering in DB plans. All this makes moving existing Pillar 2 pension arrangements to TOPS/NPSS-type arrangements a logical next step for the Dutch pension system.

- **In Australia.** There is already broad Pillar 2 coverage through mandatory participation in capital accumulation-based workplace pension plans. However, "lump-summing" these capital accumulations at retirement and spending the money on real estate, around-the-world trips, and the kids has become part of the national culture. This behavior is supported by a Pillar 1 component that is means tested. Thus, eliminating Pillar 1 means testing, and building Pillar 2 auto-pilot lump-sum-to-annuities conversion mechanisms should be high priorities in Australian pension reform.

- **In developing economies.** The TOPS/NPSS design is also a promising formula for developing countries ready to foster workplace pension arrangements as part of their development strategies. The Chilean reforms of the early 1980s are often held out as the "pension poster child" for developing economies. Unfortunately, however, the Chilean Pillar 2 system was designed with too much of an "opt-in" philosophy, rather than the "opt-out" philosophy the Turner Commission is advocating. Thus, not surprisingly, material Pillar 2 pension shortfalls are now being predicted in Chile, with the means-tested Pillar 1 component continuing to be an important backstop. These pension shortfalls are further aggravated by the six for-profit pension fund administrators

(AFPs), which charge an average 1.4 percent of contributions for their services. In a more recent example, India seems to have learned from these early Chilean mistakes. The implementation of a broadly based TOPS/NPSS-type pension arrangement is currently being debated in India's parliament.

NPSS GOVERNANCE, MANAGEMENT, AND INVESTMENT OPTIONS

The final chapter of the Turner Commission report addresses a myriad of implementation issues that arise from its recommendations. These range from the mechanics of auto-enrollment and payroll deductions, to the treatment of the self-employed, to member communications, to phase-in strategies, to minimum and maximum NPSS contribution levels and their tax treatment, to the annuitization process, to implementation time-scale, to investment options, and to NPSS governance and management. We limit our comments below only to the Commission's suggestions regarding NPSS governance, management, and investment options.

The Commission considered three institutional models for the NPSS: (1) a government agency, (2) an arm's-length agency established by statute, and (3) full outsourcing to a contracted for-profit provider. It opted for (correctly, in our view) the arm's-length agency model with its own board of directors. The Commission recognized that NPSS may well want to outsource a number of key functions.

The collection of and accounting for contributions is an obvious example. Other possibilities include member account maintenance and communications. The Commission recognized that the NPSS's "most sensitive and judgmental decisions" would relate to investment fund choices to be offered, how an auto-pilot default investment strategy would be defined, and how investment mandates would be allocated.

It is on these investment matters that we would differ with what the Commission describes as its "current but tentative thinking." The Commission foresees a range of fund choices being offered by NPSS, managed by private fund managers selected through competitive bidding processes. We instead would argue for single optimal risky and risk-minimizing choices, with the default strategy automatically assigning weights between the two, using an age-based formula. We would leave it to the required internal expertise residing within the NPSS to decide which components of the investment programs to manage internally and which to outsource to external managers.

MOVING FORWARD

The Economist reports that U.K. Chancellor of the Exchequer Gordon Brown is not enamored with the Turner Commission recommendations. This is a pity and, hopefully, upon more careful consideration, he will change his mind. Meanwhile, the rest of us should also consider the Turner recommendations carefully. They truly do represent a clear blueprint for global pension reform.[1]

---

[1]HM Treasury issued a white paper on pension reform in May 2006, supporting the general thrust of the Turner Pension Commission recommendations. The United Kingdom's National Association of Pension Funds (NAPF) is also supportive of the recommendations, but would like to see more than one agency involved in managing the new pension arrangements.

CHAPTER 44

More Pension Wisdom from Europe: The Geneva Report on Pension Reform

"Rather than following the usual two-handed approach of economists, we take a clear stance on a number of controversial issues...".

From *Dealing with the New Giants: Rethinking the Role of Pension Funds*, published jointly by ICMB and CEPR, July 2006

EIGHT HANDS, FOUR ECONOMISTS, AND ONE POINT OF VIEW

Given that the cited new study[1] on global pension reform was authored by four economists, there were actually eight hands involved in writing this powerful new analysis of global pension ills and how they could be cured. Even more remarkable is that the eight-handed four economists laid out only two possible future pension scenarios, clearly rejecting one scenario in favor of the other. Adding to our sense of wonder was the fact that the four-man team included a Brit (Andrew Roberts), a Dutchman (Lans Bovenberg), a Frenchman (Benoît Coeuré), and an Italian (Tito Boeri). Maybe there is something synergistic to this EU idea after all!

---

[1] "Dealing with the New Giants: Rethinking the Role of Pension Funds", by Tito Boeri, Lans Bovenberg, Benoît Coeuré, and Andrew Roberts. ICMB (International Center for Monetary and Banking Studies), Geneva, and CEPR (Centre for Economic Policy Research), London, July 2006.

The reason for reviewing the new Geneva Report on pension reform in this chapter is clear. The report is a logical sequel to the recent Turner Pensions Report out of the United Kingdom about which we wrote positively in the previous chapter, and other essays where we wrote on creativity and innovation (or lack of it) in the pensions field. The Geneva Report echoes some of the key pension reform ideas in the Turner Report, and applies healthy doses of clear, integrative thinking to developing these ideas further, as well as to producing some new ones relevant not only to Europe, but to the rest of the developed world as well.

And what do we mean by "clear, integrative thinking"? Let us count the ways. The report distinguishes between such micro issues as life-cycle financial planning, financial illiteracy, principal-agent issues, and pension fund governance on the one hand, and macro issues such as economic stability and growth, capital market pricing, entrepreneurship, and innovation on the other. It assesses the potential for market-, and financial engineering–based solutions to such challenges as managing asset-liability mismatch risk and longevity risk in pension arrangements. It examines the respective roles of financial capital, human capital, and labor market flexibility in stabilizing life-time consumption. Maybe most importantly, it leads to a number of clear, powerful pension policy implications.

POWERFUL PENSION POLICY IMPLICATIONS

So let us go directly to the bottom line. What are these "clear stances on a number of controversial issues" that the report authors claim to be taking? Here is how we would summarize them:

- National Pillar 1 pay-go systems should continue to offer a basic pension for workers with low lifetime incomes.
- Workers with higher incomes should supplement this basic public pension with funded private pension provisions in order to maintain their standard of living in retirement.
- For these higher-income workers, membership in a stand-alone, collective occupational pension plan should be mandatory. These pension plans should offer only limited investment choice, with well-thought-out default options for those who would prefer not to, or refuse to make choices themselves.
- Such default options should recognize that young workers are endowed with substantial human capital and have considerable capacity to bear financial risk, and thus are able to supply long-horizon, risk-bearing capital to financial markets. These risky, defined contribution (DC) claims should gradually shift into guaranteed defined benefit (DB) claims as

participants grow older and become more dependent on pension wealth for their consumption.

- Stand-alone pension plan organizations must be well governed, with a clear separation between the oversight function and the executive management function.
- "Mark-to-market" disclosure of the assets and liabilities of traditional DB pension plans should be welcomed, as it enhances market discipline, transparency, and risk management.
- In DB plan cases where asset-liability mismatch risk is currently excessive, interest rate swap overlays can and should be executed to reduce balance-sheet risk without giving up diversification and returns.
- The general move away from sponsoring DB plans by corporations should be welcomed, as in dynamic economies with competitive labor markets, most corporations are in fact ineffective, inefficient, often conflicted guarantors of pension claims.
- Countries with aging populations need strategies to protect long-run labor supply. Fertility can be enhanced by more flexible life-cycle policies that lead to a better parental reconciliation of work and family. The resulting higher effective retirement ages raise the return on human capital, and also act as buffers for absorbing financial market and longevity risks.

Having summarized the report authors' "clear stances on a number of controversial issues," we now comment on a number of these stances in greater detail.

LABOR MARKETS AND HUMAN CAPITAL

The "labor markets and human capital" part of the report is probably the biggest mind-stretcher for readers with a bread-and-butter pension fund management mind-set. Yet, from an integrative thinking perspective, it may be one of the report's most valuable contributions. Aging not only increases the need for more financial capital, but also for more investment in human capital. With increased longevity, we need to foster higher returns on human capital to increase welfare and consumption. Yet, with the historical emphasis on early retirement, human capital is depreciated early. Further, people have been concentrating their work effort in the relatively short period of time during their lives in which they also raise their children. This has increased the opportunity costs of raising children in terms of foregone career opportunities. This has been an important contributor to falling birth rates in the developed world.

How do we extend working life and get a better reconciliation of family, fertility, and career? Not an inconsequential question. One answer is to foster lifetime education so that human capital doesn't depreciate too rapidly (i.e., learned skills don't become obsolescent). Another answer is to move life course patterns toward longer, more flexible, active periods in which people are engaged in the labor market. Such a move would have powerful societal benefits. For example, it would ease career pressure at that biologically determined time when parents could create and care for young children. Later in life, fulfilling work provides stimulus, companionship, and extended health. Finally, with better-maintained human capital, older workers can bear more risk as they accumulate pension rights, thus potentially keeping costs in check and at the same time providing economies with additional risk capital.

The report's message in these matters is clear. Pension reform cannot just be about pension legislation, regulation, arrangements, institutions, and financial strategies, narrowly defined. In the broader scheme of things, education strategies and how labor markets function are just as important.

OPTIMAL RISK SHARING

On the question of optimal pension plan design, the report authors are of the view that employers, especially corporate ones, are far from ideal pension guarantors for a number of reasons. At the same time, the authors believe that collective pension funds can create considerable value for participants relative to leaving people to accumulate pension wealth on their own. Specifically, expert, arm's-length pension delivery organizations can help workers design and implement the low-cost, optimal life-cycle strategies that are critical to maintaining stable lifetime consumption patterns. In parallel, through their investment operations, these pension organizations can contribute to the stabilization of economic activity in general, and to the stabilization of capital markets activity in particular.

So far, so good—but now comes the hard part. How should pension plan participants share financial markets and demographic risks? The report authors make the sensible point that whatever risk-sharing deal is struck, it should be defined before the fact, rather than negotiated after some "bad news" shock from the financial markets, or the demographic front hits the pension plan radar screen. Another sensible point they make is that tying future generations into risk-sharing pension deals may be welfare enhancing in theory, but is problematic in practice. There are strong practical incentives for the current generation of pensioners and older workers to spend surpluses now, and to shift the negative financial consequences of asset shortfalls into future generations. So where does that leave us with regard to workable risk-sharing pension deals? Here, we found the report long on words and short on clarity. It seems to us that the bottom line is that individuals begin their working lives by accumulating claims on an optimally managed risky investment portfolio, and say 40 or so years later, end their working lives with claims on an optimally managed annuity portfolio. We don't know if the authors would agree because they don't really directly say.

OPTIMAL PENSION FUND ORGANIZATIONS

We were pleased to discover that the report contained a chapter titled "Informational Asymmetries and the Optimal Organization of Pension Funds." We were further pleased to discover that most of the authors' views in that chapter were closely aligned with our own. For example, this observation is right on the money from our perspective: "... the constellation of stakeholders gravitating towards pension funds (e.g. trade union representatives, trustees, advisors, auditors, law-makers, regulators) makes information asymmetry and conflicts of interests a key concern... ". This leads them to the logical conclusion that "agency problems are best addressed by nonprofit, collective pension funds."

In commenting on how these nonprofit, collective pension funds should be organized, we fully agree with the report's broad recommendation that there should be a clear separation between a fund's oversight function (e.g., its board of trustees or supervisors) and the fund's operational management function. However, we would quibble with some of the report's more specific recommendations and assumptions regarding fund governance and organization design such as:

- The enforcement of stakeholder rights within pension funds should be underpinned by direct plan member voting mechanisms.
- Pension funds should have investment committees to make investment decisions. This includes decisions regarding asset allocation, individual portfolio activity, diversification, and corporate control of companies the fund has invested in.
- The underlying assumption of the report writers seems to be that the nonprofit, collective pension funds they envision would fully outsource investment management, benefit administration, and related information technology (IT) services.

Counterpoints to these recommendations and this assumption might be:

- There is no doubt that the board of trustees (or supervisors) of a nonprofit, collective pension fund must be accountable to its "owners" (i.e., plan members) for achieving the fund's mission in a cost-effective manner. Consequently, there must be clear mechanisms through which this accountability is enforced (e.g., election/confirmation of board members by plan members or their representatives). However, democratic decision-making processes become dysfunctional if they lead to majorities (e.g., current pensioners and older workers) oppressing minorities and/or other parties (e.g., younger workers and future generations) through direct voting mechanisms. So functional pension fund democracy involves striking a delicate balance.

- Our personal experience is that a pension fund investment committee that leads a separate life from that of a fund's board of trustees can be a double-edged sword. On the one hand, such a committee can indeed bring specialized investment expertise to the fund's oversight function. On the other hand, the existence of such a committee raises serious legitimacy issues. Who selects its membership? Who is the committee accountable to? How is its effectiveness to be judged? The bottom line is that, ideally, the entire board of trustees acts as a pension fund's investment committee. This bottom line has two obvious implications. First, at least part of the board must be populated by people with investment experience at the strategic level. Second, the experience and skill level of the fund's internal investment management team is such that it generates a high level of trust at the board level, and thus has earned the authority to manage the details of the investment function on a fully delegated basis.

- It is not clear, ex-ante, what a nonprofit, collective pension fund with effective oversight and management functions would outsource, and what it would decide to do itself internally. Absent external rules, constraints, or agency issues, it would depend solely on an ongoing series of cost-effectiveness judgments. We know of a number of high-performance pension fund organizations that have chosen to internalize 85 percent of its investment management processes, and an even higher proportion of its benefit administration and IT support functions. The key is the availability of benchmarking disciplines that allow competent boards of trustees (or supervisors) to assess whether plan members are receiving maximum "value for dollars" (or euros) relative to the alternatives. Such benchmarking disciplines in fact exist.

A POWERFUL PENSION VISION

The new Geneva Report on pension reform makes a major contribution to an emerging powerful new vision of the role and functioning of workplace pensions in the developed world. Serious students of pension reform owe it to themselves to read this study.

PART Eight

The Case of PERS

Advice for PERS CEO Alyson Green resulting from a three-hour case discussion by 55 academics and pension professionals:

1. Brief the Governor fully on the current status of the PERS balance sheet.

2. Engage a credit agency to get an independent opinion on how the PERS balance sheet might impact State finances.

3. Develop a multistakeholder, multimedia communications strategy to get people's attention.

Key conclusions from a case study discussion held at a
Rotman International Centre for Pension Management
Colloquium, October 25, 2005

The following two chapters (including tables and figures) are based on a case description and discussion titled "PERS and the Pension Revolution: Active Participant or Passive Bystander?" Keith Ambachtsheer, Alexander Dyck, Niels Kortleve, and Hein Leenders. The case was discussed at a Rotman International Centre for Pension Management colloquium, October 25, 2005.

CHAPTER 45

PERS and the Pension Revolution: Active Participant ... or Passive Bystander?

"PERS' new CEO is facing some big challenges in the coming weeks, months and years ahead. ... "

The case of PERS, 2005

ALYSON GREEN'S NEW JOB

After considerable reflection, Alyson Green had decided to throw her hat into the ring to become the next chief executive officer (CEO) of the state's public employee retirement system, named PERS for short. The state's governor, whom she had gotten to know well before he ran for office, had been very persuasive. It was his perception that, with the retirement of PERS's long-serving previous CEO, the organization needed new, vigorous leadership. With her strong track record as a private-sector "turn-around" specialist, he thought that Alyson fit the bill perfectly. PERS's board of trustees must have agreed with the governor's assessment, as they decided that Alyson was the strongest of the three finalists for the job. They had made her an offer, and she had accepted. Now six weeks on the job, she had started to make serious preparations for her first board meeting, only two weeks away. As she felt that this first meeting would offer a unique opportunity to establish a few key strategic priorities for PERS, it was important for her to develop her own view on what they should be.

While the state had made various employee pension provisions for almost a century, the current PERS organization was established as an autonomous state agency in the 1950s. According to its most recent annual report, PERS looks after the pension arrangements of some 150,000 current and former state employees, and is fully funded, with plan assets and liabilities both valued at about $50 billion. The PERS pension contract is a typical public-sector defined benefit (DB) arrangement wherein pension payment accruals are based on years of service, final earnings, and are fully indexed to consumer prices (CPI) postretirement. Normal contributions reflecting new service are split 50-50 between the employer and employees. The allocation of any balance-sheet surpluses, or dealing with balance-sheet deficits, would follow from processes that are partially predetermined by stated pension contract rules (e.g., consistent with generally accepted actuarial principles) and partially determined through negotiation between the various stakeholder groups (i.e., state government, active employees, and pensioners).

PERS had been maturing over the course of the last decade, with the ratio of pensioners to total plan membership rising steadily over time. The ratio had reached 39 percent at the end of 2004. Benefit payments began to exceed contributions 10 years ago. In 2004, the system took in $800 million in contributions, and paid out $2 billion in benefits. To calculate its current pension liability, PERS had continued to use a real return assumption of 4 percent as the liability discount rate over the course of the last five years. Over the same time period, the yield on long-term inflation-linked Treasury bonds had fallen from 3.5 percent to 2 percent. The real return on PERS assets had been volatile over the course of the last five years, ranging from a low of −5 percent (in 2002) to a high of +15 percent (in 2003). Further historical facts on PERS are set out in Table 45.1.

TABLE 45.1 A Short History of PERS Vital Statistics

	2000	2001	2002	2003	2004
Current assets ($B)	$44B	$40B	$38B	$44B	$50B
Current liabilities ($B)	$39B	$42B	$44B	$47B	$50B
Real liability discount rate	4%	4%	4%	4%	4%
Actual long TIPS yield	3.5%	4.0%	3.0%	2.5%	2.0%
Actual real fund return	6%	−3%	−5%	15%	12%
Contributions ($B)	$0.7B	$0.7B	$0.8B	$0.8B	$0.8B
Benefit payments ($B)	$1.5B	$1.8B	$1.9B	$1.9B	$2.1B
Number of pensioners (000s)	45T	47T	50T	53T	59T

HISTORY OF WORKPLACE PENSIONS

In order to develop perspective on pension issues, a former colleague had suggested that Alyson read *The Pension Fund Revolution*, the 1996 reprint of Peter Drucker's original book *The Unseen Revolution: How Pension Fund Socialism Came to America*, first published in 1976. Now that she had finished, her notes suggested that Drucker's insights seemed to fall into four broad categories: politico-agency issues, governance-organizational issues, finance-investment issues, and pension contract–risk issues.

Drucker identified Charles Wilson, president of General Motors for much of the 1940s and 1950s, as the father of the typical post–World War II corporate DB plan. Wilson believed that his corporate pension plan design would forge a direct, strong bond between the corporation and its workforce. Further, by investing pension contributions through a segregated pension fund in equity positions in Corporate America, workers would have a direct incentive to enhance the financial health and productivity of their employers. When the new DB pension plan was introduced at GM in 1950, union leaders at the United Auto Workers (UAW) were less than enthusiastic. They viewed Wilson's initiative as an attempt to undermine union power to impact the future affairs of the corporation. So, ironically, the GM pension plan was implemented over the objections of the UAW at the time. The Wilson pension formula was subsequently adopted by many other large corporations in the early 1950s. The essence of the Wilson formula would later be codified in the United States as the Employees Retirement Income Security Act of 1974 (ERISA).

Drucker recognized that the politics and dynamics of public-sector and multiemployer industry pension plans were quite different from those of the corporate sector. While he saw nothing wrong with such arrangements in principle, Drucker saw much wrong in practice. State and local governments seemed to just make up "rules" for their pension plans as they went along, with little apparent fiscal discipline or consistency. The same seemed to be generally true for union-run industry plans, even though these plans fall under the ERISA code. As a counterpoint, the evolution of the Teachers Insurance and Annuity Association - College Retirement Equities Fund (TIAA-CREF), the national pension plan for U.S. university faculty and staff, proved that it doesn't have to be that way, with Drucker noting TIAA-CREF's "enviable record of performance and innovation" starting in 1918.

THE 1976 TO 2005 PERIOD

What has happened in the political economy of pensions post-1975? Upon reading *Beyond Portfolio Theory: the Next Frontier*, an article in the

Financial Analysts Journal in the January–February 2005 issue, Alyson noted the following important developments:

- The private-sector labor market has "atomized" making corporate DB plans now irrelevant for a significant part of this market. Ironically, the growth of DC/401(k) plans has given rise to a whole new class of agency issues driven by informational asymmetry between plan members and for-profit financial service providers. She was aware of the view of some observers that, as a result, many plan members in DC pension arrangements are paying too much for too little.

- In the part of the private-sector labor market where DB plans are still potentially relevant, such plans have become significantly less attractive as a compensation component for many corporate employers. This decline in the popularity of corporate DB plans seems to be due to the evolving complexity of the collective, shared risk-bearing element in DB plans, and the advent of "fair value" accounting principles which is forcing corporate chief financial officers (CFOs) to directly address the question of how much the mismatch risk on the pension balance sheet is contributing to the corporation's overall risk profile.

- There has been an emergence of single-purpose, arm's-length agencies investing the national Pillar 1 pension reserves in Canada, Sweden, Norway, Ireland, New Zealand, and, very recently, in Australia and France. There are also many such agencies investing Pillar 2 workplace-based pension assets in all the major pension reserves countries, including not just the list above, but also in the United States, the United Kingdom, the Netherlands, and Switzerland.

GOVERNANCE–ORGANIZATIONAL ISSUES AT PERS

Alyson noted that Drucker was predictably direct in his views on pension fund governance and organizational matters. Being free of direct conflicts with specific union, business, or government agencies would not be enough. Pension funds would also have to be well governed and managed, subject to the same competency standards as the boards and managements of the companies they invest in. This in turn suggests a need to define the ideal skill/experience set for a pension board of trustees, and a requirement to impose a matching search/implementation discipline.

Through her job interviews for the CEO position, Alyson had discovered that PERS currently does not have a formal process to impose such a discipline in the selection of its board of trustees. Instead, there is a strong "representative" orientation to the board selection process, with two board members coming from the state legislature, two from the executive branch, three from various worker groups, and one from PERS pensioners. Only the ninth position—board chair—is filled through a consensus-based search process that attempts to match a candidate's actual skill/experience set against that set out in a board chair job description. Despite the way in which the board of trustees was selected, the board seemed to be a reasonably effective body today (after all, it selected her as the organization's new CEO!). However, the question whether this outcome is the result of luck or of good management remains.

FINANCE—INVESTMENT BELIEFS

As part of her "due diligence" fact-finding research on PERS, Alyson had observed that PERS had the same 60–40 equity-debt asset mix as most other public-sector pension funds. Why was that, she wondered? Is it because all of these funds have the same return expectations and the same risk tolerance? Also, most of the organization's 50 investment mandates seemed to be of the traditional "active" type, with external money managers being asked to "beat" a specific capital market–based benchmark that reflected the money manager's "style," but without being allowed to deviate much from the composition of that benchmark portfolio. Why was that, she wondered? Is this really the optimal way to implement an investment policy? She and PERS's chief investment officer were destined to have some interesting conversations about investment beliefs, and the role that investment beliefs should play in PERS's future investment program.

PENSION CONTRACT—RISK ISSUES AT PERS

Alyson noted that, officially, surplus or deficit-related decisions were not PERS issues at this point, as the recent conventional actuarial valuation showed plan assets and liabilities to be in balance at about $50 billion each. However, Alyson wasn't convinced that this was really the case. She had been reading for some time now about the "fair value" debate taking place between members of the economics, accounting, and actuarial professions. On the one hand, most actuaries seem to believe that the plan liability they calculate should be based on the expected return of plan assets. On the other hand, most economists, accountants, and even a few "radical" actuaries argue that such calculations systematically understate the "true" (i.e., default risk-free, or insured) value of the accrued pension liability.

Why is this? They explain it is because the economic "fair value" of accrued pensions is independent of the chosen investment policy for plan assets. In other words, increasing the expected return on plan assets by taking on more risk cannot reduce the default risk-free value of the accrued payment obligations. Instead, this economic value of pension liabilities should always be based on their "best estimate" transaction value. To establish that transaction value, future pension payment obligations should be discounted using the market-based term structure of interest rates for high-quality debt instruments, and not the higher expected return on plan assets. Using such a higher discount rate would result in an understatement of the accrued "true" default risk-free pension liability.

Very recently, Alyson attended a Rotman International Centre for Pension Management (ICPM) workshop that pushed this financial economics-based line of argument even further. The critical point made at the workshop was that the only truly risk-free DB pension plans are those that (1) have plan assets equal to the economic value of plan liabilities and (2) are fully cash-flow matched on an asset-liability basis. Any DB plan that cannot meet these two conditions has risk embedded in it. This raises some interesting questions. For example, when such embedded risk exists, how does it manifest itself? In exposure to the possibility of increased contributions in the future? To the possibility of benefit reductions? To both? Further, who bears these risks? Today's taxpayers, active employees, or pensioners? Future generations of taxpayers, active employees, or pensioners? Or possibly all of the above? If so, how is total risk exposure allocated between these stakeholder groups? It seemed to Alyson that these questions were not only interesting, but also important. Further, she was quite sure that no one at PERS had good, clear answers for them.

She had been especially intrigued by a workshop presentation given by Niels Kortleve and Hein Leenders of the Dutch pension fund PGGM at the 2005 workshop, "DB Pension Plans and Fair Value: Practical Challenges" hosted by The Rotman International Centre for Pension Management. (Niels Kortleve, Hein Leenders, "DB Pension Plans and Fair Value: Practical Challenges" can be accessed at www.rotman.utoronto.ca/icpm.) They showcased a computer model that seemed to offer new insights into questions related to the embedded risk in DB plans and how they are allocated. Alyson had eagerly accepted their offer to run the PERS situation through the PGGM model. The results were both intriguing and disturbing. The first display compared the values of PERS assets and liabilities based on the recent conventional actuarial valuation as reported in the most recent PERS annual report, with their economic "fair value" counterparts (see Table 45.2). As the conventional valuation uses a market-based approach for valuing plan assets, the reported $50 billion asset value matches that of its economic "fair value" counterpart. The liability calculation, however, is a different story. The $50 billion accrued pension "liability" in the

TABLE 45.2 A Tale of Two PERS Liabilities

	Asset Value	Liability Value	Funded Ratio
Conventional valuation basis	$50B	$50B	100%
Economic valuation basis	$50B	$74B	68%

conventional actuarial report had been calculated assuming plan assets would earn a net real return of 4 percent. When the current real yield curve is substituted to discount the accrued future pension payments, an economic "fair value" liability estimate of $74 billion results. On this basis, the PERS funded ratio sinks from its reported comfortable 100 percent to a distinctly uncomfortable 68 percent.

It was important to Alyson that she was able to verbalize the additional information that the economic valuation calculations conveyed. Specifically, the calculation told her that it would take $74 billion of assets today to fully assure that all accrued pension obligations will be met in full, without needing to have recourse to additional funds or pension reductions at a later date. It now also became clearer what the conventional $50 billion "liability" calculation meant in economic terms. It is the amount of money that would be sufficient today to meet accrued pension payments if plan assets indeed earned the assumed 4 percent net real rate of return over the long term.

But, Alyson realized, the 4 percent was only an expectation. There was a material probability that plan assets would earn less than that for extended periods of time. In other words, Alyson realized that settling for a $50 billion funding target and choosing a risky investment policy involves a gamble. There is now a significant possibility that somewhere down the road, people will either have to make additional contributions, accept lower than expected pensions, or experience some combination of the two. The current cost of eliminating that gamble is $24 billion. In other words, the gamble could be eliminated by writing a $24 billion check, and arranging plan assets so that proceeds (maturities plus interest) matched promised pension payments.

IS A HIGHER CONTRIBUTION RATE THE ANSWER?

It didn't seem fair to Alyson that the entire $24 billion gamble should be loaded on the shoulders of future generations. Historically, the 15 percent of pay contribution rate into the pension plan had been shared 50-50 between employers and employees. She wondered what would happen if both parties began to pay an additional 2.5 percent of pay, raising the collective contribution rate to 20 percent of pay? Before showing Alyson the calculated PERS balance sheet implications of moving the contribution rate from 15 percent of pay to 20 percent, Niels and Hein first explained what the PGGM computer model was programmed to do.

It has the ability to very quickly calculate many possible PERS balance sheet outcomes over some future horizon (15 years hence, to 2020, in the examples) and to calculate the present value of those possible outcomes using a mathematical routine that takes into account both the magnitudes of possible future balance sheet surpluses or deficits and their uncertainty. The greater the uncertainty, the lower the present value. This discounting process is effectively equivalent to establishing the current market value (i.e., option value) of possible PERS balance sheet surpluses and deficits 15 years hence. The resulting "option deficit" is the best estimate of the amount of money that would have to be paid to an insurer today to underwrite the payment of all possible plan deficits 15 years hence. The "option surplus" is the best estimate of what a financial institution would be willing to pay today to acquire access to all possible plan surpluses 15 years hence.

The results from the PGGM model confirmed what Alyson already suspected. Moving the contribution rate from 15 percent of pay to 20 percent, while maintaining a 60–40 equity-bond mix, does not solve PERS's current financial imbalance. The calculated present value of the new inflation-indexed liabilities that will be booked over the course of the next 15 years is $71 billion, while the present value of future contributions is marginally lower at $68 billion. Thus, the cost of incurring new liabilities marginally exceeds to 20 percent of pay (in fact, it is 20.2 percent of pay). Thus, even with a 20 percent contribution rate, running the PERS current "pension deal" for another 15 years effectively raises the cost of extinguishing the financial gamble from $24 billion (i.e., current assets of $50 billion vs. current economic liabilities of $74 billion) to $27 billion (i.e., current assets plus the present value of future assets add up to $118 billion vs. current liabilities plus the present value of future economic liabilities add up to $145 billion). Stated differently, the newly calculated PERS balance sheet indicates that $32 billion would have to be paid to an insurer now to buy a "put" option that would cover all potential deficits that could exist 15 years from now. At the same time, the "call" value of all potential balance sheet surpluses that could exist 15 years from now is only $5 billion (see Table 45.3).

MORE DRASTIC ACTION INDICATED

These results told Alyson that more drastic action than a five-percentage-point increase in contributions would have to be taken if PERS's current

TABLE 45.3 The Enhanced PERS Economic Balance Sheet
(20 percent contribution rate to 2020)

Assets		Liabilities	
Current pension fund	$50B	Current liabilities	$74B
Contributions	$68B	New liabilities	$71B
Option deficit	$32B	Option surplus	$ 5B

financial imbalance is to be seriously addressed. Rather than jacking up the contribution rate even higher, consideration would have to be given to reducing the level of the pension guarantee. To get a feel for the balance-sheet sensitivity to reducing the level of the pension guarantee, she asked Niels and Hein to rerun the analysis with all assumptions the same, except that going forward, the pension guarantee would be reduced from final earnings and fully CPI-indexed postretirement pensions to a career average earnings basis, with no postretirement updates.

The new analysis showed that such a drastic measure (i.e., cutting all future pre- and postretirement indexation) would indeed shift the PERS balance sheet from a significant net deficit position to a significant net surplus, both on accrued and projected "going-concern" bases. Current pension assets remain at $50 billion, and the present value of future contributions remains at $68 billion. However, without future indexation, current liabilities drop from $74 billion to $45 billion, and new liabilities from $71 billion to $37 billion. Taken together, the massive reduction of current and projected liabilities to 2020 from $145 billion to $82 billion represents a cost to current and future pensioners of $63 billion. As a result, the balance sheet's option deficit drops from $32 billion to $1 billion, and its option surplus rises from $5 billion to $37 billion (see Table 45.4).

This material balance sheet shift from a big deficit to a big surplus gave Alyson hope that all was not lost for PERS stakeholders. While the analyses performed with the PGGM model indicated that something more drastic that a contribution rate increase from 15 percent to 20 percent of pay was needed to place the PERS balance sheet on an even financial keel, there

TABLE 45.4 A PERS Surplus at Last

Assets		Liabilities	
Current pension fund	$50B	Current liabilities (without indexation)	$45B
Contributions (based on 20% of pay)	$68B	New liabilities (without indexation)	$37B
Option deficit	$ 1B	Option surplus	$37B

appeared to be a chance that something could be worked out involving both an upward adjustment in the contribution rate up from 15 percent to 20 percent, and continuing to offer future price indexation. However, indexation updates would have to become conditional on the strength of the PERS balance sheet.

SPREADING THE PAIN EVENLY

What benefit indexation update formula combined with the contribution rate increase from 15 percent to 20 percent might spread the financial pain as evenly as possible, Alyson wondered? Niels and Hein suggested trying the following indexation update formula:

> **Indexation rate:**
> Under 100 percent funded on a current assets/liabilities basis—no indexation
> 100 percent to 130 percent funded—partial indexation (linear between 100 percent and 130 percent)
> Over 130 percent funded—full indexation
> Over 150 percent funded—catch-up indexation

The PGGM computer model showed that this indexation update formula, combined with the 15 percent to 20 percent contribution rate increase, results in a balance sheet option surplus of $24 billion versus an option deficit of $1 billion. This represents a more balanced approach than the previous run which simply eliminated all future pre- and postretirement indexation, resulting in an option surplus of $37 billion against a $1 billion option deficit. The option surplus now declines because, relative to no indexation, the conditional indexation update formula being tested adds $13 billion of indexation to current and new liabilities (see Table 45.5). With the current assets/nominal liabilities ratio at 111 percent today, the update formula indicates only partial indexation would be provided initially. However, with a 20 percent contribution rate, the indexation rate is likely to improve over time. The PGGM model estimated an expected 80 percent indexation rate over the 15-year assessment period, with most of that expected indexation coming later in the 15-year assessment period.

An important assumption behind Table 45.5 is that in 2020 (i.e., at the end of the 15-year assessment period), the prospective pension guarantee will continue to be nominal, and that any indexation beyond 2020 will also be conditional on affordability. The estimated Option Surplus of $24 billion suggests a high likelihood that the post-2020 period will indeed commence

TABLE 45.5 Finding the Right Balance

Assets		Liabilities	
Current pension fund	$50B	Current liabilities (without indexation)	$45B
Contributions (based on 20% of pay)	$68B	New liabilities (with conditional indexation on accrued and new benefits)	$50B
Option deficit	$ 1B	Option surplus	$24B

with a significant level of indexation for PERS workers and retirees at that time.

Is maintaining a 60–40 asset mix, and moving the contribution rate from 15 percent to 20 percent, combined with the tested indexation update formula, the right financial policy mix to address the current financial imbalance on the PERS balance sheet, Alyson wondered? On the one hand, would it be fair to push the contribution rate well above 20 percent, moving it above the current cost price of a fully indexed future pension? Would this not mean placing an unwarranted burden on young and future workers and taxpayers? On the other hand, implementing this conditional indexation formula would impose a very considerable value loss on current pensioners and older workers. It seems that arriving at a defensible, fair policy balance will require calculating how a particular "policy ladder" would financially impact the various PERS stakeholder groups (i.e., current and future taxpayers, workers, and pensioners) in some standardized, comparable way.

Even with such calculations, it will still be impossible to avoid making some interesting retrospective value judgments. For example, if current pensioners and the older generations of current taxpayers and workers caused today's PERS balance sheet imbalance by choosing a high investment risk/low contribution rate strategy in the past that did not work out, should they not bear the consequences? It seems that more work and careful thinking is required before any kind of specific proposal could be discussed with the board of trustees and, eventually, with representatives of the various PERS stakeholder groups.

IS RISK-SHARING AN ESSENTIAL PENSION PLAN FEATURE?

Alyson was struck by the level of complexity that risk sharing creates in traditional public-sector and industry DB pension plans when it is properly specified and analyzed in a modern financial economics framework.

The analyses performed by the PGGM model strongly reinforced the reality that risk sharing in traditional DB plans takes the form of younger stakeholder groups (present younger and future workers and taxpayers) effectively guaranteeing pension payments to older stakeholder groups (present older workers and pensioners). In options terms, the young are the "put" issuers in traditional public-sector DB plans. In theory, they are prepared to do this because they also own equally valuable "call" options on better-than-expected future outcomes. The PGGM model helped make clear the condition under which this concept breaks down. It is when a DB plan's going-concern option deficit (outstanding "puts") far exceeds its going-concern option surplus (outstanding "calls"). The PGGM model also helps establish what actions (i.e., a fair and sustainable combination of contribution rate and benefit level adjustments) need to be introduced to reestablish "put-call parity" on the pension balance sheet in such a situation.

These realities raised two important questions for Alyson. Given the general lack of understanding about the true economics of DB plans, and given the ability and apparent willingness of the current generation of plan stakeholders to financially favor themselves at the expense of future generations, are DB plans in their current form worth saving? Isn't the simplest and least game-able "policy ladder" one in which pension plan members have their own target income replacement rates, accumulate their own financial reserves over their working lives in the form of risky assets and deferred annuity payments, and vary their own contribution rates over time, with their previously set target income replacement rates as a constant compass?

Studies presented at the ICPM workshop Alyson attended recently seemed to confirm her intuition. This workshop, "Pension Plan Design, Risk, and Sustainability," included components with titles such as "Pension Fund Dynamics," "Funding Strategies for Mature Pension Plans: Can the Risks Be Contained?," "The Value of Intergenerational Transfers within DB Plans," and "DB Plans Under Siege: Can They Survive?." These presentations showed mature DB pension plans to be inherently unstable, with tendencies to either generate runaway surpluses or degenerate into unfunded pay-go systems. Only the combination of an irrevocable enforcement mechanism and integrated policy steering mechanisms involving predetermined contribution rate, benefit level, and investment policy adjustments create sustainable outcomes for mature DB plans. Alyson knew that neither mechanism existed at PERS today, nor were they likely to be put into place tomorrow. This reality made the finding in another workshop paper that the kind of individual "life-cycle policy ladder" approach she was contemplating scored well in welfare/utility terms especially intriguing. An important practical litmus test was whether this kind of approach could fly in the real world. The approach sounded a lot like the TIAA-CREF formula that Peter Drucker praised as long as 30 years ago. There is nothing new under the sun!

GETTING FROM HERE TO THERE

Of course, there was the not inconsequential matter of getting from here to there. Alyson already knew from the PGGM analysis that it would take $74 billion to keep current PERS pensioners and workers whole. In other words, it would take $74 billion to create 150,000 personal member accounts with the same values as the current accrued pension promises "owned" by the 150,000 PERS plan members, when these promises are valued on a risk-free basis. Unfortunately, plan assets amounted to only $50 billion. Allocating each of the 150,000 members his or her share of the $24 billion asset shortfall would not be a pleasant task.

And that is not all. Alyson understood that even if plan assets were $74 billion rather than $50 billion today, there would still be a transition challenge in moving to a TIAA-CREF type of formula. Why? Because in DB plans, pension accruals are backend loaded. In other words, it costs far more to "buy" a pension for a person's 35th year of service than for the first year of service. Yet, the contribution rate for young workers and old workers is the same. Thus, even in a properly costed and funded DB plan, younger workers still subsidize older workers. Given these two considerations, Alyson realized that, in the short term, it would be far easier just to keep the current system going and hope for a high-enough return on the current $50 billion plus future contributions to bail everybody out!

DEVISING AN ACTION PLAN

The ICPM workshop and her work with the PGGM model confirmed for Alyson that addressing PERS's current balance-sheet imbalance should indeed be her number one priority. However, single-handedly changing the PERS pension contract is not part of her job description. Somehow, she would have to engage the parties that should and could play some role in redefining the PERS "pension deal." Where should she start, she wondered? With the PERS actuary? The PERS external auditor? The pension regulator? Should she first discuss this issue with fellow pension CEOs in a similar situation? Should she ask Niels and Hein to do more PERS balance-sheet analyses to test other possible financial policy ladders involving investment policy, contribution rate, and benefit indexation protocols? After all, the PGGM model analyses suggested that the search for the fairest, and therefore most sustainable "policy ladder" may be not yet over. Maybe finding the least painful transition to sustainability first would be helpful to everyone. Of course, the fairness question would always be subject to debate, with different stakeholder groups likely maintaining different points of view.

Then there was the reality of the upcoming board of trustees meeting. How much of what she had learned should she share with the board? How should she go about it? Talk to the chair first and get his advice on how to introduce the topic? Regardless of where she started, Alyson realized that changes to the PERS pension contract would eventually have to be addressed and agreed to by representatives of PERS retirees, active members, and their employers. These would not be easy conversations. No doubt, by choosing to be an active participant in the much-needed pension revolution, PERS's new CEO is facing some big challenges in the coming weeks, months, and even years ahead. First among these challenges, she believed, is to play a catalyst role in transforming the PERS "pension deal" into an arrangement that is transparent, fair among various stakeholder groups, and sustainable for decades to come, and in helping find a feasible transition path to it. That would be the trigger to the PERS pension revolution she was determined to lead.[1]

---

[1] All of the papers and presentations of the ICPM workshop on "Pension Plan Design, Risk, and Sustainability" can be accessed at www.rotman.utoronto.ca/icpm.

CHAPTER 46

Advice for Alyson Green: How PERS Can Join the Pension Revolution

Advice for PERS CEO Alyson Green resulting from a three-hour case discussion by 55 academics and pension professionals:

1. Brief the Governor fully on the current status of the PERS balance sheet.

2. Engage a credit agency to get an independent opinion on how the PERS balance sheet might impact State finances.

3. Develop a multistakeholder, multimedia communications strategy to get people's attention.

Key conclusions from a case study discussion held at a Rotman International Centre for Pension Management Colloquium, October 25, 2005

CASE DISCUSSION SUMMARY FROM OCTOBER 25, 2005

If you felt some tremors on October 25, the cause may have been the animated debate at the University of Toronto's Rotman School of Management about the right financial policies for the Public Sector Employee Retirement System (PERS). The participants in the debate were the 55 attendees to a colloquium organized by the Rotman International Centre for Pension Management (ICPM). The attendees came from a variety of professional and academic backgrounds and home countries (Australia, Canada, Finland, Netherlands, Norway, the United Kingdom, and the United States). The PERS case was specifically written for the colloquium in order to create a dynamic forum for exploring the current financial challenges facing public sector DB plans in the developed world. The Dutch pension fund PGGM provided technical support with its balance-sheet valuation model based on "fair value" principles. Below are summaries of the PERS situation as described in the case and of the resulting debate it provoked.

THE PERS SITUATION

After considerable reflection, Alyson Green had decided to throw her hat into the ring to become the next CEO of the state's public employee retirement system, named PERS for short. The state's governor, who she had gotten to know well before he ran for office, had been very persuasive. It was his perception that, with the retirement of PERS's long-serving previous CEO, the organization needed new, vigorous leadership. With her strong track record as a private-sector "turnaround" specialist, he thought that Alyson fit the bill perfectly. PERS's board of trustees must have agreed with the governor's assessment, as they decided that Alyson was the strongest of the three finalists for the job. They had made her an offer, and she had accepted. Now six weeks on the job, she had started to make serious preparations for her first board meeting, only two weeks away. As she felt that this first meeting would offer a unique opportunity to establish a few key strategic priorities for PERS, it was important for her to develop her own view on what they should be.

THE PERS DEBATE

An important starting point for the debate among the colloquium participants was that in its most recent annual report, PERS had reported balance sheet assets and liabilities at $50 billion each. However, the case description raised doubts about whether the two figures are really comparable. While the $50 billion asset value was based on market valuations, the $50 billion liability value was not, as it was calculated using a 4 percent real return discount rate at a time when the term structure of default risk-free real interest rates was in the 1 percent-2 percent range.

The first specific question participants were asked to address was whether the fact that PERS has $50 billion in assets (at market) and had accrued pension payment obligations with a market value (in an insurance sense) of $74 billion (i.e., well-above the reported $50 billion "liability") was a serious issue for PERS, requiring immediate attention. Specifically, is this an issue that the new PERS CEO Alyson Green should put on the agenda of her first meeting with the PERS board of trustees? A show of hands indicated that a majority of attendees thought it was a serious issue, but there was also a significant minority who were of the view that this situation did *not* constitute a serious issue requiring immediate attention. Both groups were invited to state the reasons for their view. These views are summarized in Table 46.1.

After an hour of general discussion and debate, participants were split up into seven smaller working groups and asked to provide Alyson Green with advice about what she should convey to the board about the PERS funded status, and what PERS should do about it. With the assistance of the PGGM model, the case study had shown that the asset side of the PERS balance sheet could be shored up by a higher contribution rate, while the liability side of the balance sheet could be reduced by making pension benefits dependent on the balance-sheet funded ratio. Thus, advice for Alyson could involve some combination of raising contributions, making benefit payments contingent on the health of the PERS balance sheet, and changing investment policy. In a more radical vein, even moving to an individual life-cycle arrangement with both capital accumulation and annuitization components could be contemplated.

TABLE 46.1 PERS Has a Serious Problem Requiring Immediate Attention

Yes	No
▪ The $24B gap represents the current risk embedded in the system. Everyone should be aware it is there.	▪ The plan is not insolvent. There is time to take a slow, deliberate approach to finding a solution.
▪ There is a material probability that plan members will get less than expected or pay more than expected. This fact must be disclosed.	▪ Things may turn out okay, so let's not be alarmist.
▪ Alyson Green must make her mark at her fist meeting with the board. If she misses this opportunity, she may not get another one.	▪ Having a funding target less than the economic cost of the pension promise is part of the current "pension deal." The risk of underfunding was always there. People just need to be reminded of that fact.

In the report-back session, most groups recommended Alyson should clearly explain the current financial situation of PERS in her first meeting with the board. They also suggested that Alyson convey the view that PERS needed to move to a formal "policy ladder" involving variable contributions, variable benefits, and a variable investment policy. The groups providing Alyson with this advice realized that this would be a difficult message to "sell" to the various *PERS* stakeholder groups.

Three of the more creative "selling-the-message" suggestions provided to her were:

1. Brief the governor fully on the current situation, and develop a two-pronged strategy with him. The "inside" strategy would engage representatives of the various stakeholder groups, and see if an acceptable solution to all (or most) could be brokered. The "outside" strategy would see the governor create a public forum to explain the current situation to all concerned and to seek a satisfactory solution through a more public process.
2. Engage a credit rating agency to get an independent opinion on how PERS's current financial situation could impact the state's credit rating, and how moving to a more fiscally prudent "policy ladder" involving variable contribution rates, variable benefits, and a variable investment policy could improve that credit rating.
3. Develop a multimedia communications strategy to convey the seriousness of the current situation.

One group disagreed with these PERS strategies recommended by the other groups. In the opinion of the disagreeing group, the best solution was to stabilize the pension system by (1) moving the contribution rate to full-cost (20.2 percent of pay), (2) moving the investment policy to 100 percent inflation-linked bonds, and (3) making up the annual benefit payments shortfall on a pay-go basis out of general tax revenues.

The entire three-hour process, led by Professor Alexander Dyck of the Rotman School, was a powerful learning experience for the 55 participants. Most were persuaded that the PERS situation did indeed warrant an immediate, forceful response of some sort, and that its situation in fact reflected the current reality of most public-sector defined benefit (DB) plans around the world. The challenge is to create tipping points that lead to "immediate, forceful responses." In the Netherlands, the pension regulator has already been the catalyst for change, which is now occurring. In California, Governor Schwarzenegger has tried to create change and failed. He has promised to try again. The virtual Alyson Green and her PERS board of trustees are plotting their strategy for change as you read this. More importantly, so are some of the colloquium participants!

In Conclusion:
A Call to Arms

The 2001 to 2006 events described in the chapters of this book have created the necessary conditions for the pension revolution Peter Drucker foresaw 30 years ago. But these necessary conditions do not guarantee the revolution's success. Success demands that the decisions required to launch the revolution described in these pages actually be taken. And that in turn requires, borrowing Malcolm Gladwell's expression, "tipping point" conditions. Where do these conditions exist today, and who are the people in positions to take revolutionary decisions about changing pension design, organizational structure, investment beliefs, risk management, performance measurement, and results disclosure?

In answering this question, it is useful to first observe that "tipping point" opportunities exist both outside and inside pension organizations. Examples of the former lie in the legislative and regulatory spheres, as well as in bodies responsible for setting "generally accepted" standards in accounting, actuarial, and pension management practices. One of the chapters in the book noted that it is undoubtedly the Dutch who are showing that radical change in the pension paradigm can be effected through legislative and regulatory means. With the tabling of the Turner Commission report, followed by HM Treasury's White Paper on pension reform, the United Kingdom is now seriously contemplating material change. On the other side of the Atlantic, Quebec's pension regulator Régie des Rentes is the first North American regulator to also contemplate playing a more activist role in changing the pension paradigm. On the "generally accepted" practices front, the accounting profession appears finally ready to move pension-related financial disclosures to a mark-to-market basis. This will be an important step toward finally disentangling the murky web of contingent claims embedded in traditional defined benefit (DB) plans.

There are also "tipping point" opportunities inside pension organizations themselves. These opportunities divide naturally into corporate and industry/public-sector contexts. In the corporate sector, the noted coming changes in pension accounting will provide further impetus to the closing of traditional DB plans there. An important unresolved question is what role corporations will now play to facilitate the accumulation of adequate future retirement income for their workers. One of this book's important messages is that simply offering a traditional defined contribution (DC) arrangement is not an ideal solution, and that a TOPS ("The Optimal Pension System") arrangement offers a far better one. Very large corporations can create a TOPS arrangement themselves. Not so for the rest of the corporate sector. The logical intermediary to fill this void is the for-profit financial services industry. However, an important book theme is the fundamental conflict between the financial services industry's for-profit mind-set and the retirement income aspirations of workers. This conflict logically leads to the critical question of how to best represent the financial interests of workers. The answer is simple in principle: Create knowledgeable bargaining and monitoring processes acting in workers' best interests. This raises the question of where such processes could come from. Ideally from within the corporate sector itself, acting in its collective self-interest. The Australians have had considerable success with this solution by creating pension plans based on industry and geographical affinity groupings. These initiatives now need to be kick-started in other places as well.

The industry/public sector context presents a quite different "tipping point" dynamic for the pension revolution. Several essays chapters in the book noted that the proper valuation and cost allocation of the guarantees embedded in industry/public-sector DB plans offers a promising starting point. Indeed, that was the starting point in the book's PERS case study, where CEO Alyson Green is forced to understand the difference between pension liability estimates based on traditional "rule-of-thumb" actuarial methods and those based on the rigorous contingent claims valuation framework of financial economics. It is the latter approach which shows that in the circumstances of today, fully guaranteed, final earnings-based, inflation-indexed pension promises have become too expensive for the guarantors. Once this reality is understood and accepted, the search for a fairer, more sustainable alternative becomes a logical next step. Thus, the fundamental "tipping point" question here becomes: Where are the balance sheet whistle-blowers? In the Netherlands, it was the pension regulator. In this book's case study, it is PERS CEO Alyson Green. Fortunately, she already has a few "real-life" counterparts in Canada and the United States. Many more are needed.

There is no single shot that we can fire today to launch and win a single massive global pension revolution. There are, however, a number of promising local skirmishes taking place in various places across the globe. If enough of us join in, those skirmishes may yet become the pension revolution Peter Drucker foresaw 30 years ago.